Centring
on the
Peripheries

Studies in Scandinavian, Scottish, Gaelic and Greenlandic Literature

Other books from Norvik Press

Anglo-Scandinavian Cross-Currents (eds Inga-Stina Ewbank, Olav Lausand & Bjørn Tysdahl)
Aspects of Modern Swedish Literature (revised edn, ed. Irene Scobbie)
Paul Binding: *With Vine-Leaves in His Hair. The Role of the Artist in Ibsen's Plays*
A Century of Swedish Narrative (eds Sarah Death & Helena Forsås-Scott)
English and Nordic Modernisms (eds Bjørn Tysdahl, Mats Jansson, Jakob Lothe & Steen Klitgård Povlsen)
European and Nordic Modernisms (eds Mats Jansson, Jakob Lothe & Hannu Riikonen)
Gender – Power – Text. Nordic Culture in the Twentieth Century (ed. Helena Forsås-Scott)
Nordic Letters 1870-1910 (eds Michael Robinson & Janet Garton)
Northern Constellations. New Readings in Nordic Cinema. (ed. C. Claire Thomson)
On the Threshold. New Studies in Nordic Literature (eds Michael Robinson & Janet Garton)
Ellen Rees: *On the Margins. Nordic Women Modernists of the 1930s*
Michael Robinson: *Studies in Strindberg*
Michael Robinson: *Strindberg and Genre*
Freddie Rokem: *Strindberg's Secret Codes*
Turning the Century. Centennial Essays on Ibsen (ed. Michael Robinson)
Robin Young: *Time's Disinherited Children. Childhood, Regression and Sacrifice in the Plays of Henrik Ibsen*

Knut Hamsun: *Selected Letters*, vols I and II (ed. & trans. Harald Næss & James MacFarlane)
Erik and Amalie Skram: *Caught in the Enchanter's Net. Selected Letters* (ed. & trans. Janet Garton)
Edith Södergran: *The Poet Who Created Herself. Selected Letters* (ed. & trans. Silvester Mazzarella)

Victoria Benedictsson: *Money* (translated by Sarah Death)
Hjalmar Bergman: *Memoirs of a Dead Man* (translated by Neil Smith)
Jens Bjørneboe: *Moment of Freedom* (translated by Esther Greenleaf Mürer)
Jens Bjørneboe: *Powderhouse* (translated by Esther Greenleaf Mürer)
Jens Bjørneboe: *The Silence* (translated by Esther Greenleaf Mürer)
Hans Børli: *We Own the Forests and Other Poems* (translated by Louis Muinzer)
Suzanne Brøgger: *A Fighting Pig's Too Tough to Eat* (translated by Marina Allemano)
Camilla Collett: *The District Governor's Daughters* (translated by Kirsten Seaver)
Gunnar Ekelöf: *Modus Vivendi* (ed. and trans. by Erik Thygesen)
Kerstin Ekman: *Witches' Rings* (translated by Linda Schenck)
Kerstin Ekman: *The Spring* (translated by Linda Schenck)
Kerstin Ekman: *The Angel House* (translated by Sarah Death)
Kerstin Ekman: *City of Light* (translated by Linda Schenck)
Jørgen-Frantz Jacobsen: *Barbara* (translated by George Johnston)
P. C. Jersild: *A Living Soul* (translated by Rika Lesser)
Runar Schildt: *The Meat-Grinder and Other Stories* (translated by Anna-Lisa & Martin Murrell)
Hjalmar Söderberg: *Martin Birck's Youth* (translated by Tom Ellett)
Hjalmar Söderberg: *Short Stories* (translated by Carl Lofmark)
August Strindberg: *Tschandala* (translated by Peter Graves) (2007)
Hanne Marie Svendsen: *Under the Sun* (translated by Marina Allemano)

Centring
on the
Peripheries

Studies in Scandinavian, Scottish, Gaelic and Greenlandic Literature

edited by

Bjarne Thorup Thomsen

Norvik Press
2007

A catalogue record for this book is available from the British Library.

ISBN 978 1 870041 66 9
First published 2007

Norvik Press was established in 1984 with financial support from the University of East Anglia, the Danish Ministry for Cultural Affairs, the Norwegian Cultural Department and the Swedish Institute.

Managing Editors: Janet Garton, Neil Smith and C. Claire Thomson.

Cover illustration: photograph of the Falkirk Wheel
© Lumivision Architectural Lighting (www.lumivision.co.uk).

Cover design: Richard Johnson
Copy-editing: Rachel Wiener
Printed in Great Britain by Page Bros. (Norwich) Ltd, UK.

Contents

Dedicated to the Memory

of

Bill Findlay

1947 – 2005

Acknowledgments

First and foremost I would like to thank all the contributors very much for their incisive thoughts and for the good humour and patience they have exhibited.

Many thanks also to Janet Garton, Michael Robinson, Neil Smith and Claire Thomson at Norvik Press for supporting the project. In my day-to-day dealings with Neil Smith he has proved unfailingly enthusiastic, knowledgeable and resourceful. Claire Thomson has been inspirational and helpful as ever; it was her idea to use the Falkirk Wheel for the cover illustration, and she has compiled the index.

I am also indebted to my friends and colleagues in the Scandinavian Studies section at Edinburgh University – Peter Graves, Arne Kruse, Allan Juhl Kristensen, Karen Bek-Pedersen and, not least, Gunilla Blom Thomsen – for their spirited support and sound advice.

Many thanks also to my editorial assistant, Alan MacNiven, for his efficient work.

The editor and publishers gratefully acknowledge the generous financial support of the Nordic Council of Ministers.

This volume is dedicated to the memory of Bill Findlay – translator, critic and champion of the Scots language – who passed away in May 2005.

Bjarne Thorup Thomsen
Edinburgh, February 2007

Introduction

Bjarne Thorup Thomsen

In an essay entitled 'Center og periferi' (Centre and Periphery), the Danish literary and cultural theorist Frederik Stjernfelt imagines how cultural and natural places might be articulated in a space which does not *a priori* privilege any particular points in favour of others. Such a purely geometrical conception of space, he muses, is of relevance to phenomena ranging from biological morphosis via architecture and homesickness to state building (Stjernfelt:362). He goes on to situate this problematic in the context, *inter alia*, of geopolitical changes in Europe after 1989. In the collection of essays presented here the focus is on the complex spaces of the Nordic world and Scotland and the mulitiple articulations of core-periphery relations in the rich literatures of these lands. In sixteen studies by scholars of Scandinavian and Scottish literature the examination of literary voices, currents and traditions is set in dialogue with contemporary theoretical approaches to the study of local, national and global cultural constellations. In Cairns Craig's opening chapter the book's overarching field of enquiry is formulated, while the cultural role of Scotland is also reassessed. The chapter interrogates discourses of centre and periphery as they have developed since the 1960s in world systems theory, post-colonial studies, deconstruction, theories of nation and of postmodernism through to the resistance in chaos theory to constructing an order out of core-periphery relations and the assertion in such theory of the truths embodied in the local.

Following Cairns Craig's conspectus, the challenges, creativities and connections of the northern peripheries are considered in a sequence of studies which together consitute a trajectory from, broadly speaking, east to west through a number of 'debatable' territories and texts. The journey begins in Finland whose Swedophone areas or cultures form the focus of two chapters. In Clas Zilliacus' contribution politics of nationhood meet semiotics in the context of linguistic and cultural conflict in Finland in the decades before and after its independence in 1917. The chapter investigates the quest for a figurative language that could connect the Swedophone part of the Finnish population with its 'peripheral' strongholds on the western and southern coasts of the country and in the archipelagos and thus match the inland imagery of the majority. Whereas this chapter is centred on the Finland-Swedish 'heartland' (albeit a Finnish fringe from another perspective), Nalle Valtiala's contribution takes us to the apparent eastern remoteness of the Finnish-Russian borderland of Karelia to encounter an internationally informed Swedophone poet, Edith Södergran, whose work – at the forefront of a wave of innovative Finland-Swedish lyrical output in the early decades of the twentieth century – pre-empted and hugely impacted on the development of literary modernism in the Swedish 'mother' culture and beyond.

The next three chapters shift the focus from Swedophone Finland to the Swedish nation's own spatial and cultural complexities. Anders Öhman discusses connections between early twentieth century modernity and mobility and what he terms the nomadic cultural identity of the northern 'periphery' of Sweden, Norrland, the region that occupies almost two thirds of the country's land mass. He demonstrates the role played by Norrlandic literature in re-mapping a territory and a culture which it had hitherto been the privilege of the centre to describe and draws parallels with the workings of postcolonial literature. Anders Persson's contribution likewise centres on Norrlandic cultural identity, more specifically the considerable role played by pietistic revivalism and layman-led religious life in the region from the beginning of the nineteenth century to the present and the impact of these movements on Norrlandic literature. Using prominent writer Torgny Lindgren as his main reference point, Persson shows how oral and written genres such as sermon, parable and legend are employed and reworked in contemporary Norrlandic literature, achieving an interpenetration of local specificity and universal significance. Bjarne Thorup Thomsen rounds this 'Swedish' section off, while also opening up a wider perspective on Scandinavian territoriality, by discussing the representation and problematisation of Nordic national borderlands in texts by Nobel Prize-winning novelist and Swedish icon Selma Lagerlöf. The chapter considers negotiations or reflections in Lagerlöf of redrawings of the Scandinavian map in 1658, 1864, 1905 and 1920, tracing a dialogic notion of nationhood in the author's work.

Responses, in body, landscape and discourse terms, to questions of peripherality in Norwegian, Danish and Scottish literature are the subject of two contributions of a comparative nature. Steinvör Pálsson explores the fragmenting topography of the human body in two Norwegian novels – one set in the capital, one in a northern island fishing community, one male, one female authored, one from the 1880s, one from the 1980s – that both, however, deal with profoundly decentring and debilitating experiences of rape and sexual abuse. Claire Thomson's contribution works as a stepping stone between southern Scandinavia and Scotland in comparing discourses of marginality found on either side of the North Sea, arguing that in Denmark the dominant discourse is centripetal, homogenising and to a considerable extent tied up with the vision of the welfare state, whereas in Scotland it is centrifugal, dialogic and 'heteroglossic'. Her chapter then moves on to consider the imagining of national 'spacetimes' and the play with the peripheral in one Danish and two Scottish novels from the 1990s, by Vibeke Grønfeldt, Alan Warner and Andrew Greig.

The interrogation of modern Scottish literature and culture is continued in two chapters that centre on the interface between gender and nation and on the 'state-of-the-nation' drama respectively. Aileen Christianson discusses how to configure the relationship between the marginality of femaleness and the Scottish nation, identifying a lack of analysis of the role of gender in nationhood as a feature of seminal theories on nation. Against the assigning of a privileged role in national representation to urban, male- and masculinity-centred fiction, Christianson foregrounds the core contribution made by Scottish women's twentieth century fiction to Scotland's narrative of identity. Bill Findlay then draws attention to the involvement of Scotland's strong current of contemporary drama in the re-examining of Scottish identity in response to the political peripheralisation during the Thatcher years and in the wake of devolution and the opening of the Scottish Parliament in 1999. Through an analysis of Stephen Greenhorn's acclaimed drama *Passing Places* (1997), the chapter takes us on a northwards trajectory from Scotland's urban 'Central Belt' into the Highlands, in search of a redefined identity expressed in terms of a broader, more inclusive idea of both nationhood and selfhood.

Following the examination of modern Scottish culture conducted by Thomson, Christianson and Findlay, Ronald Jack adds a deeper diachronic dimension to the understanding of the centre-periphery relations of Scottish culture. To widen a unitary cultural paradigm which has centred on a nationalist model of the Scottish literary tradition, Jack argues that an alternative multiracial, multilingual, decorous and polymathic model of Scottishness has been presented in Scottish literature from the Middle Ages onwards.

No consideration of Scotland's linguistic and literary landscape can overlook, of course, the influence of the Gaelic language with its strongholds in the highlands and islands of western Scotland. In his discussion of twentieth century Hebridean literature, prose writing as well as verse, Donald Meek explores how the theme of enduring, powerful islands is central both to traditional literature, affirming the archipelago, and to the exile Gaelic writer, operating between cultures and languages and negotiating the demands of a variety of maps. Meek demonstrates how, in the creative processes of the 'non-traditional' poets, any meaningful distinction between core and periphery is nullified.

The problematics of language, poetry and the island community are developed further in Anne-Kari Skarðhamar's contribution which deals with the Faroe Islands, located between Scotland and Iceland in the North Atlantic. The chapter focuses on the figure of Christian Matras, who, in his twin capacities as leading twentieth century Faroese poet and as professor of

Faroese language and literature at the University of Copenhagen, was well versed in the cultural, linguistic and national dynamics of his native islands as well as in competing perspectives on their position. The chapter explores how Matras' poetry, in centring on Faroese topography, fuses the physical and metaphysical, reaches out to the cosmic and the sublime and challenges the notion of Faroese marginality.

Moving further north-west, the main themes of Baldur Hafstað's discussion are the vibrancy, connectedness and sense of tradition of the literary culture of Iceland, a nation of 300,000 inhabitants. In co-examining the ostensibly disparate textual phenomena of a medieval family saga, the novels of Halldór Laxness – the country's most prominent and most controversial twentieth century writer – and the poetry of the Icelandic-Canadian Stephan G. Stephansson, Hafstað shows how modern Icelandic literature has been engaged in constant dialogues with the country's weighty literary heritage as well as with international intellectual influences in order to address contemporary concerns of the nation. The investigation of the international involvement of Icelandic culture is continued in Daisy Neijmann's contribution. It traces the development of Icelandic-Canadian immigrant literature from strategies of cultural purity, colony building and transplantation, through processes of transformation, 'translation' and 'bastardisation' to the current embrace of multiculturalism. The chapter sheds light on the changing core-periphery relationships between 'old' and 'new' Icelandic culture in the contexts of Icelandic struggle for independence, the home rule of the inter-war period, full independence in 1944, post-war NATO entry and American military presence to today's globalisation.

Some of these themes are continued and new ones added in Kirsten Thisted's contribution, which concludes our journey through the debatable northern terrains by focusing on Greenland, its post-colonial relationship to Denmark and its prospect of becoming a full national state in a globalised world. The complex questions of identity and belonging this context implies are investigated in the chapter through the prism of the different literary voices of Ole Korneliussen and Hans Anthon Lynge: the former post-national, constructivist, bilingual and inclined to stepping off a map based on the fixity of notions of home and roots, the latter centred on Greenlandic settings and the Greenlandic language and preoccupied with the re-definition and positioning of Greenlandic identity, culture and nation in a world of multiple core-periphery and periphery-periphery relations.

Reference

Stjernfelt, Frederik (1997): 'Center og periferi. Grænsens fænomenologi, stedernes betydning – Haushofer, Lotman, Heidegger, Derrida, Poincaré', in *Rationalitetens himmel og andre essays*. Copenhagen: Gyldendal.

Centring on the Peripheries

Cairns Craig

I

Let me start by reflecting on my own past involvement with the issue of peripherality. In the 1980s I edited a multi-author, four volume *History of Scottish Literature* (Craig 1987-89). Its aim was, precisely, to centre on the periphery. In 1984, immediately before starting work on the *History*, I had written an essay entitled 'Peripheries' (Craig 1983), which was an angry attack on the central tradition of modern English literary criticism from T. S. Eliot to Raymond Williams, decrying the ways in which it reshaped the history of writing in English in order create an illusory sense of the completeness of the English tradition. The typical manoeuvre of this centrist English tradition was to claim writers from the periphery as integral elements of its own national tradition, thereby depleting and undermining the unity and coherence of the national traditions of the other countries of the archipelago. I took as a typical example Raymond Williams's discussion of Thomas Carlyle from his highly influential *Culture and Society 1780-1950*, first published in 1958:

> In 1829, in the *Edinburgh Review*, Carlyle published his important essay, *Signs of the Times*. His essay was his first main contribution to the social thought of the time [...] yet it states a general position which was to be the basis of all Carlyle's subsequent work, and which, moreover, was to establish itself in the general thinking of many other writers, and as a major element in the tradition of English social criticism. (Williams 1963:85)

Carlyle, of course, was a Scot and a Scot who, in 1829, had no direct experience of English life. This Scottish contribution 'to the social thought of the time' is merged into and becomes 'a major element in the tradition of English social criticism' – a tradition so unitary that it is, simply, *the* tradition of English social criticism. English culture and society thus become the very epitome of those universal abstractions, *Culture* and *Society*, making the adjective 'English' redundant, while Scottish culture and society, on the other hand, simply disappears – a historical absence invisible from and irrelevant to the centre.

Against that invisibility, my *History of Scottish Literature* set out to prove that Scottish culture had all the qualities that were normally associated with the centre – cultural continuity, a rich intellectual context, and forms of writing which evolved primarily *within* the culture itself rather than being borrowed from elsewhere. It also reversed Williams's strategy and – unlike many previous histories of Scottish literature – assumed that Scots who went to London to make their literary career remained not only Scottish but contributors to a distinctively Scottish literature. The 'Anglo-Scots' of the eighteenth century like Boswell and Thomson, the cultural emigrés of the nineteenth like Carlyle and J. M. Barrie, were all claimed as significant parts of Scotland's ongoing cultural history, no matter how much they might also have been participants in English literary culture. Scotland, in this construction, was not merely translated from being 'peripheral' to being 'central', but in doing so it effectively challenged the notion of *English* centrality by detaching from it one of those 'peripheries' which constituted its sphere of cultural influence. It was an argument that was given significant support in the following decade by Robert Crawford's *Devolving English Literature* (1992) and *The Scottish Invention of English Literature* (1998). The first of these reshaped the history of English literature in the modern period as a tradition of the peripheries, while the second unmasked the Englishness of English literature to reveal that the tradition on which Eliot, Leavis and Williams had rested their conception of what was central to English culture – and what made English culture central – was in fact of Scottish origin. English Literature had been born in Scotland and it was in Scotland that the discipline of 'English' gained its initial significance.

In retrospect, this literary critical revolt by the peripheries can be seen as part of a wider effort by Scottish, Irish and Welsh writers to depose and delimit the authority of English culture in the decades after the Second World War. From the late 1950s, Perry Anderson and Tom Nairn, for instance, had conducted a campaign through the pages of the *New Left Review*[1] to undermine long-standing assumptions about the specially favoured nature of English history. English historiography, they argued, of both right-wing and left-wing persuasions, had never freed itself from the sense that English history presented a model by which other nations should be judged. England stood at the centre of world history, an exemplar to those less advanced in civility. Anderson and Nairn, on the other hand, represented England as a nation that had failed to make the transition from absolutism to modernity that was typical of other nations in the developed world; rather than the epitome of the modern nation state, England, and the Britain that it had shaped around it, were characterised as a grotesque anomaly, not only peripheral to the main developments of European culture but culturally redundant in terms of its contemporary creativity. This revolt of the peripheries, conducted through the apparent universalism of a Marxist ideology (Nairn was Scottish, Anderson of Irish background), sought to undermine the relevance of modern English culture as a basis for the future of British identities. Modern English culture was, quite simply, an evasion of the modern world; a retreat from the real issues of modernity into a carefully controlled environment where 'England' could survive in the illusion of its continued centrality:

> ... all modern nations have such a myth, the key to their 'nationalism', and the common source of their political upheavals and regeneration. England does not possess one. 'Modern conditions', in the pertinent sense, have never reached her. This is certainly one of the explanations of the astonishing resistance of a fossilized and incompetent political order, through thirty years of imperial defeat and economic degeneration. Were there an alternative in the sub-strata of that system, it would surely have been summoned up to action. (Nairn 1981:296)

This conception of modern England as 'deformed' by its imperial role, rather than as the model for its subservient cultures, became integral to the 'postcolonial' theories of the 1980s and 1990s. In the fashion of Hegel's 'master-slave' dialectic, England came to be seen as dependent upon, rather than dominating over, its imperial 'others'. As Declan Kiberd put it,

> If Ireland had never existed, the English would have invented it [...] because it was necessary that Ireland should be patented as not-England, a place whose peoples were, in many important ways, the very antithesis of their new rulers. (Kiberd 1995:9)

The relation of centre and periphery is reversed: it is the peripheries, rather than the centre, that come to represent the 'authentic' cultural formation of the modern world. To be central is to be in a minority of one; to be peripheral is to represent the majority of the human race who suffer under the oppressions of colonialism. The peripheral, envisaged initially as the 'backward' and the 'underdeveloped', become, in effect, the most advanced:

> ... by the 1880s and 1890s, Ireland was in certain respects clearly advanced by contrast with England. In politics, it was confronting its national question (something which even today, the English have not done), dismantling church-state connections, and evolving a republican politics based on a theory of citizens' rights. (Kiberd 1995:24)

Reversing the traditional dependence of the peripheral on the centre, it is at the peripheries – in the Ireland that produced Yeats, Joyce, Beckett, and

Heaney, for example – that real cultural energy is generated. The centre, on the other hand, is sclerotic, and, as a consequence, English national culture is increasingly treated by both Irish and Scottish writers and thinkers as irrelevant to their own concerns. David McCrone's *Understanding Scotland* (1992), for instance, opens on this note:

> The conventional nation-state, treated as a self-contained and bounded social system is rapidly losing its *raison d'être* in the modern world. [...] the useful assumption that nation-states, at least in the developed world, had economic, political and cultural coherence – that they were self-contained 'societies' – has begun to seem less sure. (McCrone 1992:1-2)

The most conventional nation-state, of course, was England, and, as a consequence, McCrone is able to turn conventional distinctions of core and periphery on their head: it is now Scotland that 'stands at the forefront of sociological concerns in the late twentieth century'; instead of being, as peripheries ought to be, 'an awkward, ill-fitting case, it is at the centre of the discipline's post-modern dilemma' (McCrone 1992:1). Scotland's move from periphery to centre is symbolically enacted in the title of T. M. Devine's *The Scottish Empire* (Devine 2003), which makes Scotland's empire a quite separate business from the once 'British' empire, and is also proclaimed in Arthur Herman's *The Scottish Enlightenment*, subtitled *The Scots' Invention of the Modern World* (Herman 2002). Scotland is at the foundation of modernity: as central as any country could be to the history of the world we now inhabit.

The speed of this turnaround, accompanying as it did the steady progress towards the establishment of the Scottish parliament in 1999, by way of the successful devolution referendum of 1997, was staggering. What it ignored, of course, was that Scotland was still the only country in Europe whose population had declined in the twentieth century; that it was the only one of the northern European countries that had failed to produce a modern industrial organisation with global ambitions; that its economic strategy was based on inward investment by American and Japanese companies in search of cheap labour; and that its new parliament had severely restricted powers that did not allow it to claim even equivalence with Canadian provinces or German *Länder*. Modern Scotland was outshone even by its former partner in Celtic peripherality, Ireland, which had transformed itself into the 'Celtic tiger' of the modern world economy in the years during which Scotland had been shuffling towards its mousy devolution. A Scotland puffed with pride that its past was recognised as *central* to European and, indeed, world culture had, by all contemporary international standards, declined further into the periphery. And the more that past Scotland was made to appear fundamental to the emergence of the modern world, the more modern Scotland, and modern Scots, looked like children dwarfed in adults' clothes.

II

The Scottish experience points to fundamental problems with the discourse of centre and periphery as it has developed since the 1960s. It was in the work of Immanuel Wallerstein, and the so-called 'World Systems Theory' he pioneered, that the relations of core and periphery came to be seen as the decisive determinant of the pattern of modern history.[2] Challenging developmentalist conceptions of the relation between the developed and the un- or under-developed world, Wallerstein argued that models based on the assumption that the underdeveloped could catch up and reach the same stage of economic activity as the developed ignored the power relations by which the core economies of the world maintained their economic advantage – and others' economic disadvantage. For Wallerstein, core and periphery are involved in a mutually defining structural relationship: cores aggrandise and enrich themselves precisely by enforcing peripherality on those whose resources they require. A world-wide division of labour forces peripheral areas of the world economy into supplying the requirements of core areas, and the states in the periphery, as a consequence, are always relatively poorer and much more politically unstable than those of the core. Where nineteenth and early twentieth-century Marxists had seen the key to history as the inevitable conflict between the bourgeoisie and the proletariat, Wallerstein saw the key as the conflict between the core economies of the world and the rest of the world which they exploited, whether directly (by imperialism) or indirectly (through economic domination). The system of nation states that characterises the modern world works precisely because it produces a flux of conflicts that continually refine and reshape the relations of one geopolitical area to another, but do so without disrupting the *structural* relation of core to periphery.

> ...more and more 'states' operating within the interstate system have been created. Their boundaries and the definitions of their formal rights have been defined with increasing clarity (culminating in the contemporary United Nations structure of international law). The modalities and limits of group pressures in state structures have also been increasingly defined (in the sense both of the legal limits placed on such pressures, and of the rational organization by groups to transcend these limits). None the less, despite what might be called the 'honing' of this institutional network, it is probably safe to say that the relative power continuum of stronger and weaker states has remained relatively unchanged over 400-odd years. That is not to say

that the same 'states' have remained 'strong' and 'weak'. Rather, there has been at all moments a power hierarchy of such states, but also at no moment has there been any one state whose hegemony was totally unchallenged (although relative hegemony has occurred for limited periods). (Wallerstein 1984:30).

Thus in the nineteenth century the core area of the world economy was north-western Europe; after the World Wars of the twentieth century for domination of that core, the core had moved to North America. The transfer of the core to a different geopolitical location did not, however, according to Wallerstein, disrupt the functioning of a world system whose dynamic lay in the relations of the core to the periphery. The system continued to work in the same way even though the actors had changed, and precisely because of its systemic quality it was impossible, as long as the world was organised by capitalism, for peripherality to be abolished. Individual states might escape from the periphery to achieve semi-peripheral status, or even to join the core, but they could do so only as a result of the peripheralisation of some other area restricted by the requirements of the world-wide division of labour.

What made Wallerstein's theories seem like a breakthrough for the peripheries was that the peripheries could no longer be regarded as inhabiting some earlier stage of the history of world development, as being simply backward versions of the centre. Core and periphery inhabited the same historical moment – they were different ways of being, different ways of experiencing the surge of capitalist development. The assumption of both liberal and marxian thinkers that the core was more 'advanced' could be reversed: that the core was more *developed* implied only a certain relationship to the whole world economy, a relationship that did not necessarily mean that the core was culturally or morally more advanced than its peripheries. Indeed, it was possible to suggest that the core was *deformed* by the very need to play its central role, and that while its economic dominance was inescapable, the peripheries might represent a fund of alternative cultural formations which were *more* valuable precisely because they were not subject to the same deformation. Rather than representing the highest achievements of humanity, the technological advantage of the core might in fact represent a profound cultural disadvantage: peripherality became a virtue in a world where centrality had become a crushing burden. The alienation of the proletariat in traditional Marxist accounts of world history could become the alienation of the core, the spiralling intensity of its economic activity encouraging a dehumanisation of its inhabitants from which the peripheries were – to some extent at least – protected.

Wallerstein's re-reading of European history provided the backdrop for the inversions of the core-periphery binary that were to become typical of the 'postcolonial' in English language literary studies, a model that was to be taken over wholesale in the work of Irish critics such as Declan Kiberd and David Lloyd. By undermining traditional assumptions about the historical superiority of the core, Wallerstein's world systems theory provided a context for alternative ways of mapping the history of modern culture, centring on peripheries as places where the clash between modernity and the local produced the real *cultural* innovations of the modern world, innovations which would later be adopted by the core. If, for Pierre Bourdieu, the 'Field of Cultural Production' is 'The Economic World Reversed' (Bourdieu 1993:30ff) because in high culture, at least, failure – the failure, for instance, to be understood by a large audience – means success, then Wallerstein's theories allowed a similar reversal of core-periphery relations in which economic subservience at the periphery becomes the necessary basis for cultural success. While the core exported its economic innovations, the peripheries responded by exporting their cultural innovations. Readings of modernism that located its origins at the periphery – whether in the Scandinavian countries or among the black community in North America or among Jews in Eastern Europe – were typical of this 'cultural world reversed', and the explosion of 'postcolonial' literatures, as well as the South American origins of styles such as magic realism, underlined that it was no passing phenomenon. Peripherality was a cultural energy on which the centre fed for the nourishment it could not produce for itself, and, by the 1990s, claims to peripheral creativity abounded, fuelled by the rise of postcolonial studies in various parts of the former British Empire, by identity politics in the United States, by the emergence of a new and potent regionalism in the European Union and by the new nationalisms unleashed by the collapse of the Soviet Union. The peripheries, it might seem, had regained the center at the very moment when the economic hegemony of the United States was assured by the collapse of communism.

In Wallerstein's economistic model, however, there was no way of giving a value to such cultural outcomes. For Wallerstein, the core-periphery relation might have displaced the bourgeois-proletarian opposition of traditional Marxism, but whatever peripheries might *think* of their own cultural values, their only place within Wallerstein's world system was as disruptions of the hegemonic power of capitalism. Whether your cultural value was peripheral nationalism, trades-union socialism, Muslim or Hindu resistance to westernisation, or eco-politics, its *function* in the system was simply as an irritant to overwhelming capitalism. Such antisystemic movements, resisting the world system in which they were inevitably caught, might, at some future point, allow an entirely new and as yet unimaginable socialist world system to come into existence, but the individual antisystemic movements would not, themselves, be the basis of that future non-exploitative society. As Alberto Moreiras has put it: 'There is no cultural-ideological praxis that is not always already produced by the movements of transnational capital, which is to say, we are all factors of the global system, even if and when our actions misunderstand themselves as desystematising ones' (Moreiras 1998:92). As rigorously as traditional Marxism, Wallerstein envisaged the future as a future in which the nation states of the modern world, and the cultures which they had inherited from an earlier set of geopolitical relations, would wither away. The causes for which people fought *now*, as resistance movements to global capital, would be rendered redundant when capitalism was finally overthrown. Their efficacy was purely negative: they might help derail global capitalism but their positive content would be irrelevant to the ideology by which capitalism would, eventually, be replaced.

It is little wonder, then, that World Systems Theory failed to turn into an active political movement to overthrow global capital. The relentless determinism of Marxism was redoubled in Wallerstein's model, since there could be no equivalent of the traditional communist vision of an alternative world to which people could subscribe and towards which they could act. Some unknowable future socialist state would somehow come into existence as a consequence of all the antisystemic resistance to capitalism, but it would be of an entirely different kind from any of the antisystemic movements which would make its coming possible:

> ... we really do not have more than the remotest idea of what a socialist world would look like in practice, and most certainly it would require a heroic leap of the imagination to envisage its cultural parameters. It is a bit like asking the burghers of thirteenth-century European cities to sketch our twentieth-century world. (Wallerstein 1984:167)

The message, therefore, of world systems theory to those who were involved in local cultural or political resistance to capitalism was that their values were illusory. The beliefs for which they thought they were fighting were simply symptoms of the pain that capitalism was inflicting on them rather than a foundation for an alternative form of society. To fight for the autonomy of your local culture might seem to be an assertion of peripheral value; at worst, however, it was only the smokescreen behind which capitalism divided up the world into competing segments in the international division of labour; at best it was an antisystemic disruption making possible the arrival of a new world system to which your local culture would be equally irrelevant. World systems theory may have explained peripherality, may even have given it a resonance that it had not previously enjoyed, but in the end it saw peripheral cultures as being just as irrelevant to the future of humanity as they had been within the world system they were opposing.

The aftermath of the collapse of communism gave ironic justification to Wallerstein's theories, since the important issue was not the rediscovery of peripheral *cultural* value in the re-emergence of the old nations of Eastern Europe, but their rush to join the competition for a place, however marginal, in a world-dominating capitalism. Whatever peripheral nationalists might *think* they were doing when they declared their culture reborn, what they were actually doing was opening their nation to exploitation by the core areas of the world economy; their assertions of cultural *difference* were actually a demand for *equality* – the equality of exploitation they would share with all other peripheral nations. Centring on the peripheries was, in this case, no more than the re-establishment of the peripherality of those who had no choice but to play their role at the margins of the world economic system. The new arrivals in the international state system might value their political and cultural independence, but such independence could be no counterbalance to the profound dependence by which they were linked to the centres of world economic power.

The reassertion of peripheral nationalism in the aftermath of 1989 was therefore profoundly ironic, linked both to the destruction of local cultures by globalisation – effectively, the Americanisation of all cultures – and to the irrelevance of such local cultures in the perspective of a socialism like Wallerstein's, which looked forward to replacing global capitalism with an alternative but equally global set of values. It was in this context that Benedict Anderson's *Imagined Communities* (Anderson 1991), first published in 1983 and revised and updated in 1991, set the agenda for thinking about the nature of the nation and, therefore, for thinking about the relations between centre and periphery. Like Hobsbawm and Ranger's *The Invention of Tradition* (Hobsbawm & Ranger 1983), published in the same year, *Imagined Communities* reads the development of the modern world through the lens of a disillusioned Marxism. For Anderson, as for Hobsbawm, the Marxism which had been supposed to reveal the rationality of history had been defeated by the nationalisms that should have withered away under its scrutiny. Nationalism, that smoke-screen of bourgeois economic exploitation, had survived, while socialism had been rolled back into a historical irrelevance. To explain the success of nationalism was to grasp the key to the history that had failed to conform to Marxian expectations, and the key was the power of the imagination. In a rational history, the nation might be the utilitarian deliverer of social goods, but it could not attract that profound devotion, that 'deep, horizontal comradeship' that leads directly to those 'colossal sacrifices' (Anderson 1991:7) that characterize modern history. Nationalism's appeal to the imagination gave it the affective power of great art, the power to provide a transcendent sense of meaning beyond the limits of our individual lives:

> Take national anthems, for example, sung on national holidays. No matter how banal the words and mediocre the tunes, there is in this singing an experience of simultaneity. At precisely such moments, people wholly unknown to each other utter the same verses to the same melody. The image: unisonance [...] How selfless this unisonance feels! If we are aware that others are singing these songs precisely when and as we are, we have no idea who they may be, or even where, out of earshot, they are singing. Nothing connects us all but imagined sound. (Anderson 1991:145)

For Anderson, the 'imagined' in 'imagined community' has to be differentiated from the 'fabrication' and 'falsity' implied in the work of his distinguished predecessor, Ernest Gellner (Gellner 1964). 'Imagined', in Anderson's sense, is asserted to be equivalent to 'imagining' as some kind of 'creation' (Anderson 1991:6). Despite his own protestations, however, Anderson's usage moves relentlessly towards 'imagined' as 'fabricated' and 'fictional'. The unisonance of national anthems is not a *real* sense of communality but one based entirely on fiction – 'nothing' is what connects the nation together in its moments of supposed unity; '*imagined* sound' replaces any real connections between people in the national community.

This is why, for Anderson, the realist novel is a significant paradigm for his conception of the nation. The novel is both a product of the print capitalism that Anderson presents as forging language communities into nations and, at the same time, a reflection of the imagined nation which it was helping to create. In Anderson's conception of the novel, 'the novelty of this imagined world conjured up by the author in his readers' minds' is that its 'acts are performed at the same clocked, calendrical time [...] by actors who may be largely unaware of one another' (Anderson 1991:26). This simultaneity of action by actors who are unaware of their own interconnections 'is a precise analogue of the idea of the nation, which also is conceived as a solid community moving steadily down (or up) history' (Anderson 1991:26). Fiction is the best model of the nation because the nation is itself nothing but a fiction. And the ultimate fiction is the newspaper, which daily inscribes its inventions into the lives of its readers:

> ... the newspaper is merely an 'extreme form' of the book, a book sold on a colossal scale, but of ephemeral popularity. Might we say: one-day best-sellers. The obsolescence of the newspaper on the morrow of its printing – curious that

one of the earlier mass-produced commodities should so prefigure the inbuilt obsolescence of modern durables – nonetheless, for just this reason, creates this extraordinary mass ceremony: the almost precisely simultaneous consumption ('imagining') of the newspaper-as-fiction [...] The significance of this mass ceremony – Hegel observed that newspapers serve modern man as a substitute for morning prayers – is paradoxical. It is performed in silent privacy, in the lair of the skull. Yet each communicant is well aware that the ceremony he performs is being replicated simultaneously by thousands (or millions) of others of whose existence he is confident, yet of whose identity he has not the lightest notion. (Anderson 1991:35)

The transcendent power of religion is transferred to the nation as the newspaper-reader becomes a 'communicant' in its belief-system, a belief-system through which 'fiction seeps quietly and continuously into reality' (Anderson 1991:36). The first modern nations were founded on such fictions but in the developing world nationalism was the creation of 'early-twentieth-century intelligentsias' who had access 'to models of nation, nation-ness and nationalism distilled from the turbulent, chaotic experiences of more than a century of American and European history'. The illusions that made early nationalisms possible are deliberately instilled by these later nationalists, thereby helping 'to give shape to a thousand inchoate dreams' (Anderson 1991:140). If, in the original nations, fiction 'quietly and continuously' displaced reality, in later nations reality is overwhelmed by dream. Indeed, these later nations are doubly distanced from reality because they are themselves already the products of others' fiction. In places such as Burma and Indonesia, it is the maps and censuses of the imperial powers that have 'invented' the nation.

> Map and census thus shaped the grammar which would in due course make possible 'Burma' and 'Burmese', 'Indonesia' and 'Indonesians'. But the concretisations of these possibilities – concretisations which have a powerful life today, long after the colonial state has disappeared – owed much to the colonial state's peculiar imagining of history and power. (Anderson 1991:185)

If all nations are, for Anderson, merely 'imagined communities' rather than real communities, the nations of the periphery are doubly so – they are the imagined identity of peoples who have been imposed upon by another's fiction. As in a platonic theory of the real, we all inhabit 'imitations', but some of us inhabit imitations of an ultimate reality and others only imitations of others' imitations. At the periphery, everything is fiction, since the very nature of the peripheral nation should be 'traced to the imaginings of the colonial state' (Anderson 1991:163), which is incapable of describing the reality of what it encounters and substitutes for it a 'feverish imagining' which is 'guided by its imagined map' (Anderson 1991:169) of the place it has conquered. To imagine oneself as a *national* of such a nation is to live already in a second-hand fiction: to resist those external powers in the name of the nation is to live in a world where all is delusion.

For some, Anderson's work could be embraced joyfully because, if nations were imagined, then all that had to be done to change them was to imagine differently. Thus Richard Kearney, for instance, envisaged the transformation of British-Irish relations by changes in 'imaginative representation':

> This last requires us to invent, or reinvent, new images of communal identity – replacing (for example) the Four-Green-Fields with the Fifth Province. Or, on the British side, replacing the triumphalist emblems of Empire (Britannia, Sceptre and Crown, King and Country) with alternative images of accommodation: Britain as 'archipelago', as 'North-West Islands' and so on. (Kearney 1997:69)

A plethora of books about the 'invention' and 'imagining' of particular national traditions – *Inventing Ireland*, *The Invention of Scotland*, etc. – paid tribute to the effectiveness of Anderson's theories in this respect. But by degrading the national imagination to a mere fiction, Anderson's work effectively evacuated the major resource by which the peripheries could resist the effects of the saturation of international media with American culture. If the nation was a mere fiction, then it hardly mattered which nation one's imagination inhabited, though better, perhaps, to be a powerful one than a weak one.

By the late 1980s, therefore, the retreating horizon of a possible socialism had undermined the potential of Wallerstein's theories as a medium of resistance to the economic effects of core-periphery relations: peripheries were stuck with their peripherality. At the same time, accounts like Anderson's apparently bankrupted the cultural capital on which peripheral nations depended for their power of cultural if not of economic resistance. If, from the point of view of the developed world, this represented the emergence of a post-nationalist world to which traditional nationalisms – whether imperial or resistant – were irrelevant, from the peripheries the decay of nationalism as the vehicle for resistance did not portend acceptance of the new world order – rather, it led directly to the search for deeper sources of resistance in the pre-nationalist resources of religious fundamentalism.

III

The work of two of the most influential English-language literary critics of the 1980s and 1990s – Edward Said and Homi Bhabha – can be read as responses to the crisis of the nation in the core-periphery relation of the modern era. Said's *Orientalism* (1978) explicated the ways in which the centre – in this case the Occidental, imperial powers from Britain and France in the nineteenth century to the United States in the twentieth – had constructed its imperial periphery – the 'Orient' – as its submissive 'other' (Said 1978). Said's reading of the literature of the major Western cultures was a reading from the periphery designed to reveal the unconscious or latent elements in those Western traditions which Western critics themselves could not see because they already lived within the presuppositions of orientalism. It was a technique which, in *Culture and Imperialism* (1993) he described as 'contrapuntal reading':

> As we look back at the cultural archive, we begin to reread it not univocally but *contrapuntally*, with a simultaneous awareness both of the metropolitan history that is narrated and of those other histories against which (and together with which) the dominating discourse acts. (Said 1993:59)

The reader, in other words, can retrospectively position him- or herself both at the centre and at the periphery. If the economic and political impact of imperialism is to drive an enormous distance between centre and periphery, the procedures of cultural understanding can reverse that process and allow them to be understood in their mutual interaction. The destructive and disruptive forces that ravage the periphery for the aggrandisement of the centre, can be turned back into cultural harmony:

> In the counterpoint of Western classical music, various themes play off one another, with only a provisional privilege being given to any particular one; yet in the resulting polyphony there is concert and order, an organized interplay that derives from the themes, not from a rigorous melodic or formal principle outside the work. In the same way, I believe, we can read and interpret English novels, for example, whose engagement (usually suppressed for the most part) with the West Indies or India, say, is shaped and perhaps even determined by the specific history of colonization, resistance, and finally native nationalism. (Said 1993:59-60)

By reading back and forth across the core-periphery divide, a transcendent order emerges which re-establishes the value of 'culture' not as the imposition of power but as the domain of a revitalised humanism, able to envisage 'an imaginative, even Utopian vision which reconceives emancipatory (as opposed to confining) theory and performance' (Said 1993:337). This 'emancipatory' performance requires a reader who is trapped neither by the dominating culture of the centre nor the resistant culture of the periphery, a reader who has, in effect, moved beyond the cultures of either core or peripheral nations. As a consequence, for Said, 'three great topics emerge in decolonizing cultural resistance': first, 'the insistence on the right to see the community's history whole, coherently, integrally'; second, 'the idea that resistance, far from being merely a reaction to imperialism, is an alternative way of conceiving human history', a way of conceiving human history as interconnectedness rather than separation; and, third, 'a noticeable pull away from separatist nationalism towards a more integrative view of human community' (Said 1993:259-61). Who, however, can represent this post-nationalist 'human community'? Who can escape from the orders of the nation, either core or peripheral, to achieve such contrapuntal elevation? The answer is, quite literally, those who have left their nation behind but not yet acquired a new one: the utopian vision of a new humanity belongs to the migrant and the exile:

> It is no exaggeration to say that liberation as an intellectual mission, born in resistance and opposition to the confinements and ravages of imperialism, has now shifted from the settled, established, and domesticated dynamics of culture to its unhoused, decentred, and exilic energies, energies whose incarnation today is the migrant, and whose consciousness is that of the intellectual and artist in exile, the political figure between the domains, between forms, between homes, and between languages. (Said 1993:403)

By being the inhabitant of both the culture of the periphery and the culture of the centre, the exile and the migrant have the stereoscopic equipment to hear the counterpoints to which the monocultural is necessarily deaf. It is no accident, of course, that *Culture and Imperialism* announces itself in its 'Introduction' as 'an exile's book', written by someone who, by accident, 'belonged to both worlds, without being completely *of* one or the other' (Said 1993:xxx). The theoretical perspective of contrapuntal reading and its possible liberation is, in effect, the projection of a personal history which others might read as being the history of a person trapped on the margins of both cultures, rather than *belonging* to both, the history of someone alienated from rather than *at home* in both. Might not the contrapuntal 'harmony' of being at both ends of the scale be simply a means of sidestepping how pressing certain issues are when seen from inside just one of those cultures? Is the monocultural perspective necessarily and always a flawed one? Perhaps the intellectual exile and writerly migrant is able to 'transcend' the conflict of core and periphery only because s/he is not actually subject to its real pressures, pressures which inevitably generate discord rather than harmony.

Said's style of criticism is one derived from the English New Left – particularly Raymond Williams – and from the aftermath of French existentialism – especially the notion of a *littérature engagée* and the theory of 'discourse' in the work of Foucault. Since both traditions emphasize the significance of the critic's own biography to the very possibility of effective criticism, Said's biographical emphasis can hardly be held to be inappropriate to the task he has set himself. Nonetheless, to universalize the personal as not only relevant to the circumstances of the *present* but to the utopian possibilities of the *future* is perhaps to refuse to recognize that a criticism so personally based must acknowledge the equal relevance of other, very different, biographical experiences and critical stances. A nationalist who has lived her life entirely within the culture of a periphery has as much right to claim the universalisability of her values as Said does to claim the universalisability of his. And it would not be appropriate in that context to raise the old argument that nationalists cannot universalize their arguments because they are always based on the particular. Said's criticism, being based on his own personal experience of being at both ends of the core-periphery relation, is just as particular as the experience of the nationalist – who can, in any case, universalize her argument by insisting on the rights of all peripheral or minority communities to equal status and recognition.

Homi Bhabha's critical stance derives from the very different French tradition of Jacques Derrida, but Derrida is himself, in his Algerian background, as much of an example as Said of someone whose experience encompasses both core and periphery. Bhabha's use of the 'wit and wisdom of Jacques Derrida' in order to explore his 'own experience of migration' (Bhabha 1994:139) may therefore reflect back on the nature of Derrida's work as well as his own. For Bhabha, it is the exile and the migrant who make it possible for us to unravel the relations of core and periphery by deconstructing the narratives of the nation which are embedded in the culture of both core and periphery.

> The transnational dimension of cultural transformation – migration, diaspora, displacement, relocation – makes the process of cultural translation a complex form of signification. The natural(ized), unifying discourse of 'nation', 'peoples', or authentic 'folk' tradition, those embedded myths of culture's particularity, cannot be readily referenced. The great, though unsettling, advantage of this position is that it makes you increasingly aware of the construction of culture and the invention of tradition. (Bhabha 1994:172)

The 'unifying discourses' to which Bhabha points are discourses both of the imperial centres and of nationalist resistance to imperialism: Bhabha makes no distinction between them. The exile and the migrant live in a 'hybrid location of cultural value' and through their experience can be revealed what the imperial illusions of the core and the nationalist resistances of the peripheries both conceal from themselves, that 'hierarchical claims to the inherent originality or "purity" of cultures are untenable' (Bhabha 1994:173). For Bhabha this is both a theoretical truth – Derridean *différance* resists all essentialist meanings – and a historical fact, since the 'empirical historical instances' do not reveal the 'purity' of nations but 'demonstrate their hybridity' (Bhabha 1994:37). In the light of the hybrid culture of exile and the migrant, what we can see is the hybridity of all cultural formations. From the marginal and peripheral come 'counter-narratives of the nation that continually evoke and erase its totalizing boundaries – both actual and conceptual – disturb those ideological manoeuvres through which "imagined communities" are given essentialist identities' (Bhabha 1994:149). In this sense the poststructuralism of late-twentieth-century Derridean criticism has already been anticipated by the experience of those whose lives have been disrupted by imperialism:

> My growing conviction has been that the encounters and negotiations of differential meanings and values within 'colonial' textuality, its governmental discourses and cultural practices, have anticipated, *avant la lettre*, many of the problematics of signification and judgment, that have become current in contemporary theory – aporia, ambivalence, indeterminacy, the question of discursive closure, the threat to agency, the status of intentionality, the challenge to 'totalizing' concepts, to name but a few. (Bhabha 1994:173)

If the colonial past is – at a linguistic and cultural level – the mirror image of the cosmopolitan present, then the cosmopolitan present is, equally, a mirror image of the colonial past. And what is true of the temporal relations of centre and periphery is true also of their contemporary spatial relations: all are marked by the collapse of the narratives of the nation, by the impossibility of any totalizing framework, by the necessary hybridity of cultural formations. Centre and periphery are no longer at opposite ends of a spectrum of cultural differentiation: they are conjoined by their shared relationship with the minorities which inhabit them, linked by their internal relationship to cultural and political 'communities' that fissure shared national identifications:

> Community is the antagonist supplement of modernity: in the metropolitan space it is the territory of the minority, threatening the claims of civility; in the transnational world it becomes the border-problem of the diasporic, the migrant,

the refugeee. Binary divisions of social space neglect the profound temporal disjunction – the translational time and space – through which minority communities negotiate their collective identifications. (Bhabha 1994:231)

However different centre and margin might be, they are both equally defined by – and deconstructed by – their supplementary communities, so that it is not their difference that is significant but their similarity in relation to that from which they are actually different – their own minority cultures.

Bhabha defines the significance of the migrant and the exile in terms of a 'third space' which comes between the 'I' and the 'You' of any enunciation:

> The intervention of the Third Space of enunciation, which makes the structure of meaning and reference an ambivalent process, destroys this mirror of representation in which cultural knowledge is customarily revealed as an integrated, open, expanding code. Such an intervention quite properly challenges our sense of the historical identity of culture as a homogenizing, unifying force, authenticated by the originary Past, kept alive in the national tradition of the People. (Bhabha 1994:37)

For Bhabha, all nations – core, peripheral or semiperipheral – are equal before the interventionist significance of the Third Space – and equally undermined by it. In his Third Space the opposition of core and periphery is as decisively dissolved as it is in the transcendent humanism of Said, whose counterpoint will generate from a higher reality to which both should aspire. But somewhere in there the peripheries still struggle with the unequal rates of exchange that shape their cultural as well as their economic lives, and for some, at any rate, the struggle will not be towards a higher integration but towards a greater resistance, since the real integration on offer is not the higher humanism or the Third Space but mere immersion in the values of the centre.

IV

The paradox of what Frederic Jameson likes to call 'late capitalism' (Jameson 1991) is that it incorporates the whole of the world into its division of labour (and division of consumption), intensifying at economic and political levels the opposition of centre and periphery, while, at the same time, exporting an international culture which negates the differences between centre and periphery. It is what Roland Robertson describes as 'a massive twofold process involving *the interpenetration of the universalization of particularism and the particularization of universalism*' (Robertson 1992:100). The cultural distinctions on which peripheries could draw to resist the processes of 'globalisation' are thus erased: difference at an economic level turns into sameness at a cultural level; passivity within the imperious commercial domain organized from the centre turns into passivity before – or, indeed, complicity with – its cultural products. The mirror image in which peripheral cultures mimic the culture of the centre – effectively, their Americanization or their Westernization – produces the appearance of a shared rather than a divided world, what Moreiras describes as 'the homogenization of difference' (Moreiras 1998:84). Alternatively, from the perspective of Jameson's account of postmodernism, this can be represented as the fact that 'we are all marginals now' because 'globalization has meant a decentering and proliferation of differences' (Jameson 1998:66). Postmodernity generates difference as the characteristic of both the centre (with its migrants and minority cultures) and the periphery (its boundaries overwhelmed by the displaced, its ethnie disrupted by cultural division). The residually local, in this environment, does not remain outside the workings of homogenization – rather, it is transformed into a spectacle for those in search of difference, a self-conscious orientalism or what Joep Leerssen, discussing nineteenth-century Irish culture, describes as an 'auto-exoticism' (Leerssen 1996:37). In this context, 'centring on the peripheries' develops profoundly ironic overtones: the peripheries morph into miniature versions of the centre, minor monads in a world of pre-established harmonies.

Like Wallerstein's World Systems Theory, however, this version of the postmodern is based on an implicit universalism – capitalism not only dominates the world, it is inherently *singular* and everywhere the same. The technical and technological knowledge that drives its development is also universal and singular, mirrored in the spread of English as the *lingua franca* of international technical and commercial communication. They are 'systems' precisely to the extent that they are orderly, and, within the necessarily incomplete limits of current knowledge, predictable in their operation – thus the emergence of 'futures' markets which negotiate between the openness of the future and the predictability of humanity's needs for certain resources. What has to be recognized, however, is that this 'universality' is little less than an ideology. As Josué V. Harari and David F. Bell put it in their introduction to a selection of the work of Michel Serres,

> Until recently, science had convinced us that in the classification of the spaces of knowledge the local was included in the global, in other words that a path always existed between one local configuration and another, that from local configurations one could always move without break or interruption to a more encompassing global configuration. Clearly this assumption implied a homogeneous space of knowledge ruled entirely by a single scientific or universal truth that guaranteed the validity of the operation of passage. Such a space differs qualitatively from a more complex space in which the passage

from one local singularity to another would always require an arduous effort. Rather than a universal truth, in the more complex case one would have a kind of truth that functions only in the context of local pockets, a truth that is always local, distributed haphazardly in a plurality of spaces. (Serres 1982:xiii)

The local, in effect, is the habitation of truths which escape universalisation; the universal an illusion achieved by ignoring the evidence which disrupts and disturbs the applicability of a 'truth' under all conditions. Thus Newtonian physics works, but works only by ignoring its own limitations. As Ian Stewart describes it, 'One of the common idealizations of Newtonian mechanics is to consider hard elastic particles. If two such particles collide, they bounce off at well-determined angles and speeds. But Newton's laws are not enough to fix the outcome of the simultaneous collision of *three* such particles' (Stewart 1990:33). This was the problem that Poincaré showed in 1890 could not be solved within Newtonian physics (Poincaré 1890), opening the way to what has become known more recently as 'chaos theory' – the study of nonlinear systems in which the magnitudes of cause and effect do not correspond as they do in Newtonian physics. This became famous as the 'butterfly wing' account of the forces involved in the production of weather (Lorenz 1963) but what chaos theory in general asserts is that far from being the exception, such chaotic systems are in fact the normal state of nature. Michel Serres's presentation of the ways in which classical science emerges through the suppression of chaos, through the repeatability of time rather than the unrepeatability of space, presciently suggested how, in the words of N. Katherine Hayles, 'the sciences of chaos make the local/global relation problematic in a way which it was not in older paradigms', because, 'with the onset of chaos, different levels tend to act in different ways, so that locality intrudes itself as a necessary descriptive feature, defeating totalization' (Hayles 1990:210). The desire to construct an *order* out of core-periphery relations is such a totalization: it is equivalent to the effort to impose a Newtonian model on the weather. The kind of knowledge required to understand the workings of peripheries is one which acknowledges the asymmetry of the global and the local, the universal and the particular; one in which, as Serres argues, 'the global does not necessarily produce a local equivalent, and the local itself contains a law that does not always and everywhere reproduce the global' (Serres 1980:75).

Rather than try to model relations of core and periphery in a global hierarchy, we have to study them as a series of different kinds of resistance through which the powers – especially the communications – of the centre are deformed, distorted and reshaped; we have to analyse the ways in which those resistances create disturbances, turbulences, and eruptions which result in chaotic intrusions at the centre. And we have to track the ways in which the same processes discharge themselves in cultural transactions *between* peripheries as well as between the centre and the periphery. To centre on the periphery in this sense is to refuse to write our cultural histories on the model of nineteenth-century railways that run from the centre to the periphery and back again on a single track. To centre on the peripheries requires us to trace the ways in which the peripheries appropriate from each other the tools of cultural resistance, copy forms by which they can adapt to the pressures of outside forces, and remake the differences by which they can continue to live within their own value systems. To the historians and critics of the centre, these pathways will be invisible but their invisibility to the centre is the opportunity of the periphery to construct an alternative kind of history, a different kind of map of the ways in which the past has been shaped, and therefore of the ways in which the future might be shaped.

When, for instance, James Macpherson published his *Fragments of Ancient Poetry* in 1760, he was attempting to re-establish the value of the Highland culture of Scotland which was being rigorously destroyed by the British government for its support of the Jacobite Rising of 1745-46. The materials he used he had, quite literally, collected in a journey around the periphery of the nation, trying to save for posterity what was becoming ever more marginal to modern British society. Within thirty years, Macpherson's work was generally accepted as fraud – a mere fiction of peripherality that could not take its place in an authentic history of literature – and yet during those thirty years it had inspired similar searches for national myths across all of Europe[3] and, especially, had set in motion that search for the real Irish origins of the Ossianic tales whose outcome in the work of W. B. Yeats would be the Irish Revival.[4] In the history of literature written from the perspective of an English centre, Macpherson's work disappears, a mere curiosity of eighteenth-century taste. In a history of Irish literature, like Declan Kiberd's *Inventing Ireland*, it also disappears, because Kiberd is only interested in the centre-periphery relation of England and Ireland. In the relations between Scotland and Ireland, however, Macpherson's work becomes crucial to the modes of cultural survival of two countries trying to deal with their threatened incorporation into the centralizing power of English culture. The turbulence produced by Macpherson's Ossianic poetry was to prove profoundly creative as it was translated from periphery to periphery, continually disrupting the order – both aesthetic and historical – that centre-periphery hierarchies are designed to maintain.

Such creative interactions, it might be argued, become impossible in a world where the telephone and the computer are now the instruments of a universal technology of globalisation. They provide the means by which the peripheries can speak to each other but the medium destroys the very possibility of their having anything to share except their common participation in a global culture. I would like to end, however, by reflecting on Scotland's relationship to the telephone, and to the webbed world it produces, as an instance of the asymmetric interactions of the local and the global. We should bear in mind that the construction of an apparently universal scientific truth or universal technology does not come from nowhere. The fact that it can be applied everywhere does not mean it could have emerged anywhere. What, among those competing to invent the telephone, gave Alexander Graham Bell, a Scot, born in Edinburgh, who had emigrated to Canada only six years before he demonstrated the first telephone at the Philadelphia Centenary Exhibition in 1876, a decisive advantage? It was not that he was a trained scientist or engineer – indeed, in early patent disputes, his lack of a technical background was used to try to undermine his claims to the first production of an effective system. Nor did he have, like Thomas Edison, a team of engineers to work with him. What was crucial was the fact that his father, Melville Bell, had been a teacher of elocution in Edinburgh, a city culturally obsessed with the proprieties and improprieties of the sounds of the English language in Scottish mouths and the sounds of Scottish mouths in English ears.[5] The Bells had emigrated to Canada in order to promote Melville Bell's 'universal alphabet' for the visible presentation of sound, and Alexander Graham Bell was using his father's system in the teaching of the deaf. The study of the transmission of the cultural codifications of sound was gateway to the transmission of electrical energy that could be reconstituted as sound. The apparent disability of the periphery – Scotland's obsessive embarrassment with the ways in which it used the English language – provides the 'disturbance' that generates the new technology in a different environment. Indeed, we might read Macpherson's *Fragments* as representing an inherently telephonic communication, with the blind Ossian responding in a dialogue of which we can hear only one side:

> Why openest thou afresh the spring of my grief, O son of Alpin, inquiring how Oscur fell? My eyes are blind with tears; but memory beams on my heart. How can I relate the mournful death of the head of the people! Prince of the warriors, Oscur, my son, I shall see thee no more! (Gaskill 1996:16)

The notion of the ancient bard in living communication with a modern audience is like a historical telephone, in which the narration of an ancient epic turns into a fragmentary conversation about the recollection of the ancient epic whose complete narration we cannot hear. Bell's advantage over his competitors was not technical – it was that he came from an inherently telephonic society, a society excessively attuned to the ear. The telephone would have happened, of course, but it would not have happened as it did without that disruptive history and without those transfers of energy between the centre (Britain) and periphery (Canada), between periphery (Scotland) and emergent centre (the United States).

If Scotland stands as origin to the telephonic age, might the telephonic not represent the coming abolition of Scotland, and of all the cultural diversity which was founded on the spatial distinction written into the core-periphery paradigm? When the whole world is potentially no further from us than our earpiece or our computer screen, what remains of the distinctiveness of the peripheral? The telephonic, however, is the chaotic, because communication can go in any direction, any distance. And chaos, as we have seen, is the defender of the local. As Claud S. Fischer points out, it is often assumed that the telephone destroys the local, that it is 'an antidote to provincialism', but the most extensive research into the topic insists that the impact of the telephone was 'to augment local ties much more than extralocal ones and that calling strengthens localities against homogenizing cultural forces, such as movies and radio' (Fischer 1992:25).[6] No matter how much we know about the recording of speech, about wiretapping and the possible archiving of every conversation on the network, we treat telephonic communication as private, as internal, as an escape from the rule-bound hierarchies of the external world. Our telephonic voices do not need to bend themselves to the 'rules' of public broadcast, or our typing to the requirements of a public discourse. Thus the localized conventions by which text messages reduce the number of characters in a communication creates an alternative, local language that is the textual equivalent of vernacular speech. The telephonic foregrounds voice over content, interaction over meaning, as exemplified in Tom Leonard's ironically entitled 'hangup', a poem mimicking the simplicity of a digital world in which everything is reduced to only two possibilities – the binaries of yes or no.

aye bit naw

naw bit
aye bit

away
away yi go
whut

mini whur
minmalism

aw minimalism
minimalism aye

aye right
aye right inuff
aye right inuff definitely

aye bit
naw bit

a stull think yi huvty say sumhm
(Leonard 1984:138)

Despite the minimalism of its medium, the telephonic gives voice to the local, it *recalls* the local, it re-establishes the local simply by opening a channel in which you have to 'say sumhm'. The cultural effects of such a telephonic poem are then recreated and megaphoned by those local radio stations that get so much of their content from telephone calls. Through the telephone, the local is rescued from the antiquarian of the 'oriental' and 'auto-exotic' to be able to represent itself to itself.

In Scotland, the status of Scottish speech in relation to Scottish writing had always been presented as one of the stumbling blocks of Scottish literature. In 1978, for instance, Francis Hart's study of *The Scottish Novel* ('was there one?', inquired an English reviewer, condescendingly minimising Hart's extensive account) concluded with a gloomy awareness that Scottish novelists believed 'cultural survival is doomed or unlikely' and that the Scottish novel can never escape the problem of the 'uncertain narrative voice' (Hart 1978:407) produced by the conflict between 'literary' English and the local vernacular. Tom Leonard's lack of any 'hangup' about a vernacular that refused to hangup was, however, to be prologue to an explosion of vernacular literature in Scotland in the 1980s and 1990s. Only six years after Hart's study was published, James Kelman was proving, in *The Busconductor Hines* (Kelman 1984), that it was not only possible to use the vernacular in a novel, it was possible to make the vernacular the very medium of the novel. Far from being a dead literary language lingering on only in local conversation, vernacular Scots emerged in Irvine Welsh's *Trainspotting* (Welsh 1993)[7] as a language in which 'the chemical generation' worldwide could find the defining account of its condition.

The possibility of a novel in Scots becoming an international bestseller would have seemed ludicrous only twenty years earlier – indeed, would have seemed ludicrous at any time in Scotland's history. But *Trainspotting* is symptomatic of the ways in which keeping open the channels of communication with the local may, at any moment, empower artists with the means to reconfigure the present and, therefore, to imagine alternative futures – 'imagine' not in the Andersonian sense of 'create a fiction' but imagine in the sense of 'set an agenda for action'. Accepting the peripheral, maintaining the peripheral, communicating from periphery to periphery – these imply the possibility of a space from which it is possible to critique and to resist the obliterating effects of international capitalism. That the universalising thrust of international capitalism can never finally appropriate or erase the local is a function of the very chaos which it produces: the resistances which it sets in motion, consciously or unconsciously, generate new configurations of local difference that negate the universality to which capitalism aspires. To centre on the peripheries is to focus on the incommensurable relation of cause and effect – the enormous cause that is international capitalism may have effects which seem merely incidental; the 'insignificantly' local may have consequences out of all proportion to its apparent significance. Of course, if I index the significance of the peripheral by the example of a work taken up by, and approved by, the centre, I only enforce the ironies that endlessly circulate when we decide to centre on the peripheries, because by doing so we necessarily disrupt the hierarchies that have shaped our understanding of the order of history, or, indeed, of the order of things.

References

Anderson, B. (1991): *Imagined Communities. Reflections on the Origin and Spread of Nationalism* (revised edition). London & New York: Verso.

Anderson, Perry (1992): *English Questions*. London: Verso.

Bhabha, Homi K. (1994): *The Location of Culture*. London: Routledge.

Bourdieu, Pierre (1993): *The Field of Cultural Production: Essays on Art and Literature*, edited and introduced by Randal Johnson. Cambridge: Polity Press.

Chase-Dunn, C. & Grimes, P. (1995): 'World Systems Analysis', in *Annual Review of Sociology*, vol 21, pp. 387-417.

Chirot, D. & Hall, T. D. (1982): 'World Systems Theory', in *Annual Review of Sociology*, vol. 8, pp. 81-106.

Craig, Cairns (1983): 'Peripheries', in *Cencrastus*, 8; revised version in *Out of History: Narrative Paradigms in Scottish and English Culture*. Edinburgh: Edinburgh University Press, 1996, pp. 11-30.

Craig, Cairns (Gen. ed.) (1987-89): *The History of Scottish Literature*. Aberdeen: Aberdeen University Press.

Devine, T. M. (2003): *The Scottish Empire*. London: Penguin.

Fischer, Claud S. (1992): *America Calling: A Social History of the Telephone to 1940*. Berkeley, Los Angeles, London: University of California Press.

Gaskill, Howard (1991): *Ossian Revisited*. Edinburgh: Edinburgh University Press.

Gaskill, Howard (ed.) (1996): *The Poems of Ossian and Related Works*. Edinburgh:

Edinburgh University Press.

Gellner, Ernest (1964): *Thought and Change.* London: Weidenfeld & Nicholson.

Grosvenor, Edwin S. & Wesson, Morgan (1997): *Alexander Graham Bell: The Life and Times of the Man who Invented the Telephone.* New York: Harry N. Abrams.

Hart, Francis Russell (1978): *The Scottish Novel: A Critical Survey.* London: John Murray.

Hayles, N. Katherine (1990): *Chaos Bound: Orderly Disorder in Contemporary Literature and Science.* Ithaca: Cornell University Press.

Herman, Arthur (2002): *The Scottish Enlightenment: The Scots' Invention of the Modern World.* London: Fourth Estate.

Hobsbawm, E. & Ranger, T. (eds) (1983): *The Invention of Tradition.* Cambridge: Cambridge University Press.

Jameson, Frederic (1991): *Postmodernism or, The Cultural Logic of Late Capitalism.* London: Verso.

Jameson, Frederic (1998): 'Notes on Globalization as a Philosophical Issue', in Jameson, F. & Myoshi, M. (eds): *The Cultures of Globalization.* Durham: Duke University Press.

Kearney, Richard (1997): *Postnationalist Ireland: Politics, Culture, Philosophy.* London: Routledge.

Kelman, James (1984): *The Busconductor Hines.* Edinburgh: Polygon.

Kiberd, Declan (1995): *Inventing Ireland: The Literature of the Modern Nation.* London: Jonathan Cape.

Leerssen, Joep (1996): *Remembrance and Imagination: Patterns in the Historical and Literary Representation of Ireland in the Nineteenth Century.* Cork: Cork University Press, Field Day.

Leonard, Tom (1984): *Intimate Voices 1965-1983.* Newcastle: Galloping Dog Press.

Lorenz, Edward (1963): 'Deterministic Nonperiodic Flow', in *Journal of the Atmospheric Sciences*, 20, pp. 130-41.

McCrone, David (1992): *Understanding Scotland: The Sociology of a Stateless Nation.* London & New York: Routledge.

Moreiras, Alberto (1998): 'Global Fragments: A Second Latinamericanism', in Jameson, F. & Myoshi, M. (eds): *The Cultures of Globalization.* Durham: Duke University Press.

Nairn, T. (1981 [1977]): *The Break-up of Britain: Crisis and Neo-Nationalism.* London: Verso.

Poincaré, Jules Henri (1890): 'Sur le problème des trois corps et les équations de la dynamique', in *Acta Mathematica*, 13, pp. 1-270.

Robertson, Roland (1992): *Globalization: Social Theory and Global Culture.* London: Sage.

Said, Edward W. (1978): *Orientalism: Western Conceptions of the Orient.* London: Routledge.

Said, Edward W. (1993): *Culture and Imperialism.* London: Chatto & Windus.

Serres, Michel (1980): *Hermes V: Le Passage du nord-ouest.* Paris: Minuit.

Serres, Michel (1982): *Hermes: Literature, Science, Philosophy*, ed. Josué V. Harari & David F. Bell. Baltimore: Johns Hopkins University Press.

Stafford, Fiona (1988): *The Sublime Savage: James Macpherson and the Poems of Ossian.* Edinburgh: Edinburgh University Press.

Stewart, Ian (1990 [1989]): *Does God Play Dice? The New Mathematics of Chaos.* Harmondsworth: Penguin.

Wallerstein, Immanuel (1974): *The Modern World System*, vol. 1. New York: Academic Press.

Wallerstein, Immanuel (1979): *The Modern World System*, vol. 2. New York: Academic Press.

Wallerstein, Immanuel (1984): *The Politics of the World-Economy.* Cambridge: Cambridge University Press.

Welsh, Irvine (1993): *Trainspotting.* London: Martin Secker & Warburg.

Williams, Raymond (1963 [1958]): *Culture and Society 1780-1950.* Harmondsworth: Pelican.

Notes

1. The most important of these essays were collected in Nairn (1981) and Perry Anderson (1992).
2. See Wallerstein (1974, 1979 and 1984). For an account of the development of world systems theory, see Chirot & Hall (1982); for its later development see Chase-Dunn & Grimes (1995).
3. See Gaskill (1991) and Stafford (1988).
4. The connection was made explicit when the society established in Dublin in 1852 to collect and publish the ancient Gaelic texts decided to adopt Macpherson's name for the ancient bard rather than the Irish one (Oisin) and called itself the 'Ossianic Society of Dublin'.
5. See Grosvenor & Wesson (1997), especially chapters 1 and 2.
6. The quotation is from Malcolm Willey and Stuart Rice, 'Communication Agencies and Social Life' (1933).
7. See the section entitled 'The Elusive Mr Hunt' (278) for a dramatization of the intervention of the telephone between standard and vernacular speech.

The Gnarled-Pine People: Humility as Nobility in Finland-Swedish Letters

Clas Zilliacus

Finland is a highly forested country, and trees are palpably present in its literature. I propose to examine the symbolic part played by one of them – the pine – in Finland-Swedish literature, from Finland's last decades as a grand duchy and through the interwar years of the independent republic which was born in 1917. Political history will be confronted with elementary semiotics for a look at the imaged notion of the Swedish-speaking population of Finland as a gnarled-pine people. I shall try to outline the genesis and dissemination of this notion through the agency, in the main, of a number of lyrical poets.

This may sound funny, as I should hope it does; it is much funnier in Swedish and other Germanic languages which use the same word for tree-trunk and for tribe. In Swedish I would call my topic 'Martallens stam' (the gnarled pine tribe *or* trunk).[1] The pun is unsubtle yet intentional: the project I am referring to was geared to a double-exposure of tribe and tree. It was an organicist endeavour, meant to signpost a biotope and to signal rootedness in this biotope. For my proposition to gain some credibility I have selected a number of pictorial exhibits that expose the rugged charm of a Nordic gnarled pine.

The cover of Elis Selin's 1931 novel *Utskärs* (Outer Islands; *Figure 1*, overleaf) shows a pine that shouldn't be there at all – how can it take root in solid rock? Selin was a vicar in a little parish that had many more islands and skerries than parishioners, and no regular service to the mainland. The *Utskärs* tree is marked by solitude; on another cover (*Figure 2*, overleaf) the pine has been instructively provided with a human correlative. The man standing straddle-legged in front of his pilot station, telescope in hand, adorns the 1912 edition of an annual almanac published by a society called The Friends of the Swedish-Language Elementary School, a society created in 1882 for the furtherance of general education in Swedish in Finland. The pilot epitomises steadfastness in stormy weather. On his right, the artist has drawn his arboreal counterpart, a knotted pine pressed by perpetual wind against the

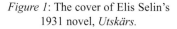

Figure 1: The cover of Elis Selin's 1931 novel, *Utskärs*.

Figure 2: The cover of The Friends of the Swedish-Language Elementary School's 1912 almanac.

granite rock. As on the previous cover, a real pine would be less likely to be growing there. But this does not matter: the pictorial purpose of the pine pressed flat is to imbue the man with uprightness.

Arvid Mörne was no doubt the chief instigator and leading purveyor of the gnarled pine symbol, from his debut at the very turn of the century. A posthumous volume of poems published in 1946 was titled *Solbärgning*, a poetic word for sunset. Its cover pine is broken, cracked, at rest at last (see *Figure 3*, opposite). My examples will have made it clear that this is a tree singled out for suffering on the threshold between land and sea – and that just happens to be the Finland-Swedish biotope, poetically speaking. The Swedophone part of the population (approximately 13 per cent in 1900) had settled on the western and southern coasts and in the archipelago but never ventured far inland. The very first instance of a concrete mapping out of these demographic demarcations is found, in black, on the 1897 cover of the almanac published by the society mentioned above (see *Figure 4*, opposite).

Nature, when touched by the human gaze, becomes infused with 'sign functions'; it becomes a source of symbols. One such resource, most appealing to man, is the anthropomorphism that he finds himself surrounded by. Human beings have no way of not trying to translate the appearance or noises of other living things into human forms or human language.

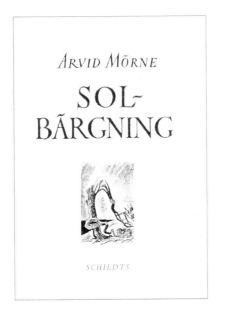

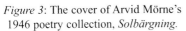

Figure 3: The cover of Arvid Mörne's
1946 poetry collection, *Solbärgning*.

Figure 4: The cover of The Friends of
the Swedish-Language Elementary
School's 1897 almanac.

Finnish artists and poets spent much of the final years of the nineteenth century charging nature with symbolic meaning, and the public duly learned to read these meanings. Much of this work came about as direct or indirect offshoots of the *Kalevala* vogue, which had been initiated in the second quarter of the century. And much of it was articulated in an Aesopian language, using the kind of artful circumlocutions that one tends to take to in the face of censorship. All of it was highly nationalistic, and seemed to emphasise the Finnishness of the country. There were calls for a counter-movement. It was becoming imperative to find ways of charging nature with meaning in Swedish as well, if that language was to have a future in Finland. The language conflict was on the agenda, and increasingly so. A decree stating that Finnish and Swedish were to be placed on an equal footing had been issued in 1863.[2] The obvious purpose of this decree was to adjust the law of the land to linguistic reality. It prescribed a twenty-year interim before taking full effect.

The Swedish-speaking population was nonetheless apprehensive of the progress of the Finnish cause. The degree of anxiety varied from region to region. The province of Nyland (Fi. *Uusimaa*), along the southern coast, had a majority of Swedish speakers, albeit very marginally so (50.2 per cent in 1880). If in what follows I shall be focusing on Nyland, it is because Nyland was the province of the capital. This made it a test area of sorts, where the gamut of social, cultural and economic differences was wide both within and between the two language groups. Nyland is where most of my literary exhibits come from.

The Swedish speakers felt threatened by what became known as the Fennoman movement, that is, the advocates of a purely Finnish-speaking Finland. To ensure the survival of their language, the Swedophones now had to assert their right to be part of that country – and preferably in a potent figurative language that offered counter-images to what had already been achieved for Finnishness. The task of this imagery-to-be was to thematise Swedishness, to link the people to the territory on which they lived by connoting both. A 'natural' or 'organic' image was badly needed, and direly so after the radical overhaul of the parliamentary system in 1906. The move to universal suffrage would bring about a steep decrease in the political representation of the Swedish-speaking segment. A new strategy had to be devised, one which involved convincing the Swedish peasantry, *allmogen*, that it had interests in common with the upper classes. And that strategy was in need of symbols.

We should not be surprised by the choice of a tree for a symbol in a country which is forested to quite a rare degree. But what tree should be singled out?

'Pan-Finnish' trees stud the writings of both Johan Ludvig Runeberg, national poet designate from the mid-nineteenth century onward, and Zacharias Topelius, the country's most popular writer in the same period. Both wrote in Swedish. Neither of the two regarded himself as Swedish, or Finland-Swedish, for that matter. The region of 'Swedish Finland', the 'Finland-Swedes', and the symbolic accoutrements that accompany and distinguish these phenomena were not brought into being until the early decades of the twentieth century.

In 1832 Runeberg had published an ethnographic essay, 'Några ord om nejderna, folklynnet och lefnadssättet i Saarijärvi socken' (Some Words on the Nature, Folk Character, and Way of Life in Saarijärvi Parish). This parish is situated in central Finland and Runeberg's enthralled little tract was instrumental in spreading a picture of the genuine Finn as a creature of his landscape: simple, honest, a man of philosophic joys, a truly authentic being. The awe-inspiring forests of this, the very heart of the country are singled out for contemplation. 'Man vandrar i dem, som på bottnen af ett haf, i en oafbruten enformig stillhet, och hör blott högt öfver sitt hufvud vinden i granarnas toppar eller de skyhöga furornas kronor' (Runeberg 2003:43) (You wander in them as you'd wander on the bottom of a sea, in perpetual uniform stillness, and all you hear, high above your head, is the wind in the spruce fir tops or in the crowns of the pines towering sky-high).[3] Spruce, here, is 'a tree you can't see for the wood', whereas the long-boled pine is a lone giant. There is a third very Finnish tree in the literature of the period, and that is the birch. In lyrical poetry, as in Topelius, the birch was known as fair, leafy and sweet.

The trees whose praise had been sung were all inland trees. Inland, heartland and genuine Finnishness had been conflated in one great manoeuvre by the nation-builder generation born c.1800. As time went by their preferences met with increasing dislike in Swedish-speaking quarters. If we jump all the way to the rather heated language conflicts of the 1930s, we can find, in Swedish-language newspapers, a series of syndicated articles on the topic of coastal region and poetry. The purpose of this series was to foster the readers' feelings for their native ground – that is, for the country's coastal land- and seascapes. Here the luminaries, Runeberg and Topelius, were accused of having spellbound Finland-Swedish poets, and of deafening them to their proper and most urgent concerns. They had strayed afield, 'lured away by the lady of the woods' (Kihlman 1931).

It was not, in fact, until the 1880s that Swedish-language poetry in Finland found its way down to the seaboard. The encounter is now regarded as pivotal in the history of Finland-Swedish literature: it takes place when the young Karl August Tavaststjerna, after what he calls a stifling summer in the smoke of inland slash and burn forest clearance, ventures out to where Helsinki meets the sea, to stand before it in awe. More often than not, the birth of Finland-Swedish literature proper has been dated back to Tavaststjerna.

Now that the coastal region had been reached, which of its trees was a proper candidate for the embodiment of Swedishness? The first writer to use verse to claim a future for the Swedish tongue in Finland was a young student poet, Josef Julius Wecksell. His 'Svenskan och Finskan' (The Swedish Language and the Finnish Language, 1860) is a dialogical poem on the question of nationality. 'Finskan' is a long-boled pine in the heart of the country; 'Svenskan' is a sturdy oak on a stormy skerry. The oak symbol, of course, is of old Germanic stock and hence, in semiotic play, odious to non-oaks. In 1896 Eino Leino, not yet the leading Finnish poet of his era he was to become, decreed that this stocky aristocrat had to go. In his poem 'Tarina suuresta tammmesta' (The Story of the Huge Oak), it is felled at the instigation of Väinämöinen, sage and singer of *Kalevala* fame (Leino 1896). This holy decree was made to the nation from the top of a giant spruce.

Leino's poem was criticised in no uncertain terms by Arvid Mörne, who called it a 'tendentious epopea, drab and strained' (Mörne 1898:256). One can almost discern a poetical plan in Mörne's critique. He wanted to find a tree that would not lend itself to bombast. What he finds, soon after this, is the pine, which in several poems he calls 'our holy tree'; the first person plural possessive standing for the Finland-Swedes. And increasingly it is the stunted version that is being extolled, the twisted and martyred pine that braves any storm because it is firmly rooted on 'the fatherstrand'. This word was coined, or at least given currency, by the poet Theodor Lindh, hailed by Mörne as the creator of Finland-Swedish sea poetry (Mörne 1939:105ff). The coinage is what Iurii Lotman would call a minus device. The model for this phrase is, as we know full well, 'Fatherland'. Here, the coast of Nyland is proclaimed a Finland-Swedish patriot's homeland.

The Swedish speakers were dangling from a ledge. This had been jeeringly noted as early as 1891 by Juhani Aho, a master of Finnish prose and an ideologue of sorts for the 'Young Finns': 'Ruotsalaiset ottivat haltuunsa rantamaan hedelmällisimmän ruokamullan, mutta kun kahden penikulman päässä merestä tuli vastaan suo ja korpi, niin siihen he seisahtuivat' (Aho 1921:7) (The Swedes secured for themselves the most fertile topsoil that the coastland had to offer. But when just a dozen miles from the sea they met with marsh and woodland, they stopped). On the other side of their narrow strip, however, there were vast expanses of water, with no borders in sight and a storm-swept vista, ready-made for heroics. And the *terra firma* closest to these expanses, it bore pointing out, was not fertile topsoil but solid barren rock. The biotope of gnarly trees and a gnarly people was a motif to which Arvid Mörne remained faithful for almost fifty years. *Solbärgning*, the posthumous collection of poems from 1946, opens with a holograph frontispiece entitled 'Bön i nyårsnatten' (A New Year's Night Prayer), an artlessly verbatim and rhymeless translation of which follows the original:

Du, som i nyårsnatten skådar ned
från dina fjärran stjärnevärldar
på vintervita öar, frusna fjärdar,
på mig, ditt dödsinvigda, torra träd,
din martall i sin skreva;
skänk mig en sista vår att leva
i några gröna barr! Du, som gör under,
låt skymta några leende sekunder
grönt barr på dödens ved!

(You who are this New Year's Night looking down
from your far-off star worlds
on winter-white islands, frozen bays,
on me, your dried-up tree, consecrated to death,
your gnarled pine in its crevice,
let me live just one more spring
in a few green needles! You maker of miracles,
for a few smiling seconds let a glimpse be caught of
green needles on the wood of death!)

Figure 5: The cover of Hans Ruin's
Ett land stiger fram (1941).

The gnarled pine, writes Mörne's biographer Hans Ruin, was his way of condensing into one image his threefold pathos – his patriotism, his Swedishness, and his love for the poor and lowly.[4] And Mörne was not alone in these thoughts. Ruin, too, joined the rank of gnarled-pine enthusiasts adopting this image for nationwide use, as seen on the cover of his post-Winter War book, *Ett land stiger fram* (1941; *Figure 5*, above). The title can be translated as 'A Nation Comes Forth', meaning that Finland found more of an identity of its own through this war. The gnarled pine grew into a symbol in common and frequent use during the first half of the present century. It has ceased to proliferate new meanings. The old ones, however, still seem to be taken for granted even when general and mixed audiences are addressed. An occasional poem, a sonnet published in 1984 in a Helsinki broadsheet, *Hufvudstadsbladet*, is a case in point. It moves with great confidence among the received connotations of dogged defiance, surly strength, asceticism, and firmness. It is called 'Utskärstall' (Seaward Skerry Pine), referred to as 'our classic symbol', and it consists of a list of these and additional qualities.[5] No strategies of persuasion are called for here: this fiction is fact.

I shall now turn to a brief survey of the main functions that the gnarled pine was to fulfil and served to fulfil. The paradigm within which a choice was to be made will in what follows be called The Tree. My reading, I should perhaps add, is a brazenly teleological one. It knows what to find.

The Tree was to be non-aristocratic, for a number of reasons. The noble oak had to go. I already mentioned the overhaul of the parliamentary system in 1906. The move towards universal suffrage meant that the image of the Finland-Swede had to be rendered more rustic, less manorial. This was important as part of a new strategy for the Swedophone population; it was useful, too, in order to qualify Finnish notions of what Swedishness in Finland implied.

Yet it is obvious that there is an air of nobility, of *pauvres honteux*, about the gnarled pine. It flaunts the haughty pride of its long-boled kin. As a phenotype it compares with, for example, stunted Sierra Nevada pines like the *aristata* or *longaeva*, which are respected by dendrologists as true aristocrats. It is, I think, hard to overrate the Germanic – or Aryan – associations offered by the gnarled pine, as opposed to the hordes of spruce come from the East. In a bard like V. K. E. Wichmann, an unmistakable Vikingophile better known under his *nom de plume*, Gånge Rolf (Rollo), these associations are orchestrated with an endearing lack of abashment. The final stanza of a 1908 poem of his addresses 'min egen folkstam af ariskt blod / med svenskens solljusa lynne' (my own tribe of Aryan blood / with the sunny temper of Swedes); the survival instinct of this tribe is on a par with the toil of a pine on a rocky skerry, or a flower in the crevice of a cliff': 'som tallen sträfvar på stenigt skär / och blomman i bergets skrefva' (Wichmann 1919:27). A similar coupling was seen on the almanac cover featuring pine and pilot: the biotope they have in common will perforce render them similar.

The Tree was to embody an idea of defiant masculinity. It was also to provide a contrast with the leafy Topelian birch, epitome of the grace and peacefulness of inland Finland. And it was to be ever vigilant, always on guard; this is why deciduous trees would not do. There are quite a number of deciduous trees – alder or rowan, for example – which are far more common on the outermost skerries than pines. But they are not evergreen. Moreover, they are bushlike, and the bush had already been claimed. The sole evergreen bush in the country was taken. It had been appropriated through Juhani Aho's 1891 definition of Finns as a juniper people, an epithet that Aho reiterated almost as diligently as Mörne repeated his. It has become part of national lore:

> Yläilmoista iskevä ukkonen musertaa pirstaleiksi korpikuusen, mutta katajikkoon se tupsahtaa voimatonna. Sotaratsut ajavat siitä ylitse, ja kanuunavaunujen rattaat saattavat taivuttaa sen maata myöten. Mutta kataja ei katkea. [...] Ja kun yliajaja huomenna hakee eilisiä jälkiään, ei hän enää niitä löydä. Tie on kasvanut umpeen, ja katajikko näyttää koskemattomalta. (Aho 1921:8)

(The lighting that strikes from on high leaves the pine of the wilds in splinters but the juniper bush is hit unharmed. The chargers speed over it, and the gun-carriage wheels bend it to the ground. But the juniper will not break. [...] And when tomorrow he who ran over it comes searching for yesterday's tracks, he can no longer find them. The road is no longer there, and the juniper seems untouched.)

Aho's subject here is how to confront a superior force, be it Swedish, Russian or otherwise. His immediate allusion was the endeavour current at the time to russify the country. His polarisation – bend or break – is a proven one. Aesop, like La Fontaine, had contrasted oak and reed. Juhani Aho now exchanges this classic pair for one with marked national traits. Trees as emblems give way to demands for realism, for images of resistance. In a way, Aho's choice of the juniper brought about the choice of the gnarled pine: the two of them are so similar that their dissimilarity is brought to the fore. We now have a polemic that allows for fine adjustment.

One of the opposites activated here is that of collectivism versus individualism. Aho's Finnish junipers are a resilient multitude. The gnarly Swede is a solitary hero, a watchman, an outpost – but also a demoted centre figure who now extols the moral superiority of the margin. He takes on all of these roles in Mikael Lybeck's 1903 poem 'Trötta träd' (Tired Trees), known as *the* definitive example of gnarled-pine poetry. The middle stanza (of three) runs:

Bryt våra stammar, storm, och bryt de sista
rötternas motstånd i gammal jord!
Natten förråder det icke,
vågorna lägga sig icke –
ingen morgon väntar oss,
endast det: att brista, ej böjas... blott brista.

(Break our trunks, storm, and break the last
roots still resisting in age-old soil!
Night will not reveal it,
the waves will not subside –
there is no morning in store for us,
only this: to break, not bend... just break.)

The poem has two motifs, political misfortune from without (Finland *v.* Russia) and language strife from within (Swedish *v.* Finnish). It is close to the concerns of the Aho text. But the symbol is a different one, and the expected outcome is different indeed: 'there will be no break of day for us'.

The pines standing sentry on their rock sing the paean of a minority to itself. Being solitary, small in numbers, forgotten – all of these are aspects of haughty self-pity. But then there is the breakability, which is also tacitly opposed to the pliability, or compliancy, of the juniper people. Lybeck's poem is an apotheosis of passive haughtiness, whether one looks at it from the pro-Swedish or from the anti-Russian angle. We might call it a *non possumus* stand, of the kind which is liable to end in tragedy. The cracked-tree cover of Arvid Mörne's *Solbärgning* showed us the scripted finale. And that is about the last we hear of the gnarled pine, as an active passive force. The Finland that emerged from the Second World War is known in Finnish historiography as the Second Republic. It was a distinctly post-war player, a pragmatic survivor, with little use for heroic antics.

References

Aho, J. (1921): *Kootut teokset* VI. Porvoo: Werner Söderström OY.

Kihlman, E. (1931): 'Vår hembygd och vår dikt', (e.g.) *Svenska Pressen*, 10 October, p. 5.

Leino, E. (1896): *Tarina suuresta tammesta y. m. runoja*. Porvoo: Werner Söderström OY.

Lybeck, M. (1903): *Dikter. Tredje samlingen*. Stockholm: Albert Bonniers förlag.

McRae, K. D. (1997): *Conflict and Compromise in Multilingual Societies: Finland*, vol. 3. Waterloo: Wilfried Laurier University Press.

Mörne, A. (1898): 'Ungfinsk lyrik'. *Finsk Tidskrift* XXXXV, pp. 249-261

Mörne, A. (1946): *Solbärgning*. Helsingfors: Holger Schildts förlag.

Mörne, A. (1947): *Vårstorm. Lyrik i urval 1899-1919*. Urv. verkställt av Hans Ruin. Helsingfors: Holger Schildts förlag.

Runeberg, J. L. (2003): *Samlade skrifter* VIII:2. *Uppsatser och avhandlingar på svenska. Journalistik*, ed. Pia Forssell. Stockholm: Svenska Vitterhetssamfundet.

Wichmann, V. K. E. (1919): *Svenskhets-sånger av Gånge Rolf* [Songs of Swedishness by G. R.]. Vasa: Fram.

Zilliacus, B. (1984): 'Utskärstall'. *Hufvudstadsbladet*, 19 August, p. 5

Zilliacus, C. (1991): 'Om uppodlingen av ett finlandssvenskt symbolträd', *Sphinx*. Societas Scientiarum Fennica Series B. Yearbook 1991. Helsingfors: SSF, pp. 49-58.

Notes

1. This is, in fact, the future title of a study in progress, parts of which are summarised in this paper. For a slightly more substantial discussion (in Swedish) the reader is referred to Zilliacus 1991.
2. A good account of the history of the language question in Finland is found in McRae 1997.
3. This and subsequent translations from Swedish or Finnish by the author.
4. Ruin, 'Företal' (Preface), in Mörne 1947:8.
5. Be[nedict] Z[illiacus] 1984. 'Bez', the acronym at the foot of the poem, was transparent to readers of *Hufvudstadsbladet*.

Edith Södergran:
When Karelia was the Centre

Nalle Valtiala

I

V. S. Naipaul most brilliantly reminds us of the fact that geographical remoteness does not preclude cultural centrality. In the Swedish literary field, voices can easily be found to support this view; all one has to do is look at the literature written in Finland. In political terms, Sweden lost Finland as its eastern province as a consequence of the so-called Finnish War of 1808-09, but in literary terms the unity is still largely unbroken. A group of some 300,000 people, comprising not quite 6 percent of the present population of Finland, have not only kept the Swedish language alive, but have constituted – and still constitute – the substratum for a statistically unlikely number of talented writers. Whether this gives the Swedish-speaking part of Finland the right to proclaim itself Centre of Swedish letters on the threshold of the third millennium is a matter upon which I will abstain from expressing an opinion.

In an earlier day, however, i.e. in the four decades from 1837 to 1877, the literary centre of the Swedish language was quite expressly located far to the east. These are the decades that coincide with Johan Ludvig Runeberg's residence in Borgå, a small town located a good day's ride east of Helsinki. Bedridden by paralysis from 1863 to his death, Runeberg was comforted not only by his status as National Poet of Finland but also by the uncontestable fact that he had by then realised Zachris Topelius's prophesy that Runeberg would 'störta tegnerismen i svenska vitterheten' (quoted in Söderhjelm 1906:54) (destroy the Tegnerism in Swedish belles-lettres). When Runeberg disappeared from the scene, the centre was shifted from the periphery back to Stockholm, only to rebound even further east, in fact to the easternmost fringe of the Swedish language domain and beyond: St Petersburg and the Karelian Isthmus. This radical disturbance in the order of the universe occurred two short generations after Runeberg's death, with the birth of Edith Södergran.

II

Edith Södergran's earthly existence was brief; she lived from 1892 to 1923. She was born in St Petersburg, where she attended school. Both her parents were of Swedish-speaking Finnish stock. Her father, a drifter by nature, had set up a prospering forestry business in the former Russian capital. For a number of years the Södergrans were well-off, but their fortune melted rapidly away in the Russian revolution. The family situation got worse when Edith's father died of tuberculosis. Before turning 16, Edith contracted the same disease from him. In spite of receiving treatment in Nummela, a sanatorium in Finland, and, especially, in Switzerland, she never regained her health. When not hospitalised, Edith lived with her mother in what remained of the family fortune, a large villa in Raivola (the Rosjtjino of today) on the Karelian Isthmus, some sixty miles north-west of St Petersburg, where they had spent their summers in earlier days. Consumption was to take her life. A constant awareness of death and the typical flushed state of a consumptive person had such an indisputable influence on her poetry it could be described as instrumental in the shaping of Södergran as a major poet.

Edith was enrolled at *Die deutsche Hauptschule zu S:t Petri*, the top German school of its kind in St Petersburg, in the autumn of 1902. Having fallen ill, she quit school after completing the autumn term of 1908-09. As a student Edith showed great promise, excelling in languages and literature. She developed crushes on some of her teachers, yet still found time to respond to the current political situation in Russia: the murky and repressive Tsarist regime caught her ire. In St Petersburg – and later in Arosa and Davos-Dorf (October 1911-March 1914) – the young girl was highly stimulated by an international atmosphere. She spoke seven languages, with German as number one, and read extensively. Edith was influenced by Russian futurism, German expressionism, aesthetic idealism, and modernism in a broad sense, as well as by charismatic thinkers such as Schopenhauer, Nietzsche and Steiner, not to mention the avantgarde of the feminist movement.

Edith Södergran's poetical career started at school. Her earliest poems, collected in the *Vaxdukshäftet* (Wax-Cloth Copybook; see Enckell 1961), are almost exclusively in German. One poem, written in Russian, seems to indicate that the young poet could easily have made her career also in the majority language. But having settled down in Raivola, Edith switched to Swedish, the language she would stick to until the end. She managed to publish four collections of poetry in her life: *Dikter* (Poems), in 1916; *Septemberlyran* (The September Lyre), in 1918; *Rosenaltaret* (The Rose Altar), in 1919; and *Framtidens skugga* (Future's Shadow), in 1920. Her last poems appeared posthumously, under the title *Landet som icke är* (The Land That Is Not).

Edith Södergran's poetry has been translated into all the major and some of the minor European languages. With his translations in *The Collected Poems of Edith Södergran* (1980), Martin Allwood raised the status of the poet in the English-speaking world; four years later David McDuff did the same with *Edith Södergran: Complete Poems*. In 1990, he was joined by Gounil Brown: *Poems by Edith Södergran*. A bilingual centennial edition, *Love & Solitude*, edited by Stina Katchadourian (also the author of a play, *The Raspberry Patch*, based on the correspondence between Edith Södergran and her literary friend Hagar Olsson) saw publication in 1992.

Edith Södergran's disease was discovered on a New Year's Day; she expired on a Midsummer's Day. From the perspective of posterity, her life span appears as only a Midsummer Night's Dream; put in another way, a tale told by a genius, full of sound and fury and deep melancholia, signifying something.

III

No serious scholar would question Edith Södergran's qualities today, but only a small group of contemporaries were open-minded enough to acclaim her while she was alive. Literary modernism in general was still alien country to the majority of common readers, who were raised on traditional poetry with rhyme and reason; and to such folk Edith Södergran was modernism personified. What especially provoked them was the grandiloquent tone in many of the poems. Consider for example 'Makt' (Might) in *Framtidens skugga* (1957:133):

> Jag är den befallande styrkan. Var finnas
>   de som följa mig?
> Även de största bära sin sköld på drömmar-
>   sätt.
> Finnes det ingen som läser hänförelsens
>   kraft i mina ögon?
> Finns det ingen som fattar, då jag med låg
>   röst säger lätta ord till de närmaste?
> Jag följer ingen lag. Jag är lag i mig själv.
> Jag är människan som tager.

(I am the commanding strength. Where are those who will / follow me? / Even the greatest bear their shields like dreamers. / Is there no one who can read the power of ecstasy in my eyes? / Is there no one who can understand when in a low voice I say / light words to those nearest? / I follow no law. I am a law unto myself. / I am the person who takes) (Trans. David McDuff).

Also Sprach Zarathustra. A moll from a one-horse town in the middle of nowhere, with the cheek to claim Nietzsche's mantle! No wonder the asses were braying. The empathetic, yet in another way patronising interpretation of Södergran's poetry as being largely the psychotherapeutic daydreams of a consumptive came later, with scholars such as Gunnar Tideström (1949, *passim*) and Olof Enckell (1949, *passim*). Latter-day specialists tend to look upon this view as being way too narrow, albeit not necessarily incorrect as such.

Without having access to the total bulk of Södergraniana, I venture the opinion that Tideström's *Edith Södergran* (1949) is the most enjoyable of the books written on the subject. Neither can I at this point suppress my memory of Olof Enckell's lecture series on the Edith Södergran of *Vaxdukshäftet*. My professor of Swedish at the University of Helsinki devoted an entire term of Saturday morning lectures to a schoolgirl's first efforts, later to be published as a book. This was in the late fifties; the lecture hall was packed with people, mostly students enrolled in other faculties – surely an absurdity in the present cybernetic twilight. Thus my interest in Södergran was launched. If Olof Enckell had dealt with Södergran's mature period as closely as with her adolescent efforts, he would have kept going until his death.

With *Vaxdukshäftet* given its due, Edith Södergran's poetry could be divided into four parts. Usually, however, the early part, consisting mostly of German poems, is left out. The common way of looking at her oeuvre is to see it split in three sections: an early, comparatively tranquil set of poems (published in *Dikter*), with femininity, sexual relations, and nature as dominant elements; an apocalyptic, Dionysian part (expressed in *Septemberlyran*, *Rosenaltaret* and *Framtidens skugga*); and a low-key, meditative, Christian epilogue (posthumously collected in *Landet som icke är*), in token of approaching death. For obvious reasons, no exact borderlines can be drawn, and some scholars refuse to take any particular account of them in the first place. For example, Ebba Witt-Brattström, in *Ediths jag* (1997), senses a strong current of superfeminism throughout Edith Södergran's career, ensuring her a top position among the feminist writers of the early nineteen hundreds, together with Lou Salomé, Ellen Key, Zinaida Hippius, Else Lasker-Schüler, Anna Achmatova, and others. On the other hand, Holger Lillqvist, in his study *Avgrund och paradis* (2001), makes a great effort to connect the poet with the aesthetic idealism of philosophers and writers such as Kant, Schopenhauer, Stagnelius, Wordsworth and Baudelaire – without losing sight of Friedrich Nietzsche. On one hand only female peers, on the other an all-male cast; yet the poet can, with no breach of logic, be linked to either sex. As Edith Södergran herself has already made perfectly clear in *Dikter*, the virginity she cultivates is of a distinctly androgynous kind. 'Vierge moderne' (1957:15) – a poem that could just as well have been written this year – shows the Tintomara of Finnish-

Swedish letters in an ego trip of unsurpassable magnitude:

Jag är ingen kvinna. Jag är ett neutrum.
Jag är ett barn, en page och ett djärvt beslut,
jag är en skrattande strimma av en schar-
    lakanssol...
Jag är ett nät för alla glupska fiskar,
jag är en skål för alla kvinnors ära,
jag är ett steg mot slumpen och fördärvet,
jag är ett språng i friheten och självet...
Jag är blodets viskning i mannens öra,
jag är en själens frossa, köttets längtan
    och förvägran,
jag är en ingångsskylt till nya paradis.
Jag är en flamma, sökande och käck,
jag är ett vatten, djupt men dristigt upp till knäna,
jag är eld och vatten i ärligt sammanhang
    på fria villkor...

(I am no woman. I am a neuter. / I am a child, a page-boy, and a bold decision, / I am a laughing streak of a scarlet sun... / I am a net for all voracious fish, / I am a toast to every woman's honor, / I am a step toward luck and toward ruin, / I am a leap in freedom and the self... / I am the whisper of desire in a man's ear, / I am the soul's shivering, the flesh's longing / and denial, / I am an entry sign to new paradises. / I am a flame, searching and brave, / I am water, deep yet bold only to the knees, / I am fire and water, honestly combined, / on free terms...) (Trans. Stina Katchadourian).

Edith Södergran's self-consciousness, which has been compared to the limitless egocentricity of Thomas Thorild, is a strong armour shielding a hypersensitive soul. When the poetess casts off her coat of mail, as she often does, the effect is quite a different one; to quote Lillqvist, 'transcendensens eufori' (the euphoria of transcendence) is transferred into 'immanensens melankoli' (2001:403) (the melancholy of immanence). In *Dikter*, there is a balance between these poles; in the three subsequent collections the euphoria becomes the dominant tone, occasionally transcending into a region of Arctic chill. I am referring to poems such as 'Världen badar i blod...' (The World is Bathing in Blood) and 'Månens hemlighet' (The Moon's Secret) in *Septemberlyran*, poems drenched in a blood mystique inspired by the Great War and the Russian Revolution, as it were endorsed by the Kantian concept of the sublime. Expertly phrased as such lyrical expressions may be, they reveal an attitude not altogether acceptable. But this can be seen as a necessary phase in a fatally sick young woman's progress towards the dark finality of the raspberry patch, evoked in her last poems; Edith Södergran seems even herself to have been revolted by her audacity. Personally, I do not hesitate to join those readers that prefer the early and the late Södergran to the raving Lady Nietzsche of the middle period.

No boisterous modernist – or, if one wishes, post-romantic – messianism can surpass the complex fragility of an early poem such as 'Dagen svalnar...' (1957:8-9) This is a poem split into four parts, each constituting a universe of its own. The first part runs as follows:

> Dagen svalnar mot kvällen...
> Drick värmen ur min hand,
> min hand har samma blod som våren.
> Tag min hand, tag min vita arm,
> tag mina smala axlars längtan...
> Det vore underligt att känna,
> en enda natt, en natt som denna,
> ditt tunga huvud mot mitt bröst.

> (The day cools toward evening... / Drink the warmth from my hand, / it throbs with spring's own blood. / Take my hand, take my white arm, / take the longing of my slender shoulders... / How wondrous it would be to feel, / one single night, a night like this, / your heavy head against my breast) (Trans. Stina Katchadourian).

Tintomara has, ostensibly, been transformed into a young woman, communicating with her male lover, who initially seems to be present, but who, in the last sentence, rather appears to wither away into wishful thinking. In the second part of the poem, the 'thou' of the intimate relation is said to have been present on an earlier occasion; he has cast 'din kärleks röda ros / i mitt vita sköte' (your love's red rose / into my white womb), which implies a sexual consummation. The lovers' tryst has not been a meeting between equals; the male protagonist is a 'härskare med kalla ögon' (master with [your] frozen eyes) offering his female subject a crown so heavy that her head is bent towards her heart. In the third part of 'Dagen svalnar...', the speaker finally recognises her master. The encounter has made her shiver, she feels the impact of his heavy hand on her light arm. Through this experience she has lost her proud female freedom, together with her 'klingande jungfruskratt' (ringing maidenly laughter). The mood has darkened; harsh reality has replaced the sweet daydreams of the young female voice.

The master figure of the poem, with his cold eyes and heavy hands, has – for obvious reasons – been the object of more or less profound speculation. Scholars with a biographical bent have made efforts to spot in him the features of Henri Cottier, Edith's French teacher at the S:t Petri Schule, as well as Dr Ludwig von Muralt, the head of the sanatorium in Davos. Edith evidently had a crush on both. A more enigmatic figure, in fact a person whose identity nobody has been able to establish, was a man, a resident of Raivola or thereabouts, with whom some scholars wish to speculate that the poetess had had a brief sexual affair. In fact, this man may not even have existed – unless he was the neighbour accused by Edith Södergran's mother of killing her daughter's favourite cat in cold blood.

There are, however, also a number of less quotidian interpretations of the male figure in 'Dagen svalnar...' The ruler could be a literary resurrection of Nietzsche, the spiritual father turned rhetorical lover. Rudolf Steiner, for a while an almost equally important source of inspiration to the poetess, is another possible model, Schopenhauer a third. Finally, there is the quintessentially sublime figure of Christ, the great comforter of Edith's terminal phase – who, in that case, makes another appearance in 'Landet som icke är': 'där går min älskade med gnistrande krona' (my beloved walks with brilliant crown). For all we know, the features hiding behind 'min herre' could be all of the characters mentioned here rolled into one – or none. Whether primarily engineered by Nietzsche's message about the Übermensch or – with reference to a trope in 'I feernas hängmatta' (In the Fairies' Hammock) in *Rosenaltaret* – the 'Dianas lampa' of superfeminism shining 'genom mina nätter' (through my nights), such influences can, I would like to suggest, also be seen as being radically altered by a filter of solipsism. If so, the male counterpart is in fact reduced – or perhaps enlarged – into the masculine half of an androgynous ego. The disappointment expressed in the fourth part of 'Dagen svalnar...' is, in this reading, turned inwards, as a reaction against an evolutionary *fait accompli*, a state of finality implying the end of personal growth. Yet I would not deny that a less sophisticated reading of part IV as a feminist woman's proud address to a male, set on objectifying her sex, may sound at least equally plausible:

> Du sökte en blomma
> och fann en frukt.
> Du sökte en källa
> och fann ett hav.
> Du sökte en kvinna
> och fann en själ –
> du är besviken.

> (You looked for a flower / and found a fruit. / You looked for a well / and found a sea. / You looked for a woman / and found a soul – / I disappoint you) (Trans. Stina Katchadourian).

I can easily think of one more interpretation (as in Shakespeare, surely the possible readings are innumerable): in this instance the poetess is directly addressing the reader. As has already been noted, the great bulk of her first-generation readers turned down their thumbs. This is hardly surprising; surely, the sublimity of the sea is too much of a good thing for someone bent on the beauty or picturesqueness of a spring; and a woman is a lot easier to handle than a soul. Yet Edith Södergran was and remains a soul, packed with the *animus* and *anima* of a complex personality. Complex, and indeed tragic, in its hectic brevity. Her poignant biography has touched the hearts of generations of readers; braving the accusation of sentimentality, I maintain that it requires a special effort to read Edith Södergran dry-eyed. As concerns *Dikter* and *Landet som icke är*, such a reaction ought not to be dependent on any facts about her life whatsoever.

Throughout her career, in her ecstatic outbursts as well as in her melancholic moods, she advanced with unhesitating strides in the avant-garde of modernism – undisputed by none in the sphere of form, casting off the fetters of tradition without a second thought. '*Jag följer ingen lag. Jag är lag i mig själv.*' Keep in mind the amazing case of Edith Södergran's almost total isolation from her own language domain – in this respect a parallel case to Franz Kafka. Thus, as Gunnar Ekelöf has noted, her Swedish was a language whose 'arkaiskt kantiga, grammatikaliskt inlärda vändningar förråder bristen på kontakt med modersmålet och dess organiska utveckling' (quoted in Witt-Brattström 1997:46) (archaically awkward, grammatically acquired phrases reveal a lack of contact with the vernacular and its organic development; my translation). With a firmness put upon a par with *The Trial* and *The Metamorphosis*, works to my knowledge conceived in Prague, on the outskirts of the German language domain, *The Land That Is Not* and the works preceding it have reversed the positions of periphery and centre.

IV

'*Jag följer ingen lag. Jag är lag i mig själv.*' Yet there is one force in the universe which will, sooner or later – in Edith Södergran's case, sooner – silence even the Titans: the kiss of Death. In her sixteenth year, the kiss was (inadvertently) offered by her father's lips. Fighting Keats's and Chekhov's disease for the rest of her life, with a spirit ranging from wild inebriation to darkest melancholia, the recluse of Raivola (*Fury's Place* in Finnish) rose from obscurity to the position of high priestess of Swedish literary modernism. The asses brayed, but Hagar Olsson and Elmer Diktonius went on pilgrimage to the holy shrine, where today a statue of Totti, Edith's favourite cat, commemorates the brief earthly existence and long-lasting triumph of its mistress. With Edith Södergran in the lead, lyrical modernism flourished in the Swedish part of Finland, including outstanding poets such as Gunnar Björling, Rabbe Enckell and R. R. Eklund, soon transforming the lyrical scene in Sweden as well. As a mark of this, Gunnar Ekelöf's *Färjesång* (1941) is generously seasoned with intertextual references to Södergran's work; and in Harry Martinson's grand space epic *Aniara* (1956) the young maiden from the Karelian Isthmus is resurrected in the figure of the blind poet in Songs 49 and 58, and *passim*. An inspired celebration of the human spirit and a homage to Edith Södergran:

> Och undret som hon förde med sig hit
> var människosjälens lek med språkens själ
> och visionärens lek med ve och väl. (Martinson 1982:48,4)

> (The miracle that she had brought along
> was human soulplay on the soul of words,
> the visionary's play on weal and woe) (Martinson 1991:80).

References

Allwood, Martin (1980): *The Collected Poems of Edith Södergran*. Mullsjö *et al.*: Anglo-American Center.

Brown, Gounil (trans.) (1990): *Poems by Edith Södergran*. Gwynedd, Wales: Zena.

Katchadourian, Stina (trans.) (1992): *Love & Solitude: Edith Södergran: Selected Poems 1916-1923*. Seattle: Fjord Press.

Enckell, Olof (1949): *Esteticism och nietzscheanism i Edith Södergrans lyrik*. Helsingfors: Söderströms.

Enckell, Olof (1961): *Vaxdukshäftet: En studie i Edith Södergrans ungdomsdiktning*. Helsingfors: Söderströms.

Lillqvist, Holger (2001): *Avgrund och paradis*. Helsingfors: Svenska litteratursällskapet i Finland.

McDuff, David (trans.) (1992 [1984]): *Edith Södergran: Complete Poems*. Newcastle upon Tyne: Bloodaxe.

Martinson, Harry (1982 [1956]): *Aniara*. Stockholm: Bonniers.

Martinson, Harry (1991): *Aniara: A Review of Man in Time and Space*, trans. Stephen Klass & Leif Sjöberg. Södra Sandby: Vekerum.

Södergran, Edith (1949): *Samlade dikter*, ed. Gunnar Tideström. Helsingfors: Holger Schildts.

Södergran, Edith (1957): *Samlade dikter*. Helsingfors: Holger Schildts.

Söderhjelm, Werner (1906): *Joh. Ludv. Runeberg: Hans lif och hans diktning*, II. Helsingfors.

Tideström, Gunnar (1991 [1949]): *Edith Södergran*. Stockholm: Wahlström & Widstrand.

Witt-Brattström, Ebba (1997): *Ediths jag*. Stockholm: Norstedts.

Norrland and the Question of Cultural Identity

Anders Öhman

To connect Norrland with the question of cultural identity seems to presuppose the existence of a Norrland quite separate from the rest of Sweden. This might give rise to a number of different reactions. Some people could perhaps associate this with a kind of musty provincialism nurturing local folklore. To others it might have a flavour of newly bred nationalism and ethnic chauvinism, not unlike the examples we meet daily from the former Eastern Bloc countries. A few people may also think of the old concepts of stable, intrinsic, identities, which are impossible to uphold in a postmodern world.

In spite of these dangers it is my belief that we must dare to start speaking about a Norrlandic cultural identity. The concept of cultural identity is, by the way, not unproblematic, and I will return to its complexity later. On a rather simple and everyday level, however, it seems easy to accept the argument that identity does not come from within, but is formed in relation to others.

If you live in Norrland, whether you were born there or have lived there for some time, you are bound to have experienced how others regard you and have prejudices against you as a Norrlander. Most Norrlanders react ironically when watching the weather forecasts on TV. These begin by giving very detailed information on what the weather is going to be like in the south of Sweden, and then finish off by saying that in Norrland, it is going to be cold. The vast and disparate Norrland, which accounts for almost two thirds of the Swedish land mass, is lumped together in a very general and vague forecast. Another example was encountered by the author in an advertising brochure while at the cinema waiting for a film to begin. The brochure contained an article on a forthcoming horror movie about five young scientists who were heading into a burnt forest in order to examine the biological changes. The headline of the article, a play on the promotional tag line for the film *Alien*, was probably meant to attract our fear of the unknown: 'I Norrland kan ingen höra dig skrika!' (In Norrland no one can hear you scream). A similar headline from *Dagens Nyheter*, one of the biggest-selling Swedish broadsheets, in August 2000 proclaimed: 'Tysk turist försvunnen i Norrland' (German tourist missing in Norrland).

These examples, as well as countless others, express a rather naive notion of Norrland as the amorphous and unknown territory, which is quite easily countered by pointing towards the specific, towards the fact that there is no one 'Norrland' common to the experience of everybody who lives there, but rather different places, districts, and landscapes.

Even if this approach seems naive, it is not all that innocent. Historically, we find that the notion of Norrland as the great unknown has a long tradition, but so have attempts to invent another Norrland. From the seventeenth and eighteenth centuries when Norrland first becomes a concept to the rest of Sweden, it is as a Norrland that lacks an identity of its own and which is an object for the central power of Sweden. It would not be too bold to label this view 'colonial'. In 1635, for example, a member of the government, the Councellor Carl Bonde, wrote to the King's advisor Axel Oxenstierna, after silver had been found in Nasafjäll, that he was hoping Norrland would become Sweden's 'West Indies' (Sörlin 1988:30). Norrland was seen basically as 'nature' and 'natural resources', i.e. the opposite of culture, and it is typical that, in a government proclamation of 1673, those who sacrificed themselves and settled in Norrland in order to help with the distribution of its natural resources, were granted freedom from taxes and military service (Sörlin 1988:33).

With only a slight exaggeration one could say that it was during this period that the standard clichés about Norrlanders being uncommunicative, tough, poor, uncultivated, and lower-class were founded. It was not just anybody who would agree to settle down in a country characterised by its thinly spread population, rough landscape (tough), lack of real industry but abundance of natural resources (poor and underdeveloped), lack of cultural meeting places and aristocracy (uncultivated). This view of Norrland still lingers on. In recent debates on the future of thinly populated areas, for example, some researchers launched the argument that because the greater part of Norrland had only been populated for about a hundred years, it would only be natural if it were to become depopulated again. Behind this kind of argument lies the belief that in relation to the centre, Norrland is just a periphery, lacking an identity of its own.

It was not until the turn of the twentieth century that an alternative to these ideas on Norrland began to develop. The reason why it happened at this moment in time was violent industrialisation and modernisation, which having began in the 1850's acquired an almost explosive speed in the last decades of the century. From 1840 to 1910 the population of Norrland more than doubled, from 400,000 to more than one million inhabitants. Between 1870 and 1900 the population increased by 100,000 a decade. However, as not all of those who settled in Norrland cared to register as inhabitants, the real number was probably even higher. These figures may seem relatively insignificant, but it should be remembered that Sweden at the time only had about three and a half million inhabitants in total.

A hundred years may have passed but not much has changed. The concept of Norrland as a repository of natural resources still dominates, even if these natural resources are painted in a more colourful way. Norrland is characterised as a Klondike with great opportunities for the self-made man who is daring and persistent enough to create a fortune of his own.

There are, as I have already mentioned, signs that Norrland was being re-invented as a place with a culture and an identity of its own, in the hands of ravenous capitalists (some of them from Scotland) from whom it had to break loose. The question of Norrland's future had become the object of much debate, and for several writers it was no longer the West Indies but Ireland which became their point of comparison. As long ago as 1894, Jonas Stadling wrote a series of articles in the Swedish newspaper *Aftonbladet* under the heading 'Vår irländska fråga' (Our Irish question). He described the population of Norrland as exposed, poor and exploited, but also prepared to either revolt or emigrate (Stadling 1987:223). The comparison with Ireland implies a similar colonial oppression by Sweden in relation to the Norrlanders as that of the British Empire in relation to the Irish, who by that time either emigrated to the United States or rebelled against their British oppressors.

It is particularly in fiction that this different Norrland is starting to take shape. Novels like Olof Högberg's *Den stora vreden* (The Great Wrath) from 1906 try to establish a Norrlandic history and mythology and consequently a cultural identity. An ambition to emphasise Norrlandicness as an identity in its own right is noticeable in other novels by writers such as Pelle Molin, Elf Norrbo, Karl Östman, Albert Viksten, and Eyvind Johnson from the end of the nineteenth century and the beginning of the twentieth.

How should one describe the Norrland which these writers try to invent, often in defiance of the established – and colonial – notions of what Norrland is? Before trying to answer that question I should say something about the theory of cultural identity. The American feminist and literary scholar Susan Stanford Friedman claims in her book *Mappings* (1998) that cultural identity presupposes some kind of movement, either literally or metaphorically. Leaving one's home produces the concept of 'home', i.e. the very sense that being at home is separated from being anywhere else. Friedman consequently argues that cultural identity must be regarded as a dialogue and a movement between what she calls roots and routes, or stability and mobility. She writes:

> [E]xperiencing identity as roots requires some figurative or material engagement of routes through a contact zone of intercultural encounter. Conversely, identity developed through routes involves an experience of leaving roots, of moving beyond the boundaries of 'home' (however that is defined or problematized). (Friedman 1998:154)

Friedman also claims that narrative is of crucial importance in this context. Cultural identity is constructed through the stories that a society and its members tell about themselves. And these stories almost always consist of a movement between roots and routes, between home and beyond. Another scholar, Madan Sarup, expresses this thought more eloquently when he writes that cultural 'identity is not about *being*, but about *becoming*' (Sarup 1994:98). That is to say, cultural identity is, in several respects, a process. To acknowledge that one has an identity of one's own, one has to see oneself in relation to something or someone else. On a historical level this means that one's identity always evolves and changes in the meeting with others.

If one now tries to adapt this reasoning to a possible Norrlandic cultural identity, it is conceivable, especially when it comes to Norrlandic literature from the end of the nineteenth century and a few decades on, that many authors try to construct such an identity in their writing. These are attempts to invent a Norrland which relates to, and is at conflict with, the centre's established views on Norrland.

However, Susan Stanford Friedman's theory on cultural identity as a movement between roots and routes could also be used in a very concrete way as an image for an essential feature in early Norrlandic literature. The reason is that no stable and uniform cultural identity can be found in Norrlandic literature. Instead, it is an identity created through routes, deeply affected as it is by the large-scale immigration to Norrland at the time.

One could therefore speak about a nomadic identity for Norrland during this period of violent industrialisation and modernisation. Most jobs were seasonal and mobile. They consisted of work in the saw mills, timber-felling, log-driving, railway-building, mining and so on. The relatively small number of farmers who lived in Norrland before this modernisation were very likely to be displaced, due to the forestry industry's hunger for land and timber. This meant that there were a large number of workers, often with their roots in other parts of Sweden or Finland, moving through large parts of Norrland. The resulting meetings between people from different backgrounds, but with joint experiences of poverty, hard work and constant departures and travelling, are perhaps the most prominent feature of a Norrlandic identity.

Most of the early Norrlandic writers, i.e. from the end of the nineteenth century and beginning of the twentieth, deal with nomadic identity and the importance of meetings between people from different backgrounds. A good example of this is Gustav Hedenvind-Eriksson, characteristically called 'the philosopher of the road', and his first novel *Ur en fallen skog* (From a Fallen Forest) from 1910, in which initial contradictions between the settlers and the nomadic workers are resolved in a mutual insight when the settlers lose their homes one by one.

Unfortunately, I have no space in this discussion to delve into the many fascinating aspects of Hedenvind's novel. Instead I have to focus on two distinct and peculiar features concerning its thematics and narrative form.

To begin with, there is a strange gap between the first and second chapters concerning the novel's principal character, or rather, the loss of what one expects to be the principal character. The first chapter starts with a conversation taking place in the south of Sweden, probably near Gothenburg on the west coast. One of the two men participating in the conversation is small and fat and called 'boss'. He is trying to convince the other, who is described as a huge, strong man called Bertil, to work for him by moving to the North and rescuing his timber which has drifted the wrong way. Bertil, however, is very reluctant to move to Norrland. He finds it cold and unfriendly and has no desire to get lost 'däruppe' (up there) (Hedenvind-Eriksson 1923:8).[1] But in the end he cannot resist the money offered by the boss and accepts moving to the north.

In the next chapter the reader is directly transferred to a Norrlandic landscape. But it is only with an observant reading that one is gradually able to spot Bertil, the person one would imagine should be the main character of the novel. He is only one of a collective of workers, and is not even called by his real name, Bertil. Instead, he has a nickname, like most other workers. He is called 'Domkapitlet' (Chapter) due to his fair-mindedness. The loss of Bertil as the main character emphasises the theme of the nomadic identity in the novel. He is just one of a crowd fooled, like the others, by unscrupulous bosses.

The other feature concerns the narrative form, which complements the theme of nomadic identity in a number of ways, and contains the knowledge that – in the words that Marshall Berman borrowed from Karl Marx for the title of his book on modernity – *All that is Solid Melts into Air*: that is, all homes are temporary and the only stable things are values and ideas like that of solidarity (Berman 1982). In a way, one can label this work a collective novel, beacuse there is no real main character and the plot circles around a number of people and their stories. And yet, the representation of the collective is not what one feels is the most typical feature of the novel. The collective novel as a literary genre is usually reserved for the representation of a collective of workers, and even if there is a changing collective in *Ur en fallen skog*, it is the movement in time and space which, I argue, is the most distinctive feature of the novel.

The organisation of time and space in this novel, its chronotope, to use Mikhail Bakhtín's concept, is exceptional and distinctive. The first thing one notices is that time is very concrete and closely connected to space and place. There are no common time markers like, for example, 'last year', 'In the year 18**' etc. Instead, those time markers which do appear are related to a certain kind of weather or a certain kind of place, for example, 'Det var en sövande sensommarkväll' (Hedenvind-Eriksson 1923:7) (It was a soothing late summer evening); and 'En vacker sommarnatt ej långt därefter' (Hedenvind-Eriksson 1923:15) (A beautiful summer night not long after); or, when larger measures of time are marked: 'Det är uti den drömfulla skymningstid, vilken gick ned i dunklet före vindfällenas stora dag, som denna härva har sin trådända' (Hedenvind-Eriksson 1923:34) (It is in the dreamy time of twilight which sank in the gloom before the day the forest fell, where this tangle has its end of thread).

The reason why time is so closely connected to place is also partly the reason for the gap between the first and second chapters, and why Bertil, whom one expects to be the principal character, almost 'disappears'. There is no information about how much time has passed since we met Bertil in the first chapter, and we are not even told how long he has been staying in Norrland as a worker. Consequently, there is no abstract time in the novel which could help the reader to organise the things that happen. Instead, focus lies on the whereabouts of Bertil and his comrades, and their meetings and movements in the Norrlandic landscape. This also applies to all of the other stories in the novel, which, incidentally, happens to be another distinctive feature of the novel; there is not just one main storyline, the plot moves between different characters and their different stories. One could take the story about Margret, the mistress of one of the exploiters in the novel, Torkel, and her illegitimate child as an example. The narrator initiates her story by stating where she came from: 'Margret skulle hon hetat och var kommen någonstädes från kusttrakten av Ångermanland' (Hedenvind-Eriksson 1923:35) (Margret she would have been called and she came from somewhere on the coast of Ångermanland). The narrator also tells us that she has taken a position at Torkel's house, and that he has an eye for her. Then there is a time marker which relates time to the season, but there is no indication of the year in which the incident takes place: 'När våren kom, tog hon ansvaret över boskapen och flyttade den till den ensligt liggande sätern bortom de två höga bärgen' (Hedenvid-Eriksson 1923:35) (When spring came, she took the responsibility for the herd, and moved it to a lonely place beyond the two high mountains). And then follows the story about her child, the changeling in the forest, who would later become 'Philosopher', one of Bertil's comrades.

In addition to the connection of these concrete time markers to space, another important feature of this novel is the fact that almost every story in it takes place outside: the story about the dangerous road across the swamps to the 'North Drive', the life of Changeling on the island, the transportation of timber along the river, the feast in the meadows outside the houses. It is only in exceptional cases that anything happens indoors. It is as if the primary function of the story is cartographic. In this respect at least, the stories and the fates of the characters can be seen as mappings of the landscape.

This is also emphasised the few times the narrator appears in the novel and addresses the reader. However, not even in these cases is there anything abstract about the narration. It serves instead to help visualise movements and transportations. And it is these transportations which form the core of the stories. When, for example, the narrator asks the reader to notice the lines which might not be seen because they are too close at hand, he declares:

> För att få det så redigt som möjligt, skall jag nysta från början. Inom ramen av detta ligger en hård uppgift, nämligen att berätta om något som är så vanligt och ligger så nära, att man icke ser det för den skull. I städernas utkanter kan man fatta historien i ett enda ögonkast, om man bara har ögon och vill se. (Hedenvind-Eriksson 1923:35)

> (To have it as clear as possible, I shall take it from the start. Inside the scope of this there is a difficult task, namely to tell about something so common, so plain, and so close to yourself, that you can't see it for that sake. At the edge of towns it is possible to grasp the story in just a glimpse, if one only has eyes and is willing to see.)

Here the narrator also hints at a contradiction between centre and periphery. It is on the periphery that one is able to see clearly, to see the story as it were. Another interesting aspect of this passage is that it is the beginning of the story about Margret, and the narrator in the continuation of the story chooses rather abruptly to focus on a special element of that story: 'Men den här gäller "Bortbytingen" och kommer direkt från de blå bärgen' (Hedenvind-Eriksson 1923:35) (But this is about 'the changeling' and originates directly from the blue mountains). The narrator turns the eyes of the reader towards the story of the changeling and, as if to emphasise the concrete nature of the story, states that it is not 'about' but rather 'derived directly from', in other words that it is very concretely associated with the blue mountains, it springs from them in terms of place and nature.

It is my belief that the concrete relationship between time and space and the visualisation of the different stories in *Ur en fallen skog* are due to the fact that it is trying to map a territory which has hitherto been the privilege of the centre to describe. Hedenvind-Eriksson's novel thereby bears a resemblance to postcolonial literature. Parts of it also resemble postcolonial literature in the way that they affirm what I would like to call nomadic identity, although it is not insensitive to the suffering and pain which forced departures from one's native home also means.

What Hedenvind-Eriksson expresses in his novel is that an identity which is based solely on property and ownership runs the risk of degeneration into greedy selfishness and destruction. Against this way of living stand the 'strangers', the 'brothers', the 'comrades' – Chapter, Philosopher, Professor, and Changeling – who above all else have their place of residence not in material homes, but in the *ideas* of compassion, solidarity and intellectual curiosity. As Salman Rushdie declares about the experience of nomadism in his *Imaginary Homelands*:

> The effect of mass migrations has been the creation of radically new types of human being: people who root themselves in ideas rather than places, in memories as much as in material things; people who have been obliged to define themselves – beacuse they are so defined by others – by their otherness; people in whose deepest selves strange fusions occur, unprecedented unions between what they were and where they find themselves. The migrant suspects reality: having experienced several ways of being, he understands their illusory nature. To see things plainly, you have to cross a frontier. (Rushdie 1991:124-5)

This is remarkably similar to what Hedenvind-Eriksson's narrator says: 'I städernas utkanter kan man fatta historien i ett enda ögonkast' (Hedenvind-Eriksson 1923:35) (At the edge of towns it is possible to grasp the story in just a glimpse). This nomadic theme is not only central to Hedenvind-Eriksson's novels, but continues to characterise a lot of Norrlandic literature to the present day.

Nomadic identity is also one of the most prominent features of the modern, global experience; millions of people being either forced into exile or having to leave their native districts in order to find work and money to feed themselves. Because Norrland was affected by the consequences of modernity at an earlier stage than the rest of Sweden, one could perhaps assume that this might be one reason for the prominent role played by writers from Norrland in Swedish literature during the twentieth century. From Nobel Prize winner Eyvind Johnson and Lars Ahlin to contemporary writers such as Sara Lidman, Per Olov Enquist, Torgny Lindgren and Kurt Salomonson. There has always been a productive tension in their writing between the routes into the world in order to meet other people, other cultures and the discovery of roots, their Norrlandic homes. And ironically, it is in the Norrlandic landscape, in the small Norrlandic villages, they have recognised the world.

References

Berman, Marshall (1982): *All That is Solid Melts Into Air: The Experience of Modernity.* New York: Simon and Schuster.

Friedman, Susan Stanford (1998): *Mappings. Feminism and the Cultural Geographies of Encounter.* Princeton N. J.: Princeton University Press.

Hedenvind-Eriksson, Gustav (1923 [1910]): *Ur en fallen skog.* Stockholm: Svenska Andelsförlaget.

Rushdie, Salman (1991): *Imaginary Homelands.* London: Granta.

Sarup, Madan (1994): 'Home and Identity', in George Robertson *et al.* (eds): *Travellers Tales. Narratives of Home and Displacement.* London: Routledge.

Stadling, Jonas (1987 [1894]): *Vår irländska fråga. Bref till Aftonbaldet från en studieresa genom Norrland.* Östersund: Jämtlands läns museum.

Sörlin, Sverker (1988): *Framtidslandet. Debatten om Norrland och naturresurserna under det industriella genombrottet.* Stockholm: Carlssons förlag.

Note

1. Translated by Anders Öhman. If no other source is indicated in the following, translations of Swedish passages into English are by Anders Öhman.

Norrlandic Revivalism in the Novels and Short Stories of Torgny Lindgren

Anders Persson

In a short presentation of Torgny Lindgren's oeuvre, Ian Hinchliffe calls the county of Västerbotten an 'empty corner of Sweden' (Hinchliffe 1985:5). But one thing Hinchliffe states that Västerbotten has, 'which few other parts of the country can lay claim to – at least in terms of quantity and quality – is authors!' (Hinchliffe 1985:5). He mentions Per Olov Enquist, Sara Lidman and Torgny Lindgren, who all come from the northern part of Västerbotten, the area around Skellefteå. However, one could add Anita Salomonsson, Kurt Salomonson and Åke Lundgren, among others, to this list.

Beyond this common geographic origin we meet a number of distinct oeuvres that in many respects should not be compared. On the other hand, one can find common themes and motifs that these authors use to catch a local or regional identity or mentality. One such thematic similarity in the novels of Enquist, Lidman and Lindgren is the frequent representation of the religious revivalist movement in Västerbotten.

Influences from the German pietistic movements became noticeable in Sweden in the late seventeenth century and continued to play an important role throughout the eighteenth century. In the beginning of the nineteenth century a Pietistic-Moravian revivalism occurred in the northern part of Sweden. It was strongly rooted in the counties of Västerbotten and Norrbotten, and in Church history it is often called *Norrlandsläseriet*, 'Norrlandic revivalism'. The early leaders of this revivalism were mostly laymen and often very critical of the Swedish Church, although they never left. Their clarion calls were: 'Back to the Bible', 'Back to Martin Luther' and the Reformation creed. From this Norrlandic revivalism of the early nineteenth century developed two revivalist movements in the middle of the century, namely Laestadianism with its stronghold in Norrbotten, and Rosenianism with its stronghold in Västerbotten. The movements are named after the clergyman Lars Levi Laestadius (1800-1861) and the lay preacher Carl Olof Rosenius (1816-1868). Both movements are very interesting from a literary point of view, but on this occasion I will deal only with the Rosenian movement in Västerbotten.

Rosenianism was organized in 1856 under the name of Evangeliska Fosterlandsstiftelsen (EFS). Its impact is evident during both the nineteenth and twentieth centuries and up to our own time. In almost every village there was a small chapel, visited regularly by lay preachers. Hymns were sung from EFS's own hymnal and the sermons shared their specific characteristics. It is clear that Rosenian revivalism has played a central role in the creation of local and regional identity. This role is also clearly indicated by the many novels and short stories from the region that have revivalism as an important theme.

I will concentrate on some of Torgny Lindgren's short stories and novels and focus on some aspects of the representations of Rosenian revivalism. In *Merabs skönhet* from 1983 (*Merab's Beauty*, Eng. tr. 1990) the first four short stories deal in different ways with the themes of the preacher and the sermon. In the introductory story 'Skräddar Molin' (Tailor Molin), Lindgren brings our attention to the significance of the written word. Molin is not a very successful tailor and so he starts making wall hangings. On the first of his wall hangings one can read the words from Psalms 2:11 'FRÖJDEN EDER MED BÄVAN' (Lindgren 1983:9) (REJOICE WITH TREMBLING; Lindgren 1990:10). And those who bought this wall hanging could read the words every day directly from the walls of the kitchen or the living room. So, on one hand, these wall hangings show the importance of the written word. The members of Norrlandic revivalism were called not pietists but *läsare*, 'readers'. They read the Bible, the hymn book, the sermons by Luther and later on by Rosenius. Wall hangings with quotations from the Bible became very popular in many homes in Västerbotten and are documented by the photographer Sune Jonsson in his book *Bilder av nådens barn* (Images of the Children of Grace) from 1963.

Returning to tailor Molin, his text-based wall hangings become popular. This is due in no small part to Molin's ability as a storyteller:

[D]et var ju detta med berättelserna hans, folket hade vant sig vid dem, mångenstädes köpte dem bonaderna endast för berättelsernas skull, och det gjorde ingenting att det var gammberättelserna, att dem snart kunde dem lika väl som skräddar Molin själv.

Det var om Isabella Stenlund och predikanten.

Och det var predikningarna som han påstod att han kunde ordagrant. Och folket intygade: jo, det var ordagrant. (Lindgren 1983:30)

([T]here were of course those stories of his; people were accustomed to them – in many places they bought his hangings just for the sake of two stories, it didn't matter that they were old stories, that they soon knew them as well as Tailor Molin himself.

One was about Isabella Stenlund and the preacher.

And there were sermons that he said he knew word for word. And people certified that yes, it was word for word.) (Lindgren 1990:21)

This is a second aspect of Norrlandic revivalism. The pietists may have been 'readers', but they were also storytellers. And here, Lindgren associates the lay preachers' sermons with an oral culture in a broader sense:

> In the Västerbotten of my childhood, practically no one seemed to write. Most people restricted themselves to signing the income tax forms that had been filled in on their behalf by the village scribe, but even this was an agonizing process during which one's very name had to be questioned and was open to doubt.
>
> On the other hand, they all told tales – grandmother and grandfather and mother and father and neighbours and preachers and farm workers all told their tales continually and slowly and unstoppably, and they fell silent only when their work in the forest or the cowsheds or the fields prevented them from talking; they told tales to themselves and for the benefit of others. About their own deeds and those of their forefathers, about Biblical figures who were also a kind of forefather, about sickness and death and annihilation and about miracles and wonders which seemed to refute death and annihilation. Everybody knew all the tales. (Lindgren 1985:4)

The lay preachers told tales. And this is also tailor Molin's approach to the sermons: 'Och det var predikningarna som han påstod att han kunde ordagrant. Och folket intygade: jo, det var ordagrant.' (Lindgren 1983:30) (And there were sermons that he said he knew word for word. And people certified that yes, it was word for word; Lindgren 1990:21). Tailor Molin's wall hangings and his stories, the mixture of the written word, especially from the Bible, and the oral tradition from the storytellers, including the lay preachers, are the core of the entire book.

After this prologue follows the story of 'Störstorden' (The Biggest Words), in which a peasant girl and a lay preacher meet each other in a simultaneously religious and erotic experience. The preachers travelled from village to village and this preacher was staying overnight at Stenlund's house. In the middle of the night he visits Isabella's chamber and they start talking:

> Störstorden är värst, sade han. Förgängelsen. Och Evigheten. Och Vilddjuret. Och Nåden. Och Helgelsen. Och Pånyttfödelsen. Och Härliggörelsen. Och Återlösningen. Och Arvsynden.
>
> Jo, sade hon. De orden är väldiga.
>
> För att icke tala om Kärleken, sade han.
>
> Jo, sade hon. Kärleken.
>
> Och nu kröp han opp diti sängen hennes, hon lät honom göra det, det var icke bara detta med orden, han frös ock.
>
> Och två ord bortur andra Korintierbrevet nämnde han just då han kröp opp dittill henne: Köld och Nakenhet. (Lindgren 1983:39-40)

('The biggest words are the worst,' he said. 'Corruption. And Eternity. And Wild Beast. And Mercy. And Sanctification. And Regeneration. And Beatification. And Redemption. And Original Sin.'

'Yes,' she said. 'Those words are tremendous.'

'Not to mention Love,' he said.

'Yes,' she said. 'Love.'

And now he crept up into her bed, she let him do it, it was not only the words, he was cold too.

And just as he was creeping up to her, he named two words from the Letter to the Corinthians: Cold and Nakedness.) (Lindgren 1990:25-6)

I think that Lindgren in this short story is referring to the anecdotes about preachers, the common oral traditions about preachers and sermons that have been widespread down to our own days and related sometimes as proverbial sayings, sometimes as humorous ironic stories. Lindgren shares this interest in the anecdote with Per Olov Enquist, Sara Lidman and others. In Enquist's 1978 novel *Musikanternas uttåg* (*The March of the Musicians*, Eng. tr. 1993), there are several anecdotes about lay preachers; some of these anecdotes are fictional, but some of them are attributed to famous lay preachers and form part of a common oral heritage. The novel mentions, for example, the mild and emotional Gabriel Annerscha who in his sermons regularly and with a dialectal touch repeated the appeal to: 'Hörrje återigen mina vänner' (Enquist 1978:99) (Listen once again my friends).[1] As a consequence, the expression 'once again' became a signature for this well-known preacher. When he celebrated his ninetieth birthday he thanked the congratulators with the following words: 'Det gläder mig mycket att se er här i dag, då jag nu återigen fyller 90 år' (Stenlund 1959:97) (I am delighted to see you here today, when I now once again have reached the age of ninety). In Enquist's 2001 novel *Levis resa* (*Lewi's Journey*, Eng. tr. 2006) these anecdotes still play an important role in the description of a local identity and mentality (Enquist 2001:309-310).

If Lindgren claims that the preacher is a storyteller, however, he also describes the author as a preacher. In an essay he writes: 'Mina texter är alltså skrivna som predikningar och bör läsas som sådana. Precis som mina förebilder tillämpar jag en syntetisk predikometod, vilket innebär att vi använder oss av liknelser och metaforer och paralleller' (Lindgren 1978:25) (My texts are written as sermons and should be read as such. In the same way as the lay preachers I use the synthetic mode of preaching, which means that we use parables and metaphors and parallels). In the next two short stories in *Merabs skönhet* the connection with the sermon is very obvious. The two stories are interconnected by the overall title 'Två predikningar' (Two Sermons). The first is named 'Ordet' (The Word), and the second 'Nåden' (Mercy). The 'Word' of God and the 'Mercy' of God are both keywords for revivalism in general. In the writings of Carl Olof Rosenius they are extremely important and are interpreted again and again. The connection with the sermons held by lay preachers is especially significant in the first story 'The Word'. Like any sermon it begins with a text:

> Vad såningsmannen sår är ordet.
> Den som föraktar ordet hemfaller åt dess dom. Och mången talar i obetänksamhet ord som stinga likasom svärd, men de visas tunga är en läkedom. Det är ock skrivet: Han sände sitt ord och botade dem. (Lindgren 1983:47)

> (The sower soweth the Word.
> Whoso despiseth the Word shall be destroyed.
> There is that speaketh rashly like the piercings of a sword.
> But the tongue of the wise is healthy.
> It is also written: 'He sendeth His Word and healeth them'.) (Lindgren 1990:31)

Here we find quotations from Mark, Proverbs and the Psalms which all deal with the effect of the Word. So even if the quotations are taken from different parts of the Bible they must be considered as the text for the sermon. After the text, however, there follows a very sudden shift from the preaching to the practice: 'I Storholmträsk bodde det en karl som hette Samuel Burvall, han dödde för några år sedan oppå sanatoriet, det var en blodstörtning' (Lindgren 1983:47) (At Storholmträsk there lived a man called Samuel Burvall. He died some years ago at the sanatorium; it was a haemorrage of the lungs; Lindgren 1990:31).

The text and the example about Samuel Burvall are not parted by a new paragraph. So the passage is meant to be read without any pause. In stylistic terms one can talk about an ellipsis. An ellipsis is an 'omission of a part of an utterance or a grammatical structure, which can be readily understood by the hearer or reader' (Wales 1989:138). In this case the theological part of the sermon is left out so all that remains is the text and the example. I think that Lindgren is referring to the revivalist tradition with lay preachers. In this tradition where the extemporised sermon was preferred, the example was often very important. The importance of the example is also very clearly pointed out in the following passage:

> Jo, jag vet att ni allihop har hört mycket talas om Samuel Burvall, att ni allaredan vet huru det var, men jag lyfter upp honom, jag håller fram honom och lyser oppå honom så att självaste meningen ska vara uppenbar, jag gör en predikan bortur honom. (Lindgren 1983:52)

> (Yes, I know that you have all heard much talk about Samuel Burvall, that you already know how things were. But I shall lift him up and bring him forward, and shine a light on him so that the very meaning itself may be revealed. I shall make a sermon out of him.) (Lindgren 1990:33)

This is the only passage where the story is told in the first person. Of course the 'I' and 'you' in the story can be related to Tailor Molin and his listeners, but more importantly, they can at the same time be related to the lay preachers and their listeners in a small chapel somewhere in Västerbotten.

In the second of Lindgren's 'Two Sermons', called 'Mercy', the importance of the example is even more stressed. Here, the order between the text and the example is reversed. The story begins with the example: 'Jag minns en själ som jag frälste. Han hette Lundgren och var barnfödd i Granträskliden' (Lindgren 1983:70) (I remember a soul that I saved. He was called Lundgren and was a native of Granträskliden; Lindgren 1990:45). Hereafter follows the text from the Bible, but being very short and placed as an interlude within the example, it gives the impression of a hint or an allusion rather than a quotation: 'Genom orden kommer nåden oss till del. Det var oppå ett eftermöte i Lakaberg, däri Holmgrens köket. Han hade kommit dit som dräng, han var främmen' (Lindgren 1983:70) (Through the word cometh mercy unto us. It was after a meeting there in the Holmgrens' kitchen. He had come there as a farm-hand, he was a stranger; Lindgren 1990:45).

Lindgren's 1982 novel *Ormens väg på hälleberget* (*The Way of a Serpent*, Eng. tr. 1990) is also strongly influenced by the revivalist sermon. The novel is characterised by a clearly circular composition. In the first chapter, one of the principal characters formulates this prayer: 'Jag ska draga allt för dig Vårherre. Jag ska draga alltihop för dig Vårherre, från början och till slutet, och sedan ska jag fråga dig om detta som jag icke förstår' (Lindgren 1982:7) (I will tell you the whole story, Lord, I will tell you the whole story from beginning to end, and then I will ask you about the things that I do not understand; Lindgren 1990:9). Similar formulations can be found in the following chapter as well as in the four concluding chapters: 'Ända ifrån början och till slutet' (Lindgren 1982:136) (Right from the beginning and on to the end; Lindgren 1990:93). 'Alltihop från början och till slutet' (Lindgren 1982:148) (Everything from the beginning to the end; Lindgren 1990:102). In recent research this has been interpreted as a recurrent theme in a musical sense (Pehrson 1993:32-33). I have no objections to this inter-pretation but I also think that the recurrent theme can be understood in reference to the revivalist sermon of the lay preachers. In *The Great Code. The Bible and Literature* from 1983, Northrop Frye states that the Bible is interested in 'Heilsgeschichte, in the history of God's actions in the world' (Frye 1983:47). In this word *Heilsgeschichte* or 'Salvation history' lies that the story proceeds from the beginning to the end, from genesis to apocalypse. In this sense the Rosenian revivalist sermon is also interested in Salvation history. The sermons often describe a course from beginning to end and the preacher probably won't stop half-way. He will start with the creation and then proceed with the fall, the redemption and all the way to the apocalyptic events. When this perspective of Salvation history is applied to the individual in the so-called *Nådens ordning* (the order of grace, *ordo salutis*), there is the same description of a whole course from the beginning to the end. In the second of Lindgren's 'Two Sermons', called 'Grace', there is a thorough exposition of all the psychological phases in this process of conversion:

> Och sedan drog jag nådens ordning för honom, nådens ordning ska man kunna utantill fast i de här trakterna är det icke vanligt. Man ska aldrig lämna något åt slumpen.
>
> Kallelsen, då Ordet hugger tag i dig och skakar dig.
>
> Upplysningen, då Anden håller fram ljuset sitt mot synden din.
>
> Pånyttfödelsen, då Vårherre öppnar ögonen dina och skänker dig livet åter.
>
> Omvändelsen, då han fyller dig med viljan sin och giver dig hjälpen att glömma av vad du själv ville. (Lindgren 1983:72-3)

> (Then I described the laws of mercy to him, the laws of mercy that men must know by heart, though in these parts it isn't common. One must never leave anything to chance.
>
> 'The call, when the Word seizes hold of you and shakes you.
>
> Enlightenment, when the Spirit holds out its light towards your sin.
>
> Regeneration, when Our Lord opens your eyes and bestows life on you once more.
>
> Conversion, when He fills you with His will, and helps you to forget what you yourself want.) (Lindgren 1990:46)

And the preacher continues with the remaining stages in the *ordo salutis*, righteousness, sanctification, steadfastness and blessedness. The same words we also heard in the conversation between Isabella Stenlund and the preacher. This was a given pattern in the revivalist sermon, the same as in *Ormens väg på hälleberget*, that is, 'from beginning to end'. Another anecdote about two famous lay preachers from Västerbotten also illustrates this characteristic feature of the revivalist sermon:

Two well-known lay preachers were visiting a small village. One of them, Tjernqvist, began with his sermon and the second, Zakrisson, waiting for his turn, went outside the chapel and fell asleep. Suddenly Zakrisson woke up and feared that he had overslept. He went inside and with a sigh of relief he heard that Tjernqvist was still preaching. His text was from St Luke, chapter sixteen, about the rich man and Lazarus who were separated by an abyss. And therefore Zakrisson in connection with this text said with a high voice so that everyone in the chapel could hear: 'Ja, har du inte hunnit över svalget, da gar i å laigg mä' (Marklund 1990:95) (Since I hear that you still haven't passed the abyss, I will go out and continue my sleep.)

The meaning of this anecdote is clear. The sermon was describing the whole salvation history or the whole process of conversion and Zakrisson knew that the other preacher would not stop half-way. So he could calmly sleep on. In the same way, *Ormens väg på hälleberget* is told like a sermon 'from beginning to end'. Like the sermon it is also permeated by quotations from the Bible and from well-known hymns, which also contributes to Lindgren's characteristic prose style.

In an essay, 'Sånger från tre byar i Västerbotten' (Songs from Three Villages in Västerbotten) from 2001, Birgitta Holm finds an interplay in the works of Sara Lidman, Torgny Lindgren and Per Olov Enquist between the local and the universal. Holm makes use of Susan Stanford Friedman's distinction between roots and routes. In *Ormens väg på hälleberget* the addressee is God, always addressed 'O Lord'. The route, that is the global aspect, is to be found in the reference to worldwide Christendom, and at the same time the specific Swedish word *Vårherre* (Our Lord), with its dialectal touch, points to roots in Västerbotten. Holm also claims that the book title, a quotation from Proverbs, is deeply rooted both in Västerbotten's local Bible tradition and in Christendom as a whole, the local and the universal are closely connected with each other (Holm 2002:32-3).

In this discussion I have tried to point out one side of the local situation, the significance of the Rosenian revivalist movement in some short stories and novels written by Torgny Lindgren. The same could be done with a number of works by Per Olov Enquist and Sara Lidman. I am convinced that these local contexts can deepen our understanding of their writing, especially if we are aware of the interdependence between the local and the universal, between roots and routes.

References

Enquist, Per Olov (1978): *Musikanternas uttåg.* Stockholm: P. A. Norstedt & Söners Förlag.
Enquist, Per Olov (2001): *Lewis resa.* Stockholm: Norstedts Förlag.
Frye, Northrop (1983): *The Great Code. The Bible and Literature.* London, Melbourne & Henley: Ark Paperbacks.
Hinchliffe, Ian (1985): 'Torgny Lindgren', in Laurie Thompson (ed.): *Swedish Book Review* 1985:2 supplement, pp. 5-12.
Holm, Birgitta (2001): 'Sånger från tre byar i Västerbotten', in Anders Öhman (ed.): *Rötter och rutter. Norrland och den kulturella identiteten.* Umeå: Umeå Universitet, pp. 30-37.
Lindgren, Torgny (1978): 'På tal om att skriva', in Rune M Lindgren (ed.): *I egen sak.* Bjästa: CEWE-förlaget, pp. 24-28.
Lindgren, Torgny (1982): *Ormens väg på hälleberget.* Stockholm: P. A. Norstedts & Söners Förlag.
Lindgren, Torgny (1983): *Merabs skönhet.* Stockholm: P. A. Norstedt & Söners Förlag.

Lindgren, Torgny (1985): 'Writer or Wrestler?', in Laurie Thompson (ed.): *Swedish Book Review* 1985:2 supplement, pp. 3-4.

Lindgren, Torgny (1990): *Merab's Beauty and other stories* (translated by Mary Sandbach). London: Colin Harvill.

Lindgren, Torgny (1990): *The Way of a Serpent* (translated by Tom Geddes). London: Harvill Press.

Marklund, Göran & Marklund, Hans (1990): *Väckelsen Var Väldig*. Uppsala: EFS-förlaget.

Pehrson, Ingela (1993): *Livsmodet i skrönans värld. En studie i Torgny Lindgrens romaner Ormens väg på hälleberget, Bat Seba och Ljuset*. Uppsala: Uppsala Universitet.

Stenlund, Josef (1959): *Boken om Gabriel Andersson*. Stockholm: Evangeliska Fosterlandsstiftelsens Bokförlag.

Wales, Katie (1989): *A Dictionary of Stylistics*. London & New York: Longman.

Note

1.   Translated by Anders Persson. If no other source is indicated in the following, translations of Swedish passages into English are by Anders Persson.

Nordic National Borderlands in Selma Lagerlöf

Bjarne Thorup Thomsen

Approaching the nation as intermediate space

The beginning of the twentieth century saw a reorientation in Scandinavian literature and culture towards the foregrounding of national issues. This cultural turn is particularly evident in the work of Swedish novelist Selma Lagerlöf (1858-1940). In a recent discussion Vivi Edström suggests that, if Sweden has a national epic, it is probably Lagerlöf's first book *Gösta Berlings saga*, published in 1891, and quotes the contemporary critic Oscar Levertin's claim that this text is 'det mest svenska, som någonsin diktats' (Edström 2001:61) (the most Swedish that was ever written). The spatial focus of *Gösta Berlings saga* is, however, strictly limited to the local universe of Värmland, the rural western district of Sweden in which Lagerlöf grew up. In comparison, Lagerlöf's two main works from the first decade of the twentieth century, *Jerusalem* (1901-02) and *Nils Holgerssons underbara resa genom Sverige* (Nils Holgersson's Wonderful Journey Through Sweden, 1906-07), foreground a dialectic between local, national and international. At a time when the deterioration and eventual dissolution of the union relationship between Sweden and Norway accentuated the question of national belonging in both countries, these texts contributed in different ways to the focalisation and negotiation of the Swedish nation space.

In *Jerusalem*, a novel on emigration, a transition from a local to a national understanding of place and home is begun from the foreign perspective that dominates the novel's second volume, *I det heliga landet* (In the Holy Land). In this, both the religious 'colony' which a group of Swedish emigrants join and develop in Jerusalem and the longed-for landscape of their native rural parish in the central Swedish district of Dalarna[1] are gradually imbued with national symbolism. In the adventure novel and travelogue *Nils Holgersson*, a work commissioned as a textbook for use in Swedish schools, the national orientation that is suggested symbolically in *Jerusalem* as a possible position between the dominant poles of local and foreign is made manifest. The dimensions of the textbook's setting and its main concerns in constructing place are entirely governed by what Franco Moretti terms 'the typically *intermediate* space of the nation-state' (Moretti 1998:22). *Nils Holgersson* depicts a young peasant boy, its eponymous hero, from Sweden's southern-most district of Skåne (Scania) discovering his native land from, primarily, the air, as the travelling companion of a flock of wild geese migrating the length of the nation towards their breeding grounds in furthest Lapland. The ingenious means through which a national focus is constructed in the text is thus the alignment of the protagonist's perspective to a literal and mobile bird's-eye-view which shrinks the nation space into perceivable dimensions and binds its different districts together as stages of equal significance on an overriding national trajectory. Just as the text creates contacts, exchanges and cohesion between the regional constituents of the national terrain, thereby negotiating the internal borders of Moretti's intermediate space,[2] it pays particular attention to the nation's external borderland interaction with other domains such as Denmark and the European continent to the south, and Lapland to the north.

Thus, in the first decade of the twentieth century the theme of the nation and the challenging question of the status of its borders gradually gain significance in Lagerlöf's work. While these issues are more covert in *Jerusalem*, they move centre stage in *Nils Holgersson*.[3] This prominence will be reflected in the following discussion which shall centre on the peripheries of the nation space by investigating aspects of the representation and interpretation of Nordic national borderlands in a small cluster of thematically related Lagerlöf texts, factual as well as fictional, with *Nils Holgersson* at its core. With one exception, which has been made to widen the perspective to include the Danish-German borderland, the texts originate in the seminal period around the dissolution of the Swedish-Norwegian union.

Separation as joining together

In the months preceding the break-up of the union in October 1905 and Norway's consequent gaining of independence, the prospect of discontinuing an association that had existed since 1814 (before which time Norway had been in a union with Denmark for more than 400 years) was not perceived as desirable in all quarters of contemporary Sweden. Among those who voiced an initial resistance to the severance of the ties of the union were some sections of the country's cultural circles. Thus, in early March 1905 the prominent Swedish publisher Karl Otto Bonnier wrote a letter to Selma Lagerlöf in which he asked her to sign a public statement in the Norwegian question. The message of the petition was that, by displaying generosity, Sweden should strive to keep Norway in the union. Lagerlöf, however, immediately rejected this idea. In a letter of 7 March she presented the following argument to Bonnier:

Tack för Ert bref, men jag vill inte vara med om att underteckna detta upprop därför att jag inte står på fullt samma ståndpunkt som inbjudarna. Jag är nämligen sedan åratal tillbaka af den åsikten att Norge bör få bli ett eget rike. Att få se det gamla norska kungadömet återupprättadt och bevittna ett helt folks jubel öfver att åter få räknas med bland själfständiga stater har länge varit en af mina drömmar. Likaså tror jag, att nationellt medvetande skulle stärkas härhemma, alla skulle bli glada öfver att befrias från denna pinsamma union och en period af kraftansträngning och lyftning skulle inträda. Och till sist skulle vi verkligen komma att bli riktiga vänner, så som vi känna oss gentemot danskarna. (Lagerlöf 1969:28)

(Thanks for your letter but I won't be party to signing this petition because I don't completely share the views of the instigators. For years I have been of the view that Norway ought to be a country in its own right. It has long been one of my dreams to see the old Norwegian kingdom re-established and to witness the jubilation of a whole nation at once again being numbered among the independent countries. I also believe that national consciousness will be strengthened here in Sweden – everyone will be glad to be free of this painful union, and a period of real effort and inspiration will follow. And, finally, we shall come to be real friends, just as we are with the Danes now.)[4]

Interestingly, a few months later the publisher seems to have been won over to the author's line. In late June 1905, Bonnier proposed an alternative proclamation that contains clear echoes of the ideas formulated in Lagerlöf's letter. It was published the following month with 180 signatories, including a considerable proportion of the Swedish cultural elite. After having stated how demeaning it would be for Sweden to attempt to coerce the Norwegian people into remaining in 'en union, som aldrig förmått närma, endast fjärma de båda nationerna' (a union which has never been capable of bringing the two nations closer, only of distancing them from one another), the proclamation concludes in an appeal to the Swedish parliament to decide on

...en sådan afveckling af unionsförhållandet mellan Sverige och Norge, att lugn och grannsämja kunna bli rådande på den skandinaviska halfön och därmed möjlighet skapas för Sverige att, med alla sina krafter ändtligen samlade, beträda den väg, hvilken allena kan leda ett litet folk fram till varaktig storhet: den inre utvecklingens väg. (Bonnier 1956: insert between pages 104 and 105)

(...the sort of dissolution of the union between Sweden and Norway that will lead to the existence of calm and neighbourly harmony on the Scandinavian peninsula and thereby create the possibility for Sweden, with all her energy finally gathered, to enter on the only road that can lead a small nation to lasting greatness: the road of inner development.)

Thus, the tenets of the argument contained in the published petition arc identical to those that inform Lagerlöf's analysis: (a) the expectation of a future *rapprochement* between the nations through the clearer demarcation of boundaries that the dissolution of the union represents (replacing their actual distancing from each other within the confines of their artificial proximity as union partners), and (b) the ambition of offsetting what could be perceived as an external loss for the Swedish nation by internal gain and growth.

Bread and border

At the same time as Selma Lagerlöf expressed her vision of separate countries in close coexistence on the Scandinavian peninsula, she was experiencing a breakthrough in the creation of the novel-cum-textbook that was to become the key literary vehicle for the mapping of the Swedish territory post-1905. *Nils Holgersson* was brought out by Bonniers publishing house in two volumes appearing in November 1906 and December 1907 respectively. By displaying the multifarious resources – natural, cultural, industrial – of the homeland and by carefully delineating its extent and diversity, *Nils Holgersson* became one of the weightiest textual contributions to what Lagerlöf's biographer Elin Wägner has termed the Swedish renewal after the end of the union (Wägner 1954:44). The national focus the work was designed to instil was widely disseminated: within half a year of its first publication, the textbook was reportedly being used in 2000 primary school classes up and down the country (Wägner 1954:51). While soon being incorporated into the Swedish literary canon and retaining its place in the popular consciousness to this day,[5] the nation-oriented *Nils Holgersson* has in addition struck an international chord and been translated into a number of languages. It was a contributing, yet not uncontroversial factor[6] in Lagerlöf being awarded the Nobel Prize for literature in 1909 as the first woman winner.[7]

That the dissolution of the union directly influenced the design of *Nils Holgersson* has since been made probable by an interesting find. In 1959 the literary scholar Erland Lagerroth published in *Bonniers Litterära Magasin* (Bonniers Literary Journal) a hitherto unknown Lagerlöf manuscript entitled 'Brödlimpa' (Loaf of Bread), which he had discovered in the Royal Library in Stockholm. It seems clear that the manuscript was intended as a chapter in *Nils Holgersson* since its full title, written in the author's handwriting, is 'Läsebok. Brödlimpa' (Lagerroth 1959:560) (Textbook. Loaf of Bread). In a recent article Ulla-Britta Lagerroth even argues that the chapter was intended as an overall introduction to the work (Lagerroth 2000:141). What, then, is the content of the manuscript and why was it left out?

The chapter constitutes an allegory of the geological genesis of the

Swedish-Norwegian peninsula and is thus in keeping with a recurring endeavour in *Nils Holgersson* itself to attribute – in addition to embracing the modernity of Swedish society – a 'deep' or diachronic temporal dimension to the nation space. The chapter is conspicuous by claiming an almost organic symbiosis between the neighbouring countries. By means of an imagery which, not untypically for Lagerlöf's texts, is rooted in the sphere of domestic female production, the prehistoric emergence of 'Norway' and 'Sweden' is perceived as a result of God's not entirely successful attempt at baking bread:

> En annan sak åter var inte alldeles riktig, och det var att den [limpan] hade kommit att jäsa ihop med en annan limpa, som hade legat för nära på plåten. De hade grott samman så fast, att det inte var någon möjlighet att skilja dem utan att förstöra dem både två. (Lagerlöf 1959:557)

> (There was something else that wasn't quite right, too, and that was that it [the loaf] had risen and stuck to another loaf which had lain too close to it on the tray. They had grown together so firmly that there was no possibility of separating them without destroying them.)

Here, it is claimed that the degree of interconnection between the loaves/countries is so high that it is most of all reminiscent of that of conjoined twins: to separate them is to destroy them – a strikingly different view of the relationship between Norway and Sweden than the one Lagerlöf formulated in her letter to Bonnier. The decision not to include the chapter – which, in Erland Lagerroth's assessment, was written in early 1905 (Lagerroth 1959:561) – into the end product of *Nils Holgersson* can meaningfully, then, be placed in the context of the break-up of the union. This turning point in the history of the Scandinavian territories made it highly inopportune to realise an idea of a transnational continuum in relation to the newly divorced neighbours (cf. also Lagerroth 2000:141).

At a personal level the border between the countries seems likewise to have become a barrier for the author. According to Francis Bull in his article 'Selma Lagerlöf og Norge' (Selma Lagerlöf and Norway), the Swedish author – who later in life returned to her native district of Värmland that borders on Norway – seems never to have crossed the frontier to the nearby nation after 1905, thus taking her own idea of territorial divorce quite literally (Bull 1958:59-60).

The periphery as centre

If Lagerlöf's contacts with Norwegian soil were minimal, she had a considerably more intimate and dynamic relationship to the Danish terrain. She visited Copenhagen and Zealand on numerous occasions, not least during her twelve years (1885-97) as a school teacher (1885-95) and writer in the 'peripheral' southern Swedish coastal town of Landskrona, only a short ferry journey from the 'central' conurbation of the Danish capital.[8] Aspects of the author's relationship to the Danish nation space are discussed in an autobiographical article she published in 1920, 'Ett minne från stridsåren' (A Memory from the Years of Conflict).[9] Here, Lagerlöf centres on another disputed dividing line pertaining to the Scandinavian area, namely the border between Denmark and Germany. The article celebrates the establishment of the current border that was drawn in 1920 following two referenda[10] in the aftermath of the First World War. Between 1864, the year of Denmark's crucial and symbolically charged defeat by Prussia, and 1920, the border had followed a more northern line, along the stream of Kongeåen in Jutland. In the 1920 article Lagerlöf describes a visit she had made 25 years previously, in 1895, to Askov Folk High School, an institution which had been established in 1865 immediately north of the then new border.[11] Thus Lagerlöf's article could be seen as connecting two polar positions in the history of the Danish territory, that of its 'division' and that of its 'reunification'. The text may be read as a celebration of the national periphery as the core area for the national struggle and its constructive processes. Its 'topography' is characterised by a number of complex tensions and connections: between the fatherland 'up here' and the foreign or occupied land 'down there', between north and south, country and city and, not least, between core and margin.

The retrospective piece depicts how the author undertakes a journey of discovery into a different Denmark from that of Copenhagen and North Zealand. Initially, Lagerlöf informs the reader that, after a decade in Landskrona, she could consider herself familiar with the high culture and central places of the neighbouring country. She was ignorant, however, of what her friends term the 'real' Denmark, which the rural folk high schools are said to represent. When she received an invitation from the principal of Askov to visit his establishment in September 1895, she did not hesitate, therefore, to embark on the expedition. From this point on, the elegantly composed piece is structured as an attempt to solve the *riddle* which the folk high school represents to the newcomer. The core of the riddle is the fact that the remote school radiates an aura of national significance which would normally be expected of a capital and its decision-making institutions. Only towards the end of the text can the true identity of Askov be disclosed:

Efteråt under natten låg jag och tänkte på allt vad jag hade fått höra, och då kom jag äntligen till att förstå.

Detta Askov, sade jag till mig själv, är alls ingen folkhögskola. Det är en fästning.

Det är en fästning, rest här på Danmarks gräns för att understödja dem, som där nere i det erövrade landet kämpa för danskheten. [...]

Det är härifrån, som de krafter utgå, som bibehåller folket där nere som danskar. Här ger man dem danska hjärtan, danska seder, dansk bildning. Här få de lära sig Danmarks stora minnen, som också äro deras, här ställer man för deras ögon vad Danmark har ljuvast och bäst, så i dikt som i bild.

Danmarks bästa män komma hit för att understödja arbetet, därför att detta är en stridsplats, och den som strider här, han strider för fosterlandet. (Lagerlöf 1945:36)

(Afterwards, during the night, I lay and thought of everything I'd got to hear and then at last I began to understand.

This Askov, I said to myself, isn't a folk high school at all. It's a fortress.

It's a fortress, erected here just inside Denmark in order to give support to the people down there fighting for their Danishness in the conquered land. [...]

This is the place that radiates the forces that keep the people down there Danish. This is where they are given Danish hearts, Danish customs, a Danish education. This is where they get to learn the great annals of Denmark which are also their own. This is where they are shown everything that is loveliest and best about Denmark, both in literature and in art.

Denmark's finest men come here to support the work, because this is a battlefield, and the man who fights here is fighting for his fatherland.)

Thus, the remote folk high school is reinterpreted as a bastion for the protection of the nation and as a powerhouse[12] for the generation of Danish energies, minds and values south of the border.

This understanding of the borderland as a battle zone, and of the national and the foreign as antagonistic, is, however, not Lagerlöf's final say in the matter. Instead, the article concludes with a pronounced equalising of national differences. As Lagerlöf brings her perspective up-to-date, i.e. to 1920, it is striking that she conceives of the new border demarcation not only as a boundary between independent nations but also as instrumental in unifying what she terms the Germanic peoples:

Sådan tedde sig för mig bilden av sønderjyders och danskars gemensamma strävan år 1895, nu tjugufem år efteråt är den förd till seger.

Och allt Norden fröjdar sig [...] över att den orätt, som skilde germanernas stammar, nu är utplånad. Jordlotten, som vållade brödrastriden, är kommen till den rätte arvingen, och den långa, bittra frändefejden kan avlysas. (Lagerlöf 1945:37)

(That is how the picture of the common endeavour of the South Jutlanders and the Danes appeared to me in 1895. Now, twenty-five years later victory has been achieved.

And all of Scandinavia rejoices [...] that the injustice that divided the Germanic peoples has now been eradicated. The plot of land that caused fraternal strife has come to the right heir and the long and bitter family feud can cease.)

In the light of the conclusion of the First World War, these lines can be read as a message of reconciliation to defeated Germany. They express a subtle double-understanding of the reunification as a phenomenon which is played out at both a national (Danish) and a supranational (Germanic) plane. The notion of separate nations that one interpretation of the concept implies is instantly supplemented by another interpretation of unification which suggests the existence of a transnational continuum connecting the Nordic countries and the European continent.

Characteristic, then, for the treatment of the questions of Scandinavian territoriality in the Lagerlöf texts we have investigated so far is (a) a focusing on borderlands rather than on traditional centres, and (b) the employment of double-perspectives that acknowledge new border demarcations as the foundation for the (re-)establishment of independent nation-states while also insisting on the existence and importance of transnational continua. The texts are engaged in both evoking and transcending national boundaries. It must be asked whether similar approaches to nationhood are operative in *Nils Holgersson*, this most nation-focused of Lagerlöf's texts. In so doing we shall turn our attention to a third Scandinavian borderland, namely Skåne, Sweden's southern end which was part of Denmark until 1658,[13] and which constitutes the starting and finishing point of the novel's wonderful journey. We shall consider a couple of intriguing aspects – one early and one late in the novel – of the representation of this region in the text.

The writing on the wall

A passage in the opening chapter of *Nils Holgersson* gives one of those pictorial signals that tend to convey particular meaning in Lagerlöf's texts. It provides, with the protagonist as observer, the following insight into the interior of the cottage which is his family home:

> Han lät blickarna vandra från liggsoffan till slagbordet och från slagbordet till spisen. Han såg på grytorna och kaffepannan, som stodo på en hylla bredvid spisen, på vattenspannen vid dörren och på slevar och knivar och gafflar och fat och tallrikar, som syntes genom den halvöppna skåpdörren. Han såg upp till fars bössa, som hängde på väggen bredvid de danska kungligas porträtt, och på pelargonierna och fuksiorna, som blommade i fönstret. (Lagerlöf 1906:13)

> ([Nils] let his gaze wander from the sofa to the table, from the table to the fireplace. He looked at the kettles, then at the coffee-pot which stood on a shelf near the fireplace; on the water bucket near the door; and on the spoons and knives and forks and saucers and plates, which could be seen through the half-

open cupboard door. He looked at his father's gun, which hung on the wall, beside the portrait of the Danish royal family, and on the geraniums and fuchsias which blossomed in the window.)

Even though the pointing out of the portrait is somewhat counteracted by its position in a subordinate clause and as part of a longer listing, it has an arresting effect within the context of a narrative that has Swedishness as its central concern. Earlier readers also noticed it. Alfred Dalin, chairman of the committee set up by the Swedish Teachers Association to co-ordinate and monitor the development of the textbook, commented sceptically to the author in 1906 when scrutinising her script: 'I en bok för *hela* vårt land?' (Ahlström 1942:58) (In a book for the *whole* of our country?). Lagerlöf, though, was not inclined to remove the reference to the foreign royalty; rather, she highlighted in her reply to Dalin that a careful writing strategy lay behind it: 'Just karakteristiskt för skånska förhållanden. Observandum non est imitandum. Just skrivet med avsikt' (Ahlström 1942:58) (Precisely characteristic of the conditions in Skåne. *Observandum non est imitandum.* Written with intent).

The reply suggests that the reference should be understood in the context of the interplay between regional and national orientation that Lagerlöf had proposed as the textbook's main narrative method to Dalin already in her first outline of the project in November 1901: 'Jag hoppas [...] blifva i stånd att skildra mitt land genom små *lokaliserade berättelser.* [...] Och alla berättelser skola vara infogade för att bilda ett led i det stora hela.' (Lagerlöf 1967:252-53) (I hope [...] to be in a position to depict my country through small *localized stories.* [...] And all the stories will be fitted together to form links in the overall whole). In other words, it was the author's ambition to turn internal differences into a story of the nation. Her reply five years later, when Dalin calls for unity, implies that she remained true to the idea that the narration of the nation must be based on a consideration of regional variations, also in cases where local loyalties may not be regarded as exemplary. The portrait functions, then, as a contribution to signifying the particularities of Skåne as a 'chronotope', to use the critic Mikhial Bakhtín's term (Bakhtín 1996 and 1986). In a region in which the nation's internal and external borders tend to coalesce, these particularities involve Denmark's historical hegemony and the residual allegiances that may stem from this. The quoted passage makes a non-contemporaneous aspect of the country visible and demonstrates Lagerlöf's 'ability to read time in space', as Bakhtín phrases it (Bakhtín 1986:53; see also Moretti 1998:38). And as Moretti observes, it is particularly in the proximity of the border that space becomes time (Moretti 1998:38).[14]

Thus, the writing on the wall of Nils Holgersson's home can be connected to conceptualisations elsewhere in Lagerlöf's work of borderlands not (only) as cut through by a frontier but (also) as continua or as reflections of other places. A particular connection can be made with the text we considered in the previous section: As the author in 'Ett minne från stridsåren' looks down into the 'occupied' Southern Jutland from her elevated position in the school's power station (cf. note 12), she interestingly decodes the landscape featured in front of her not as distinctly Danish but as reminiscent of Skåne: 'Jag tror, att jag hade väntat, att det skulle vara något säreget över landet, men det bredde ut sig under mina spanande ögon [...] likt denna skånska slättbygd, som jag nu sedan många år tillbaka var förtrogen med' (Lagerlöf 1945:31) (I think I had expected there to be something quite special about the country but it spread out in front of my observant eyes [...] just like the flatlands of Skåne that I had already been familiar with for so many years). Here, by means of what may be read as an example of topographic pan-Scandinavianism, a linkage and a dialogue is established between the two disputed borderlands. In this instance Swedishness (albeit historically disputed) is read into the Danish terrain, thereby reversing the 'importing' and 'exporting' roles allocated to the countries in *Nils Holgersson*'s opening chapter, but resulting in similar territorial complexities.

In conclusion to this section, then, the effect of the pictorial component featured early in *Nils Holgersson* is to imply overlapping margins or porous borders between countries. The portrait is symbolic of the idea that the nation does not exist by itself alone, but is contingent upon the 'foreign' place. 'Other' realms do not exist solely beyond the border, but have a presence within the nation itself. A consequence of figuring local characteristics of Skåne in *Nils Holgersson* is therefore the addition of an international dimension to the dialectic between regional and national that Lagerlöf identified as her text's main method.

An insight into the outside

The mapping of the interior of the hero's home discussed in the previous section happens just before an elf transforms Nils Holgersson into a carbon copy of himself, a reduction which both represents punishment for the maliciousness that has characterised the protagonist's behaviour hitherto and creates the physical precondition for his involvement in the ensuing airborne travel adventures. During these, a series of national regions are illuminated by means of the mobile gaze of the hero, and the most prominent role of the protagonist is that of an *eye witness* (cf. the key role attributed to his gaze already in the passage quoted above). As a result of Nils *seeing* Sweden, the country comes into being in the text, and the hero himself is transformed in the process from an obstinate peasant boy into a loyal member of the flying *flock*, which can be understood as a representation of the *folk*, the people. Just as the protagonist develops into an exemplary citizen, the topography of the text becomes a model for the understanding of the nation – and even, as we shall conclude by demonstrating, for the imagining of the foreign.

When the textbook, deep into its second volume and more than 600 pages after the opening chapter, reintroduces Skåne, a key function is now performed by the gaze not of Nils (who knows the area) but of a new generation of goslings, born during the summer stay in Lapland and since incorporated into the flying formation of the novel's collective of characters. As the text approaches the limits of the space it occupies, it provides an interesting indirect insight into what lies beyond its horizons. This insight is triggered by the thirst for knowledge expressed by the goslings, who (like Nils) could be seen as emblematic of the core target audience of the text: Swedish school children in the younger classes. The text relates that several times since the beginning of the southbound migration the goslings have asked the more experienced members of the flock what the foreign places look like. Though not until the border into Skåne is crossed does the female leading goose, Akka, give the young ones the, perhaps surprising, answer that they should look to the ground to find out, because '[s]å här ser det ut i utlandet' (Lagerlöf 1907:472) ([t]his is what abroad looks like). In order to reinforce this idea of the borderland terrain as a mirror image or model of the foreign, Akka then takes the flock past different segments of the region's landscape: ridge, plain, coast, town – a 'serialising' method of narrating the national territory that is typical of *Nils Holgersson*.[15] In each case the content of Akka's 'teaching' is as the following summing-up of the relation between the Scanian plain and the extensive foreign field: '"Se nu ner! Titta väl efter!" ropade förargåsen. "Så här ser det ut i utlandet ifrån Östersjöns kust ända till de höga bergen, och längre än till dem har vi aldrig farit"' (Lagerlöf 1907:472) ('Look down now! Take a good look!' shouted the leading goose. 'This is what abroad looks like all the way from the Baltic coast to the high mountains, and farther than that we have never travelled'). Even when a variation in size is noticeable (similar to the one articulated by the different stages on the generational series of geese), the notion of underlying or prospective congruity remains constant: '"Så här ser utlandets städer ut, fast de är mycket större," sade förargåsen. "Men dessa kan väl växa, de som ni"' (Lagerlöf 1907:473) ('This is what towns abroad look like, though they are much bigger,' said the leading goose. 'But these can grow, just like you').

Nearing the completion of its comprehensive survey of Sweden and on the foundation of the national ground that has been textually claimed, the novel thus opens up an international vista. Whereas in the introductory chapter the foreign appeared solely and briefly as a symbolic sign noted in passing, a whole chapter (LIII) is now devoted to the theme. By using Skåne as a screen upon which the features of central Europe are projected, this third to last chapter figures the borderland as a topographical palimpsest of national and foreign. This figuring communicates the (nationalist) message that the native country can hold its own against any any other country: 'Och pojken kunde inte låta bli att tro, att hon [Akka] den dagen hade rest fram över Skåne för att visa honom, att han hade ett land, som gott kunde mäta sig med vilket som helst ute i världen' (Lagerlöf 1907:473) (And the boy could not help believing that she [Akka] had travelled over Skåne that day in order to show him that he had a country that could measure up to any other country out in the world). In so doing, however, the topographical palimpsest seems – by a levelling gesture that we can now recognise as a recurring feature in Lagerlöf's texts – to express the (internationalist) view that home and away are connected and related positions. Underpinning both positions is an insight not dissimilar to Benedict Anderson's understanding of nations as forming an open series of sovereign systems that are equal in principle and therefore comparable: 'The nation is imagined as *limited* because even the largest of them [...] has finite, if elastic, boundaries, beyond which lie other nations. No nation imagines itself coterminous with mankind.' (Anderson 1991:7)

Thus, as the novel draws to its close, it does not bounce against the national border as a barrier or treat the foreign as an empty space or a *terra incognita*. Instead, it prefigures both the encounter with continental Europe that the goslings are about to experience and the internationalisation of subject matter and the large-scale transgression of borders that the core readership of the textbook would be educated about in one of the follow-up volumes to *Nils Holgersson* planned by the Swedish Teachers Association, a volume tellingly entitled 'Från pol till pol' (From Pole to Pole) (see Hedin 1911).

In *Atlas of the European Novel 1800-1900* Franco Moretti argues that, as borders in nineteenth-century Europe were both hardening and being challenged as unnatural by nationalist movements, the need for literary representation of the territorial divisions of Europe grew stronger (Moretti 1998:35). We have seen how Selma Lagerlöf in a Scandinavian and somewhat later context rises to a similar literary challenge. The majority of the texts considered above contain representations of or constitute reactions to redrawings of the Scandinavian map in 1864, 1905, 1920, with reflections in one instance of changes in sovereignty occurring as early as 1658 (see note 13). Taken together the texts constitute a debate about Scandinavian borderlands, viewing these not only or primarily as demarcated by a line that separates the familiar from the foreign, but also or rather as liminal and ambiguous places in which nations overlap, interact and connect. Underlying this is a dialogic notion of nationhood and an awareness of the contingent nature of nation space – a vision, more specifically, of the Scandinavia countries in communication both with each other and with terrains stretching further afield. Or as Ulla-Britta Lagerroth puts it in her consideration of 'Nordism' in Lagerlöf's life and work: : '...kanske detta är själva det fundamentala i hennes nordism som i så mycket annat: viljan till överskridande!' (Lagerroth 2000:146) (perhaps this – the will to transgress boundaries – is itself the fundamental element in her Nordism as it is in so much else).

References

Ahlström, Gunnar (1942): *Den underbara resan. En bok om Selma Lagerlöfs Nils Holgersson.* Lund: C. W. K. Gleerups förlag.

Anderson, B. (1991): *Imagined Communities. Reflections on the Origin and Spread of Nationalism* (revised edition). London & New York: Verso.

Bakhtín, M. M. (1986): 'The Bildungsroman and Its Significance in the History of Realism (Toward a Historical Typology of the Novel)', in *Speech Genres and Other Late Essays*, ed. Caryl Emerson & Michael Holquist. Austin: University of Texas Press, pp. 10-59.

Bakhtín, M. M. (1996 [1981]): 'Forms of Time and of the Chronotope in the Novel. Notes toward a Historical Poetics', in *The Dialogic Imagination. Four Essays*, ed. Michael Holquist. Austin: University of Texas Press, pp. 84-258.

Bonnier, Karl Otto (1956): *Bonniers. En bokhandlarefamilj. Anteckningar ur gamla papper och ur minnet,* vol. V: *Firman Albert Bonnier under det nya seklet.* Stockholm: Albert Bonniers förlag.

Bull, Francis (1958): 'Selma Lagerlöf og Norge', in *Lagerlöfstudier*, 1958, ed. Nils Afzelius & Ulla-Britta Lagerroth. Malmö: Selma Lagerlöf-sällskapet, Allhems förlag, pp. 47-64.

Edström, Vivi (2001): 'Selma Lagerlöf – en nationell ikon', in *Vad är Sverige? Röster om svensk nationell identitet,* ed. Alf W. Johansson. Stockholm: Bokforlaget Prisma, pp. 61-72.

Hedin, Sven (1911): *Från pol till pol,* vols 1-2. Stockholm: Albert Bonniers förlag.

Lagerlöf, Selma (1906): *Nils Holgerssons underbara resa genom Sverige* (= *Läseböcker för Sveriges barndomsskolor,* I, ed. Alfr. Dalin & Fridtjuv Berg), vol. 1. Stockholm: Albert Bonniers förlag.

Lagerlöf, Selma (1907): *Nils Holgerssons underbara resa genom Sverige* (= *Läseböcker för Sveriges barndomsskolor,* I, ed. Alfr. Dalin & Fridtjuv Berg), vol. 2. Stockholm: Albert Bonniers förlag.

Lagerlöf, Selma (1945 [1920]): 'Ett minne från stridsåren', in *Från skilda tider. Efterlämnade skrifter,* vol. II, ed. Nils Afzelius. Stockholm: Albert Bonniers förlag, pp. 22-37.

Lagerlöf, Selma (1956 [1950]): *The Wonderful Adventures of Nils,* trans. Velma Swanston Howard. London: J. M. Dent & Sons.

Lagerlöf, Selma (1959): 'Brödlimpa. Ett okänt Nils Holgersson-kapitel', ed. Erland Lagerroth, in *Bonniers Litterära Magasin,* vol. 28, no. 7, pp. 557-59.

Lagerlöf, Selma (1967): *Brev,* vol. 1: *1871-1902,* ed. Ying Toijer-Nilsson. Lund: Selma Lagerlöfsällskapet, Gleerups förlag.

Lagerlöf, Selma (1969): *Brev,* vol. 2: *1903-1940,* ed. Ying Toijer-Nilsson. Lund: Selma Lagerlöf-sällskapet, Gleerups förlag.

Lagerroth, Erland (1959): 'Geologiskt brödbak. En kommentar till Selma Lagerlöfs berättelse', in *Bonniers Litterära Magasin*, vol. 28, no. 7, pp. 560-62.

Lagerroth, Ulla-Britta (2000): 'Nordism i Selma Lagerlöfs liv och författarskap', in *Nordisk tidskrift för vetenskap, konst och industri*, vol. 76, issue 2, pp. 129-46.

Lund, Jørn (ed.) (1994-2001): *Den Store Danske Encyklopædi*, vols 1-20. Copenhagen: Gyldendal.

Moretti, Franco (1998): *Atlas of the European Novel 1800-1900*. London & New York: Verso.

Ravn, Jørgen (1958): 'Selma Lagerlöf i Landskrona og København', in *Lagerlöfstudier*, 1958, ed. Nils Afzelius & Ulla-Britta Lagerroth. Malmö: Selma Lagerlöf-sällskapet, Allhems förlag, pp. 139-156.

Thorup Thomsen, Bjarne (1998): 'Terra (In)cognita. Reflections on the search for the sacred place in Selma Lagerlöf's *Jerusalem* and *Nils Holgerssons underbara resa genom Sverige*', in *Selma Lagerlöf Seen from Abroad*, ed. Louise Vinge. Stockholm: Kungl. Vitterhets Historie och Antikvitets Akademien, pp. 131-41.

Thorup Thomsen, Bjarne (2004): 'Lagerlöfs relative landskaber. Om konstruktionen af et nationalt territorium i *Nils Holgersson*', in *Edda. Scandinavian Journal of Literary Research*, 2004/2, pp. 118-35.

Wägner, Elin (1954 [1943]): *Selma Lagerlöf*, vol. II: *Från Jerusalem till Mårbacka*, in *Valda Skrifter*, ed. Holger Ahlenius, vol. 12. Stockholm: Albert Bonniers förlag.

www.bif.se/ (accessed 30 January 2007).

Notes

1. In 1897, Lagerlöf moved from Landskrona in southern Sweden (see later in this chapter) to the town of Falun in Dalarna. Vivi Edström suggests a connection between this event and the national 'turn' in the author's work, as the national in Sweden around 1900 was increasingly identified with Dalarna (Edström 2001:62). If, however, this district and its people operate as a synecdoche for the nation in *Jerusalem*, it is not so much in the form of the traditional Dala society, which is torn apart during the course of the novel's first volume *I Dalerne* (In Dalerna), as in the transposed shape of the new colony abroad and in the imagined landscapes of home.

2. For a closer examination of the 'internal' fabric of the nation space in *Nils Holgersson*, see Thorup Thomsen (2004).

3. For further consideration of the relationship between the two novels, see Thorup Thomsen (1998).

4. Translated by Peter Graves. If no other source is indicated in the following, translations of Swedish passages into English are by Peter Graves to whom I am grateful.

5. In a poll which was conducted in the autumn of 1997 by the journal of the Swedish public libraries, *Biblioteket i fokus*, and in which c. 21,000 votes were received, *Nils Holgersson* was placed fifth on a list of Swedish books of the century. See www.bif.se/ (accessed 30 January 2007).

6. Vivi Edström documents that a contributing factor in Lagerlöf – in spite of public opinion in favour – not being awarded the prize in 1908, the year of her 50th birthday, was reluctance in a section of the Swedish Academy, the body responsible for the prize, to make an award that, due to the proximity in time to *Nils Holgersson*'s publication, could be perceived as a tribute to this particular work of whose ideology the members of the section were sceptical.

7. Lagerlöf received the award two years after Kipling, whose *Jungle Books*, according to Lagerlöf's own statements (1969:40), formed a source of inspiration for *Nils Holgersson* – in particular for the idea of placing the protagonist in a borderland between the animal

and the human world.

8. Vivi Edström observes that Lagerlöf, when living in Landskrona, 'var minst lika mycket vänd mot Danmark som mot Sverige' (Edström 2001:62) (looked towards Denmark at least as much as towards Sweden). Ulla-Britta Lagerroth likewise emphasises that in this period the author had 'tät förbindelse med det rika kulturlivet på andra sidan Sundet och därmed också med sådana kretsar och institutioner, där den nordiska tanken hölls synnerligen levande' (Lagerroth 2000:130) (close connections with the rich cultural life on the other side of the Öresund and consequently with the kind of circles and institutions in which the pan-Scandinavian ideal was particularly kept alive). Similarly, Jørgen Ravn argues that the author's connection with Copenhagen and its intellectual life in the 1880s and 1890s had 'en overordentlig betydning for hele hendes udvikling som forfatterinde' (Ravn 1958:150) (an extraordinary importance for the whole of her development as an author).

9. The article was originally published in *Nordens årsbok*, 1920, pp. 67-81, and reprinted 1945 in the posthumous collection *Från skilda tider* (From Various Times) to which the passages quoted here refer.

10. The first referendum, on 10 February 1920, involved the northern zone of the disputed area, Schleswig/Slesvig, and resulted in a Danish majority of 74%. The subsequent referencum in the central zone took place on 14 March and gave a German majority of 80% (Lund 1994-2001: vol. 7 (1997):366).

11. The establishment of Askov Folk High School was the result of a relocation of Denmark's first folk high school, founded 1844 in the village of Rødding which became part of Prussia after 1864 (Lund 1994-2001: vol. 2 (1995):73).

12. The notion of a powerhouse should be taken quite literally. One major turning point in the text sees the author invited up into the school's own power station in which experiments with the exploitation of wind energy are carried out. The building is thus embedded in the national complex in a country that, as the text has it, possesses no coal or water power 'men en sådan ofantlig rikedom på blåst' (Lagerlöf 1945:28) (but such enormous resources of wind). It is from this vantage point and by means of the views into the disputed territory it offers that the author realises that the seemingly remote and isolated school is in fact carefully and precariously positioned in a larger (inter)national geography.

13. Following the conclusions of peace between Denmark and Sweden in 1658 and 1660, the Danish districts east of the Sound, the regions of Skåne, Halland and Blekinge, were transferred to Sweden (Lund 1994-2001: vol. 17 (2000):375).

14. Moretti's observation is made in connection with his analysis of the spaces occupied by historical novels and concerns the nation's internal borders. It seems possible, however, to widen his argument as attempted here.

15. And, according to Benedict Anderson in *Imagined Communities*, typical of the 'grammar' of the national imagination as such (Anderson 1991:184-85).

The Fragmented Body: Transgressing the Periphery. Two Novels by Herbjørg Wassmo and Christian Krohg

Steinvör Pálsson

Herbjørg Wassmo's critically acclaimed debut novel *Huset med den blinde glassveranda* (*The House with the Blind Glass Windows,* Eng. tr. 1987) was written in 1981. The first volume of a trilogy about the adolescent girl Tora, it won the Norwegian Critics' Prize and has been translated into numerous languages. Wassmo was born in 1942 in the north of Norway, near the Lofoten islands, on the island of Skogsøya. *Huset med den blinde glassveranda* takes place in a parallel setting: an isolated fishing community on an island off the north-west coast of Norway in the 1950s.

Christian Krohg was born in 1852 in Aker, near Norway's capital of Kristiania, as it was known then. When he wrote his novel *Albertine* he was already a highly respected and well established painter. When the book came out, it was considered obscene and was immediately seized by the authorities and confiscated. Krohg was brought to trial, although he had many supporters, especially in the women's movement and the newly-formed workers' movement. In contrast to the rural setting of Wassmo's book, Christian Krohg's novel, written almost 100 years earlier in 1886, takes place in the town of Kristiania.

We could say, then, that Wassmo's novel is situated on the periphery, in geographical terms. Through the eyes of its protagonist, we see the northern landscape, we witness the effects of its climate and we glimpse the lives of its people. Krohg's novel, on the other hand, is located in the country's centre: in its capital city. Very much an urban novel, it depicts the plight of the city worker, in this case the female worker: the seamstress Albertine. The urban landscape serves as a backdrop to the tragic human story that unfolds, depicting the protagonist's passage into prostitution. It was the human landscape that preoccupied Krohg, both in his painting and his writing. He referred to people as 'den levende natur' (Gauguin 1932:109) (living nature).[1]

In this discussion, it is the landscape of the human body that I shall be attempting to explore; more specifically, the transgression of the boundary – or if you like, the periphery – of the female body and how it is represented in these texts. I shall be concentrating mainly on the patterns of focalization and fragmentation that occur in the depiction of sexual abuse and rape in each of these two novels.

In her thesis on point of view in writings on childhood sexual abuse, Ellen Klosterman writes:

> Paradoxically, it is not the detail itself which defines the action as abusive within the text – it is the emotional tone of the point of view used for narration . . . (Klosterman 1997:189)

In a narrative concerning sexual violation, point of view is crucial in determining the reader's interpretation of events and in influencing his or her attitude towards the characters involved. How, for example, does the writer portray the rapist? What are the stylistic indices that signal a particular character's perspective? How does the writer depict a rape from the victim's viewpoint?

The rapist

I would like to begin by exploring the portrayal of the rapist: Tora's stepfather Henrik in *Huset med den blinde glassveranda* and the police officer Winther in *Albertine*. In both novels, the narration, when filtered through the consciousness of the female protagonist, fragments the male into specific body parts, as in the following excerpt from Wassmo's novel, where Henrik's hands function as tools of abuse:

> Hender. Hender som kom i mørket. Det var farligheten. Store, harde hender som krafset og klemte. (Wassmo 1981:6)

> (Hands. Hands that came in the dark. That was the dangerousness.[2] Large, hard hands that groped and squeezed.)

Here, the narration is in the third person but it is *focalized* through the eyes of the child Tora. In his discussion on point of view in fiction, Roger Fowler gives a very clear and succinct definition of the term 'focalization':

> A novel may be narrated from the pervasive viewpoint of a single narrator, or it may be told in the third person as if by a narrator, but focalized through the eyes of a character within the narrative. (Fowler 1996 :161)

In the earlier extract from Wassmo's novel, the deictic verb *kom* indicates that the disembodied hands are depicted from the protagonist's perspective: they are looming towards her, seemingly from nowhere. Implicit in this description is Tora's tactile perception of her abuser. She cannot see the hands, for they come 'in the darkness'. The full import of this image becomes apparent when the reader later discovers that Henrik has the use of only one arm, the result of a war injury. The diametric interplay between aggression and passivity is exemplified in the contrast between his two limbs:

> Den veltet seg enormt under klærne. Neven og armen var en eneste bunt av trassige muskler i rastløs bevegelse. Men på venstre side hang hånden og armen underutviklet og passiv og var en hån mot hele Henriks vesen. (Wassmo 1981:12)

> (It was huge, tossing around under his clothes. The fist and arm were a single knot of defiant muscles in restless motion. But on his left side the hand and the arm hung, underdeveloped and passive, an insult to Henrik's entire being.)[3]

The contrast between impotence and force, passivity and aggression, that is so powerfully expressed in this extract, alludes not only to the conflicting characteristics of Henrik's arms but also to the extreme difference in the balance of power between the abuser and the abused. As Rakel Christina Granaas observes, the depiction of Henrik's crippled arm provides a rare insight into 'an otherwise one-dimensionally evil literary persona' (Granaas 2000:17). It is true to say that the narration is never related from Henrik's perspective. The scenes depicting Tora's abuse are either related from the narrator's viewpoint or focalized through Tora herself. Throughout the novel, the corporal fragmentation of the male perpetrator is a powerful linguistic device in the depiction of sexual abuse as experienced by the young female protagonist. These fragmented body elements are a part of *farligheten* – 'the dangerousness' – Tora's term for her stepfather's sexual abuse of her. The representation of Henrik by his body parts: fingers, hands, mouth, and other isolated aspects of his being: his voice, breath, laughter, presents Henrik as a grotesque, monstrous entity, a gothic villain typified by his inhumanity, which is forcibly illustrated in the following excerpt from the novel:

> Henrik beregnet verken dørkarm eller dør. Han hadde ikke skritt, han subbet bare inn. Men Henrik hadde andre skritt inni hus om han ville. Skritt som nesten ikke hørtes. Lydløse, men full av grov pust. (Wassmo 1981:6)

> (Henrik didn't take into account either doors or door frames. He just shuffled in. But Henrik had other footsteps inside the house if he chose to. Footsteps that could hardly be heard. Silent, but full of coarse breathing.)

Like Henrik, the police officer Winther in Christian Krohg's novel *Albertine* is what E. M. Forster would have termed a 'flat character' (Forster 1990:73), i.e.

a character lacking development and unaltered by circumstances. In the key chapter of *Albertine*, which takes place in Winther's apartment and culminates in his rape of the young seamstress, we see Winther through Albertine's eyes. Her observations of him are minimal, reflecting not only the implicit imbalance of power between a middle-aged, senior male police officer and a young working-class woman in the late nineteenth century, but more significantly perhaps, the sexual intent on the part of the male and the absence of desire on the part of the woman. In the entire chapter, a physical description of Winther occurs in only two instances, both of which are relatively brief. The first of these is focalized through Albertine, as she sits in a chair facing Winther:

> Hun så hans kortklipte, mørke isse bøyet over mandelen, de korte hvite hendene som plukket det lyserøde skallet forsiktig av. (Krohg 1994:86)[4]

> She saw the cropped, dark crown of his head bent over the almond, the blunt white hands that carefully plucked off the pale red shell.

Winther, the focalized object, is fragmented through Albertine's gaze. As the theorist Mieke Bal points out in her work on narratology, 'the image we receive of the object is determined by the focalizer' (Bal 2001:100). In *Albertine*, the description of Winther's 'blunt' hands suggests an aversion to the focalized object and creates a striking contrast to the activity in which the hands are engaged. Implicit also in this image we are given of Winther is a fascination on Albertine's part with the peeling of the almond. Winther's movements are almost clinical in their precision, his fastidiousness suggesting a skilled operation. The man's delicate handling of an inanimate object in contrast to the subsequent brutality and violence of his rape of Albertine, serves to highlight his callous and indifferent attitude towards women; Albertine is a replaceable commodity. The specific action in which Winther is engaged at this point anticipates also his impending act of rape and Albertine's enforced gynaecological examination later in the novel, which could be interpreted as a second 'rape'. Winther's action of 'plucking' the shell from the almond suggests here Albertine's imminent 'deflowering'. The almond, symbolically associated with virginity, is stripped of its protective casing. As Albertine's focus shifts from the crown of Winther's head to his hands and finally to the 'pale red shell', the latter becomes the focalized object shared by both characters.

The second description of Winther, again focalized through Albertine, occurs immediately after she has been raped by him. This time, her viewing position is from the bed where she has been sexually violated:

> Om en stund trengte et flakkende skinn inn under øyelokkene. En fyrstikk ble tent, og hun så Winther stå foran den store vaskevannsbollen med stearinlys ved

siden av seg. – Hodet med den svarte, kortklipte nakken var bøyet forover, og nedenfor den gulgrå jegerskjorten stakk de to stygge, lodne, hjulbente benene. Gud, hvor hun hatet ham! (Krohg 1994:88)

(In a while, a flickering light pressed in underneath her eyelids. A match was lit, and she saw Winther standing in front of the large washbasin with a paraffin candle at his side. – The head with its black, closely-cropped nape was bent forward, and below the greyish-yellow undershirt, protruded two ugly, hairy, bandy legs. God, how she hated him!)

Having just raped Albertine, Winther is now observed by her to be in the process of what can only be assumed to be a post-coital wash. As in the previous description, Albertine's focus is directed at his head, but on this occasion his back is turned to her in a final gesture of contempt towards the object of his abuse. He is framed by the light of the match, his image static and grotesque. Albertine is no longer able to see his hands as in her earlier observation of him. They are now hidden from her, although again engaged in activity. As in the previous description, the representation of Winther is fragmented, but this time it is a reverse image of her earlier observation of him. Now, his back turned towards her, she sees the nape of his neck, where previously, seated opposite her, he had presented to her the crown of his head. Albertine's observation of Winther is cursory and crude, her feelings of repugnance and contempt manifest in the sequence of derogatory adjectives depicting Winther's unattractive legs and in her final, heartfelt exclamation.

A notable aspect of Winther's depiction as focalized through Albertine in the only two instances that occur in the text is the fact that no description of his face is given. As we have seen, he presents only the 'crown,' or the 'back' of his head. In the following excerpt from *Huset med den blinde glassveranda*, taken from a scene where Henrik sexually abuses his stepdaughter Tora in her bath, the abuser's 'facelessness' emphasizes the inhumanity of his actions:

Mannen hadde ikke noe ansikt. Fatet veltet. Den friske armen var villig til å greie opp for to. (Wassmo 1981:53).

(The man had no face. The tub overturned. The healthy arm was willing to do the work of two.)

'The man' referred to in this extract is depicted as a mindless, faceless 'machine' that blindly knocks down anything in its way. The image of the abuser is again fragmented, represented here as a disembodied arm. Wassmo's use of deviant collocation highlights the depravity of the situation being described and conveys also the wanton greed that motivates the arm into action.

The rape

I shall now look at the rape scene in each novel, beginning with Herbjørg
Wassmo's *Huset med den blinde glassveranda*. In the following depiction of
Henrik's savage invasion of Tora's young body, the narration is focused on the
physical experience of the victim:

> Myk, myk var motstanden. Bare til å sette tommelen i øyet på. Den ba for seg,
> og ga nok etter. Så revnet det. Tora kjente det et sted utenfor seg selv. Visste ikke
> hvor det begynte eller endte, det hang ikke fast med resten av henne. Likevel
> smertet det så. (Wassmo 1981:152)

> (The resistance was soft, soft. Just enough to press the thumb into its eye. It
> begged for its life, and gave in. Then it tore. Tora felt it somewhere outside
> herself. Didn't know where it began or where it ended. It wasn't attached to the
> rest of her. Yet it hurt so.)

There is a sense here of the point of view shifting from the narrator to Tora,
this transition signalled by the mental process verb 'felt'. From this point, the
narration is focalized through the female protagonist. The profound pain and
trauma of her rape is beyond the limits of her experience. It is simultaneously
without and within her experiencing self, the boundaries of her body ruptured
through Henrik's brutal violation.

As in *Huset med den blinde glassveranda*, the rape in Krohg's novel is
focalized through the female protagonist:

> ...Med engang blev den lysegule Striben mellem Portièrerne borte, og der kom
> noen ind. En kom hen og klappet hende paa Hodet og kyssede henne paa Panden.
> Eau de Lubin! Der var noen, som klædte af sig – først dunkede en Støvle blødt
> mod Gulvtæppet ossaa om lidt en til. Hun hørte et Uhr bli' trukket op, og saa blev
> det hængt op paa Væggen over Sengen. Hun fikk et Kys paa Panden, og hun
> bøjede Hodet bagover for bedre at kjende den fine Lugten – og saa fik hun et
> langt paa Munden – et langt og saa flere bagefter og saa endda flere.
>
> Hvad var det, hvad var det, hvor var hun? Hun følte en knugende Vægt paa
> Brystet, saa hun var nær ved at kvæles. Der var noget, som gjorde forfærdelig
> ondt. Et skrig – det var hendes, og ædru og angst til Døden forstod hun med
> engang alt og klorte og slog og krafsede og skreg. – 'Hysch, hold Kjæft', sa en
> forpustet Stemme lige i hendes Øre – det blev en lang Kamp som for Livet, men
> to Armer af Jern holdt henne fast, og hun lukkede Øjnene.[5]

> (Suddenly the pale yellow stripe between the drapes disappeared and someone
> came in. Someone came over and patted her on the head and kissed her on the
> forehead. Eau de Lubin! Someone was getting undressed – first a boot thumped
> softly against the rug, then after a little while, another one. She could hear a watch
> being wound up, and then it was hung up on the wall above the bed. She felt a
> kiss on her forehead and she tilted her head back so that she could get a better

smell of the fine scent – and then she felt a long kiss on her mouth – a long kiss followed by several more and then even more.

What was it, what was it, where was she? She felt a crushing weight on her breast so that she was on the verge of suffocating. There was something that was hurting her terribly. A scream – it was hers, and alert and afraid for her life, she suddenly understood everything and scratched and hit out and tore and screamed. – 'Shh! Shut your mouth', said a breathless voice right in her ear – there was a long struggle as though for her life, but two arms of iron clutched her tightly, and she closed her eyes.)

Like Tora, Albertine seems to experience her rape both within and beyond her own body. The scream happens before it is identified by its source: 'A scream – it was hers ...' The sound is foreign to Albertine herself and she perceives it as occurring outside her body. In its nominal form, the scream is concretized, an embodiment of Albertine's suffering. Nominalization eliminates the process of screaming, which in this case effectively conveys the sudden, intense nature of her scream. As in the earlier excerpt from Wassmo's novel, the verb 'felt' conveys the physical pain of Albertine's rape as she is experiencing it. Sara Mills suggests that 'focalization can manipulate the reader's sympathies' (Mills 1995:181) and Krohg achieves this by representing to the reader the consciousness that experiences the rape.

A predominant aspect of the narration concerning the rape itself, which is also manifest in Wassmo's novel, is the omission of any physical description of the rapist. When Winther enters the bedroom where Albertine is sleeping, he is represented by the indefinite pronoun, indicating that Albertine is unable to identify the intruder in the darkness of the room, or that she is still drowsy. We could perhaps make the observation that in his depiction of the rape scene Krohg was being faithful to his painter's gaze. His objective was to present only 'the impression of the moment' (Thue 1968:10).[6] Unable to portray that which was concealed by the darkness, he had to find other means of conveying the protagonist's impressions.

The recurrence of the indefinite pronoun in the passage quoted above establishes an atmosphere of mystery regarding the identity of the person entering the space. The reader can of course deduce that it is Winther, but it is Albertine's perceptions that must be conveyed in order for the reader to gain an insight into her thought processes: i.e., to share her *impressions*. The anonymity of the rapist creates an atmosphere of intrigue which is then unexpectedly attenuated by the ordinary, everyday actions of a person getting ready for bed. To Albertine, the actions are immediately identifiable but their agent is not. As the scene rapidly progresses, there is a dramatic shift in this relationship between agency and identity; the intruder's mundane actions, which hitherto have involved inanimate entities as objects (the boots and watch, for example), are suddenly transformed into the act of rape inflicted upon the female body, as the male agent is eventually identified by his victim.

The concepts of centre and periphery in the context of sexual abuse and rape are highly complex, and by no means easy to articulate. They are eloquently conveyed in the following quotation from an article by Rhonda Capelon entitled 'Surfacing Gender: Reconceptualising Crimes against Women in Time of War':

> Every rape is a grave violation of physical and mental integrity.
> Every rape has the potential to profoundly debilitate, to render the woman homeless in her own body and destroy her sense of security in the world. (Capelon 1998:76)

References

Bal, M. (2001): *Looking In: the Art of Viewing*. Amsterdam: G & M Arts International.
Capelon, R. (1998): 'Surfacing Gender: Reconceptualising Crimes against Women in Time of War', in L. A. Lorentzen and J. Turpin (eds): *Women and War Reader*. New York: New York University Press.
Forster, E. M. (1990 [1927]): *Aspects of the Novel*. London: Penguin.
Fowler, R. (1996): *Linguistic Criticism*. Oxford: Oxford University Press.
Gauguin, P. (1932): *Christian Krohg*. Oslo: Gyldendal Norsk Forlag.
Granaas, R. C. (2000): 'Den kroppen som ikke var hennes', in R. C. C. Krogsveen (ed.): *Født av spindel og jern*. Oslo: Cappelen.
Klosterman, E. F. (1997): *The Music She Hears: Point of View and Technique in Women's Writing about Childhood Sexual Abuse*. Ohio: Bowling Green State University. (Dissertation in partial fulfilment of PhD: Microfiche edition.)
Krohg, C. (1994 [1886]): *Albertine*. Oslo: Gyldendal.
Mills, S. (1995): *Feminist Stylistics*. London: Routledge.
Rimmon-Keenan, S. (1983): *Narrative Fiction: Contemporary Poetics*. London: Methuen.
Thue, O. (1968): *Christian Krohg: En Bibliografi*. Oslo: Universitetsforlaget.
Wassmo, H. (1981): *Huset med den blinde glassveranda*. Oslo: Gyldendal.

Notes

1. Gauguin's biography gives a full and fascinating account of Christian Krohg's life.
2. The author does not use the word for danger, *fare*, but has instead coined a new term to depict the specific type of danger facing Tora. I have gratefully borrowed Randi Eden's translation of *farligheten* as 'dangerousness'.
3. Unless otherwise stated, all translations are by the author.
4. Included in the 1994 Gyldendal edition is Krohg's defence speech to the Supreme Court on 18th October 1887, which was printed in its entirety in the newspaper *Verdens Gang* the day after the trial.
5. I have taken this extract from Christian Krohg's defence speech (Krohg 1994:116-17).
6. Thue writes: 'Både som maler og forfatter ville han gi øyeblikkets inntrykk, unngå all utpensling og bare gjengi det som momentant hadde grepet ham.'

Stille Eksistenser:
Silence, Language and Landscape in Grønfeldt, Greig and Warner

C. Claire Thomson

Geometries of language and silence

The late makar Norman MacCaig asks, in a poem called 'Centre of Centres', 'How many geometries are there / with how many circles / to be a centre of?' (MacCaig 1990:271-73). In focusing on Scotland and Denmark as nations[1] on the margins of Europe, I am all too aware that these marginal nations also function as national centres for various ethnic and social peripheries. Marginality, it goes without saying, is relative, subjective, and culturally constructed. To continue the same poem: 'Grassblade, cathedral, hero – / strawberry jam-pot – each / is a centre / of innumerable circles.' A nice way to think of the concentric circles that coalesce in the ongoing re-creation of national margins and centres.

The focus of this chapter is the 'silence' of the peripheries: how is the liminality of landscape and language troped in texts written from these shifting, concentric 'margins'? Silence, too, is shifty: it is both metaphor and strategy, and thus says something about the ambiguity of marginality. The neo-Marxist discourse of internal colonialism tends to draw not only on the metaphor of the 'silencing' of peripheral languages and cultures, but also on that of 'voice' as a strategy of resistance (Tägil 1995:19).

Scotland and Denmark, I want to argue, are both engaged in a *discourse* of marginality. I am hinting, firstly, at discourse in Foucault's sense: a network of writings and pronouncements in a field of specialist knowledge, limited to a qualified fellowship. One Danish political commentator has recently joked: 'Det specielt danske er, at have den slags specialister' – what is especially Danish is to have the kind of specialists who analyse Danishness! This kind of (post)national ironic analysis is itself, of course, part of the helix of obsessive self-definition; or, as my Granda would have put it, 'it's meant half in fun, hail in earnest'.[2] In the postcolonial context, marginality is a kind of knowledge, and thus power: by slipping in the Scots adage in the previous sentence, am I attempting to establish my own linguistic liminality – and thus a spurious authority stemming from lived experience? For power, as Foucault also insists, is all tied up with resistance: 'Where there is power there is resistance, and yet, or rather consequently, this resistance is never in a position of exteriority in relation to power' (1978:95). Neither power, nor resistance, can ever be centred, or settled.[3]

Discourse has an earthier sense, as well: speaking, holding forth, conversing. Cairns Craig writes of the 'dialectics of dialect' (1999:75-116 and *passim*), the negotiation in text of the profusion and perplexity of communication between different generations and different regions of Scots:

> Scots displaces English into being the supplementary language because it remains the origin of the nation's literary culture, though it can do so only by allowing Gaelic in turn to assert its founding claim upon the nation's 'throat'. This constant displacement of the source of Scottish identity requires a process of unending translation that makes it impossible for the father to understand his son, or for the child to know its mother tongue. (Craig 1999:76)

And Andrew Greig's recent poem 'Scotland' (2001:54-55) deals with much the same issue:

> Oh blethering seannachie
>> skiving on the machair
>>> clutching mongrel polyglottal
>
> tatters of languages
>> which we once wore
>>> in elegant style n'est-ce pas

This linguistic dimension of the Scottish national imagination is crucial, for it resists any centripetal dynamic; in this respect it is the antithesis of the Danish national language (for reasons which I'll come back to). Identity in Scotland – and I was vaguely aware of this even as a child, code-switching between playground, classroom and living-room – seems to be constructed along the faultlines of language, in the liminal spaces between dialects, sociolects and standards. In literature, especially, what Greig calls 'tatters of languages' dance around the empty centre of a national written standard.

Mikhail Bakhtín's concepts of 'dialogue', 'heteroglossia' and 'carnival' are fruitful approaches to Scottish texts of the late twentieth century, whose polyphony is, increasingly, a matter of jostling varieties of Scots, rather than the traditional interaction of Scots (usually as dialogue) and standard English (usually as omniscient narratorial voice) (Wesling 1993; Craig 1999; Hart 2002). Obvious examples of this newer dynamic are James Kelman, Irvine Welsh, and Suhayl Saadi. And yet reading the textual representation of a Scots

-lect (dia-, socio-, ethno-, or idio-) is an *uncanny* experience: precisely because one reads silently. Reading aloud is a suspect practice (Huang 2001:165ff), and yet, this non-standard English requires to be sounded out before it can make sense. I listen, but I don't hear my own mother tongue: is this because my mother brought me up to reject her language, or because the dialect of my village in deepest darkest Lanarkshire has not yet been committed to paper – or, in fact, do most Scottish readers only hear their differentiated linguistic identity in the *gaps* between other(ed) 'Scots' demotics?

In a more abstract sense, we can perhaps also think of silence as the sublime – not *merely* the absence of language, but as Jim Crumley describes his one 'sacred' experience of absolute silence in the Scottish mountains, 'that wondrous, symbolic nothing, a mountain heartbeat, or a glimpse of nature asleep' (2001:59). This is a kind of 'otherside' of language[4] beyond or before our means of expression; these gaps, these perplexed silences beyond and between the telling of the nation.

Time and landscape

> This is not about geography but time. [...] It has to do with time and weather; cloud level, altitude, the transformation of water to ice, ice to water. It's the point where the material world; its crystals of snow and rhyolote, the gnarled branches of heather, shifts through us. (Fellows & Prentice 2001:115-19)

The national imagination is easily seduced by the conaturality of topography and national character. Scotland's heteroglossic 'tatters of languages' have their analogue in the diversity of Scottish landscapes: mountain and machair, highland, island and lowland. Thinking now of the imagined territory of the nation, there is the same double movement: a discourse of marginality that tends to be centripetal and homogenising in Denmark, and centrifugal and dialogic in Scotland.

This impulse can be illustrated, in the Danish case, with the modern refrain of the Danes, their politicians and their tourist offices: 'we are a small country, but... our welfare state / football team / liquorice is the best in the world'. This compensation complex is often traced back to the traumatic defeat of 1864 at Dybbøl, which resulted in the cession of the duchies of Slesvig-Holsten to the German Bund, some fifty years after the Congress of Vienna had deprived the Danish state of the mountainous expanse of Norway. The national catch-phrase in the rump-state of Denmark became: *hvad udad tabes skal indad vindes* (Østergård 1992:40-41) (what is lost to the outside shall be won on the inside). And one of the national discourses of the nineteenth century, curiously enough, became one of *flatness*, or, rather, a lack of mountains – a crucial trope in the ongoing 'forging' of a socio-cultural cohesion and linguistic homogeneity. The national priest and bard, N. F. S. Grundtvig, wrote many a popular hymn proclaiming: 'We are not born to heights and gales: / It suits us best to remain on earth' (Borup Jensen 1993:148, my translation, and Østergård 1996). The sentiment was echoed in Michael Falch's chart-topping pop hit *I et land uden høje bjerge* (In a Land without High Mountains, 1986), which links the landscape to an alleged lack of bombast in the expression of modern Danish dreams (Borup Jensen 1993:153-54). This imagined landscape is as contingent, constructed and, ultimately, as 'colonial' as any other, and the interplay of centre and periphery here is fascinating: it was (mostly) the middle-class writers and artists of Golden Age Copenhagen who 'discovered' and tried to conserve Jutland, its heaths and its rolling hills and dales. Perhaps most tellingly, Hans Christian Andersen, in the wake of Walter Scott's enormous popularity in Denmark, proclaimed Jutland 'our very own Scotland' (Scavenius 1994:174-85).

If the (realist) novel, as Benedict Anderson's seductive but problematic thesis suggests, is the perfect conduit for national imagining (Anderson 1991:25ff), then the topography of the national landscape must be considered a palimpsest, a doubly- (or multiply-) layered construction. It must exist in text (it is also tempting to say: on celluloid) as well as in soil and rock. Moreover, a *national* topography must be a *historical* one – it must include the temporal dimension of landscape. Thus the 'real' and the 'textual' landscapes are also collective – and individual – memoryscapes. The nation is imagined synchronically as well as diachronically; the peripheral limits and borderlands are important for the former dynamic, and the nation's mythic origins and destiny are important for the latter, though the two can hardly be separated. Homi K. Bhabha describes the dynamic and multidimensional process of mapping the nation in time and space thus:

> For the political unity of the nation consists in a continual displacement of its irredeemably plural modern space, bounded by different, even hostile nations, into a signifying space that is archaic and mythical, paradoxically representing the nation's modern territoriality [...] the difference of space returns as the Sameness of time. (1994:149)

'This is not about geography but time'

G. F. Dutton also observes how human, botanical and geological chronologies merge in the Scottish mountains: 'You climb through "Deep Time" – beside you, last week's seedling roots itself into strata weathered before life began [...] and often only the brute compulsion of your lower centres hauls you back from the junkie delight of dissolving into the O-so-caressing Infinite' (2001:157).[5]

The 'recurrent metaphor of landscape as the inscape of national identity' (Bhabha 1994:143) weaves its way through time, place and text in the national imagination. The mythic mountains – or, equally, the mythic *lack* of mountains – are tropes of political, cultural, linguistic and territorial discourses. Such an iconographic approach to the complex imaginary of the nation is useful in the early twenty-first century, when Anderson's notion of the nation's steady, linear movement 'down (or up) history' (1991:26) may have been superseded in the popular imagination by new spacetimes inspired by relativistic physics and cyberspace (Middleton & Woods 2000).

In the twentieth century, the imagining of Scotland's space and history has been complicated by the nation's role in the construction of the British Empire, as Cairns Craig has argued:

> The space of the [Scottish] nation extended tentacularly around the world, and like the ships launched on the Clyde to carry much of the world's trade around the globe, took the ground of Scotland only as a launching place [...] There can be no coherent narrative of the nation not because the nation lacks narrative development but for precisely the opposite reason: its narrative spills out over many territories; it cannot be accommodated within the continuities demanded by the genre of a national history. (Craig 1999:236-37)

If, indeed, the spacetime of Scottish history is experienced as dissipating and coalescing with other spaces and times, then this very lack of 'coherence' can itself be the myth around which the nation is performed and negotiated. David McCrone's analysis of Scotland as a 'stateless nation', where 'civic' neo-nationalism takes precedence over the older 'ethnic' nationalism (1998:128-29), provides the parameters within which shifting *linguistic* loyalties and usages can be seen to mirror the 'political resource' (1998:129) of multiple identities: local, regional, Scottish, British.

It can be argued that the projected history of the Danish nation has been, in the twentieth century, to a considerable extent tied up with the utopian future of the welfare state. Now, after the apex of the Welfare State, the nation looks *backward* to a Golden Age of Welfare, the 1950s and 60s.[6] As Lars Trägårdh (1997:283) argues, the Nordic welfare state is as much cultural as social: 'from the outset [it] was an order that more perfectly than others fulfilled the ideal of the symmetrical alignment of cultural nation, civic state, and political economy'. In post-1864 continental Denmark, where the limits of state, territory, nation, language and *ethnie* have coincided almost perfectly, the territoriality of the welfare state is part and parcel of its culturality; all the more so because a direct line of descent from Lutheranism, through Grundtvigianism, to Danish Social Democracy is not only a fantasy of pedagogic myth-history (McCrone 1998:51) but is also seriously analysed by historians of a post-national bent (Østergård 1998:336-68). The spatio-temporal functioning of the welfare state as an inclusive 'imagined community' is best summed up by the Swedish Social Democratic vision, where state and hearthfire coalesce in the iconic *folkhem*: the people's home.

'Lurking beautiful mountain'[7]

How does contemporary literature imagine these new (and old) national spacetimes? MacCaig's remembered mountain lurks at the centre of two recent Scottish novels which play with the peripheral and the peripatetic. Andrew Greig's *Electric Brae* (1992) journeys to the outer and upper limits of the Scottish topography, while Alan Warner's *Morvern Callar* (first published 1995) skirts the extremes of dialect and idiolect, merging body and landscape. In both novels, a peripheral place sits at the centre of the text, and identity is constructed at the edge of language: in the immanent difference of dialects, and in the tension between speaking and silence.

Andrew Greig is a poet, novelist and mountaineer. His first novel, *Electric Brae* (1992), is concerned with mapping out the many centres and peripheries of Scotland; in a sense, the novel's 'centre' is to be found not only at the end of the text but at land's end: a figure standing on the rocky pinnacle of The Old Man of Hoy, looking south and musing '[o]n a better day you can see Scotland clear' (Greig 1992:312). The novel covers the Thatcher years, moving from Glasgow to Edinburgh to Stirling and all points in between – even Shotts, 'the end of the world' (96)! For, moving between centres, the journey to the 'peripheries' can lead inland, and can trace the routes and roots[8] of earlier Scots:

> [W]e bombed through the guts of Glasgow. It was a sudden dislocation from high silence of Rest and be Thankful and I thought, this is part of us too – the fast roads, the driving music, jeans and tower blocks and women's hands reaching for the steering wheel. But still under the motorways the old roads persist and like our fathers lay out the road we go, if not the style we go in. (95-96)

The Scottish landscape, as palimpsest and patchwork, is troped and excavated in this novel by dint of geological and archaeological motifs. The strata-effect is also borne out formally, for the ludic logic of 'Kim's Game' and 'Scissors, Paper, Stone' overwrites any linear chronology of the eighties. The past rears up through this text like the ancient rocks of the north-west, in metalanguage and ekphrasis, forming a bedrock of cultural cynicism beyond which the narrator will seldom venture:

> I was wabbit. My father's word, still popping up like an outcrop of enduring, harder rock. (10)

> There are foregrounds and backgrounds, layers of history like he's been excavating the canvas, digging away at the foundations with a palette knife instead of a trowel. A kind of naked archaeology. *Naked archaeology ma arse*, he hears his father say. (62)

This deep past – and its igneous patriarchy – is there to be surmounted, and its controlling metaphor is the Old Man of Hoy: 'In Scotland there are several Old Men, but the Old Man of Hoy is the boss – 450 feet of sheer prick. A lonely, exposed and rapidly eroding one' (11). The faultlines that run through Scottish identity are as much generational as they are regional or dialectal; the sites of negotiation between fathers and sons, for example, or between Scots born on either side of the late seventies' political watershed,[9] are also the meeting points of differentiated language, politics and place:

> My dad respected manual labour as the real thing. He'd worked with his hands for twenty years. He also saw manual labour as a dead end. His attitude to work was confused and Scottish and contradictory. Mine too. [...] His accent was moving in and out of focus like his finger. Who are we? I wondered. We don't even speak consistently. We'll say 'yes' and 'aye' and 'yeah' in the same conversation, alternate between 'know' and 'ken', 'bairn', 'wean' and 'child' and not even know why. Even the old man did it, and I've lost half his tongue, the better half. We're a small country with blurry boundaries. (56)

The text's compulsion to map the political and cultural multiplicity of 1980s Scotland gives it a centrifugal dynamic. Topographical extremities are reached *in extremis*: 'He sailed to Shetland near the edge, looking for shelter or a place to fall off' (184). Beyond Shetland, there is only the sublime chaos of the sea; at the other extremity of Scotland, the borderlands. At both ends, the idea of a homogeneous 'Scottish' culture is stretched thin, as suggested by the debatable national semiotics of 'pseudo-English public school' rugby (27) or the 'defensive huddle' of Berwick (41), or by the remnants of the Norse language in Shetland (186).

As in Greig's later novel *That Summer* (2000:176-83), climbs are turning points, times out of time in which introspection and resolution can unfurl and other battles can be played out against the elements. I would argue that time on the mountainside is illuminated by Bakhtín's description of his literary *chronotope*: 'Time, as it were, thickens, takes on flesh, becomes artistically visible; likewise, space becomes charged and responsive to the movements of time, plot and history' (Bakhtín 1981:84):

> I eased away from my temporary security [...]. Time passed – the hardest, the best. Serious play. My world narrowed to textures of snow, opacities of ice, spikes of black rock inches from my face, the axes dirling in my mitts, the red and green ropes swooping down between my feet. (Greig 1992:166)

Like the 'ancient grudges and betrayals' that still haunt Glencoe (162),
different times and places in the national (and international) imaginary of
Scotland coalesce in the mountains, that most national of Scottish landscapes
that exists for most Scots only in text or on film. Climbing avails itself of an
exclusive language, but this is not to say that *Electric Brae* de-mystifies the
mythic landscape. Naming the landscape (on maps or on the radio) is still a
heteroglossic litany whose deeper meaning lies in the silences between
sounds, sights and sites:

> Jimmy spread out the map. Nearby: Grind O da Navir, The Holes of Scraada,
> Hamnaure, The Villains of Hamna Voe. Give them a wide berth for sure. Where
> else? Zoar, Tonga, Swarta, Giltarump. Whit? Quoy, Quarff [...] It was like
> listening to Shonagh's Gaelic, a foreign tongue and yet the deep sense one once
> knew what this meant, and on some level still do... (1992:189)

The names of Scotland's landmarks are often foreign to English speakers and
must be translated, or doubly-named. The Electric Brae itself is another place
in another litany (94) that embodies the contingencies of gravity, compass and
perspective, on land and in text. As Cairns Craig points out, Scottish culture
and literature has often been evaluated as 'fragmented', a function of its
development as a 'peripheral' culture, at least from the perspective of the
ostensibly unified, core English culture, our national Other. However,
drawing on MacMurray (though the idea is not a million miles from
Bakhtínian 'dialogue', either), he argues: 'A Scottish culture which has
regularly been described as "schizophrenic" because of its inner divisions is
not necessarily sick; it is engaged in the dialogue with the other, a
conversation in different dialects, a dialectic that is the foundation not only of
persons but of nations' (Craig 1999:115).

Greig expresses much the same in the poem 'Orkney/This Life'
(2001:64): 'It is the way sea and sky / work off each other constantly [...] It is
the way you lean to me / and the way I lean to you, as if / we are each other's
prevailing'. In its compulsion to trace the 'mongrel polyglottal' culture,
language and landscape of Scotland, *Electric Brae* engages in this 'dialogue'
with the other(s) within. The thematic – as opposed to chronological –
dynamic of the text, and the kaleidoscopic shifts in narratorial voice between
first, third, and occasionally second person privilege the connectedness of all
things, of places and temporalities in Scotland. The echo of the *Electric
Brae*'s dual perspective is heard in the narrator's old engineering textbook:
'The plane of severance is also the plane of connection' (Greig 1992:312), a
pleasing geometry of which MacCaig, 'enriched by geometries / that make a
plenum of more / than the three dimensions' (1990:273), would have
approved.

If *Electric Brae* is encyclopedic and peripatetic, Alan Warner's debut novel, *Morvern Callar*, is claustrophobic. Strategies of silence cluster around the eponymous narrator, whose voice skirts the peripheries of language. The name Morvern Callar itself encompasses landscape – the granite mountains of the Morvern peninsula – and silence: *callar* is a Spanish verb which, in various conjugations, can suggest 'to silence' and 'to be silent' as Morvern finds out when she gets beyond the limited horizon of her existence in a nameless West Coast town (Oban?) and goes to Spain. Morvern is naturally silent: 'I'm taciturn' 'What's that?' 'It's a word my boyfriend told me. It means you don't really say much' (Warner 1996:36). But Morvern is the narrator, and her language goes beyond an identifiable Scots dialect: her idiolect betrays a slightly off-centre, 'foreignised' ontology: 'There were bad sinking feelings' (119); 'I stopped the going-up every time my heart was really banging in my throat' (89); 'I switched on Nighttimeness' (51). Her reaction to hearing Spanish de-familiarises the intolerable distance between all languages: 'The taxi driver started *saying words* [...] The taxi driver *says something in his words*' (122, my italics).[10]

Morvern is also an agent of silence: her boyfriend is a writer, who has committed suicide at the beginning of the novel. His last letter asks her to publish his novel for him: 'I'll settle for posthumous fame as long as I'm not lost in silence' (82). A nice postmodern wink at the death of the author, this makar of standard, written English: we never know 'His' name, and Morvern sends the manuscript off with her own name on it. The boyfriend has a train set in the attic, arranged on a scale model of the town and the hillside it stands on. In a curious passage, Morvern lugs his dead body up to the attic, hoists it up to the ceiling, and brings it crashing down on the model:

> [H]is toes at the far end of the pass. His face beyond the railway line. His body crushed the hotel with its pointing up tower at the top of the stairs. The Tree Church on the sgnurr above where he lay back upon the land. (52-53)

The dead body of the author, lying back upon the same land that Morvern later buries bits of him in; a fate echoed in an inscription she later observes in Spain: 'The words All Hills Are Calvary were over the top of the wooden doors with other words for this in all different languages' (153-54).

Morvern's claustrophobic litany of the trappings of small-town boredom (nail varnish colours, obscure song titles, methods of packaging severed limbs) is translated into a finely-honed dialogue between micro- and macro-perspectives whenever she finds herself in a landscape, be it West Highland or Balearic. Inserted into the body of the text is a hand-drawn map of the limited, provincial landscape that Morvern exists in and that exists in simulacrum in her attic, and in the text, and, with her, we look down upon it panoramically during one of her burial expeditions:

> I looked out at the landscape moving without haste to no bidding at all. I yawned a big yawn. Two arms and a leg were buried on the cliff above the sycamore tree and higher up the torso and leg would be helping flower the sheets of bluebells below the dripping rocks. (91)

Again, we can appeal to Bakhtín's chronotope, as the temporal dimension (the time of nature) of this mountainside becomes 'visible', and as space becomes 'charged' with the imminent movement of plot which will take Morvern away from the familiar prospect(s) she surveys from the mountain.

The deadpan grotesquery of the dismemberment and burial is here elided by an almost magical realist revelation of the body's place in the landscape, of the natural cycle. In this novel, the sense of connectedness is not so much a question of dialogue with the Other within, more a meeting of the Body and what is external to it. Compare Morvern's sensual, cosmic account of swimming, in Spain:

> All was made of darknesses [...] I let my legs sink down; my nudeness below in the blackwater; legs hung in that huge deep under me and the layer on layer and fuzzy mush of star pinpricks were above with the little buzz of me in between. (208)

Cairns Craig (1999:239-40) has already commented on this 'otherside', the double perspective on the Scottish historical landscape, which obtains in *These Demented Lands* (1997), the sequel to *Morvern Callar*. For all that Morvern repeatedly travels along the single railway line out of town, to London and to Spain, the other landscapes she sees tend to be mapped onto, or read against, the same, enclosed world-in-the-attic: returning to her home-town after a long stay abroad, Morvern navigates by her memory of the model village in her loft (Warner 1996:227), and her description of a Spanish town intensifies the Chinese box-effect:

> Where you would expect a jumble of hills and a circular folly above a port: none. Where you would expect piers with a seawall between and an esplanade of hotels beyond: none [...] The resort I was looking at was really another place. (151)

Again, in this text, where the controlling metaphor seems to be translation and transmutation, the 'other within' and the other without, where language threatens to fall off the edge into incomprehensibility and silence, the compulsion to trace the outer and upper limits of the Scottish landscape, to make them a centre, but a complex centre, is paramount. The mountains are always somewhere, lurking.

Jarring witnesses

> It comes clear: time doesn't flow, it drips. And here's eternities between the drops. 'Down by the Riverside' (Greig 2001:19)

In the Danish text, how can 'marginality' be expressed when the national discourse and national written language is one of homogeneity and conformity? How can a perspective on the lie of the land be gained, if not from high ground? In the 1990s, the prevailing orthodoxy in the human sciences has been to de-doxify the contingency and constructedness of their own grand narratives (questioning the nation-state is one symptom of this). Many historians now choose to emphasise the stories of what Robert Holton (1994) calls 'jarring witnesses', those versions of (national) history that do (or did) not chime with a national, schoolbook history, and which therefore were silenced: the testaments of marginal ethnic and social groups. The 'stille eksistenser' (quiet existences) in my title could be the Danish version of this concept, coined by a turn-of-the-century author, Herman Bang, who himself was rather interested in borders and liminality.[11] Clearly, the balance of power between silence and voice within a nation is constantly in flux, a situation grasped at by Homi K. Bhabha when he writes of the double-time of the nation: the constant telling and being told of the 'pedagogical' and the 'performative' versions of the national narrative:

> [T]he people are the historical 'objects' of a nationalist pedagogy, giving the discourse an authority that is based on the pre-given or constituted historical origin or event; the people are also the 'subjects' of a process of signification [...] The scraps, patches, and rags of daily life must be turned into the signs of a national culture, while the very act of the narrative performance interpellates a growing circle of national subjects. (Bhabha 1994:145)

Vibeke Grønfeldt's novel *I dag* (Today, 1998) consists of a series of short text fragments chronicling the living memory (1952-1996) of a nameless, rural Danish community, where history is experienced from the margins: a place out of time. Grønfeldt has achieved a good deal of critical (if not popular) acclaim since the late 1970s for some fifteen novels; she tends to be categorised as a chronicler of the disappearance of Danish rural life, and to be lauded for the precision and poetry of her descriptions of landscape and weather.[12] Her subjects are usually described as *randeksistenser*, marginal or peripheral existences, for these are anachronistic lives lived not only outside the metropolitan centre of Denmark, but also at the edge of history. Formally, though, *I dag* fits into the paradigm of 1990s literature in Denmark, which has emphasised both the encyclopedic novel and the shorter text 'fragment'. The question of who is telling and who is told intrigues the reader of *I dag*, for shifts in tense, and the regular italicised interjection in the narrative of what seems to be a voice from the future, suggests a tension between the free-for-all of everyday, quiet existences, and an organising power, a textual centre:

> Pressens radioavis slutter. Hun trykker på kontakten uden at have hørt et ord om Konrad Adenauer, Grauballe-manden eller de tordenbyger, som nærmer sig bakkerne vest for byen, hvor ungkreaturerne græsser. *Hvor rigmandshusene og de låste låger siden breder sig, skyder op overalt* (Grønfeldt 1998:8, italics in original)

> (The radio news ends. She flicks the off-switch without having heard a single word on Konrad Adenauer, the Grauballe Man or the thundery showers approaching the slopes west of the town, where the young cattle are grazing. *Where, later, the posh houses and the locked gates will sprawl, springing up everywhere*) (my translation).

The text's rootedness in the landscape expands into the same kind of cosmic consciousness we see in *Morvern Callar*, though this unfolds primarily in time in *I dag*, rather than in space:

> I femogfyrre år har der været orden og ro af en anden verden ind i kraniets stilhed. Den bløde, muslingeformede substans har med samme sikkerhed udført store og små opgaver til gavn for manden. En konstant proces bestående af livets samlede erfaring. Sekund lagt på sekund i millioner af år. (63)

> (For forty-five years order and otherworldly peace have reigned in the stillness of his skull. The soft, mussel-like substance has performed tasks great and small with the same reliability for the man's benefit. An ongoing process, the accumulated experience of life. Second piled upon second over millions of years.)

'Second piled upon second': the most poignant feature of *I dag* is its fragmented chronology. Every 'story' takes place on a specified date, and *part* of each story is a detailed account of a few minutes of the day in question. These 'close-up' sections of the text are narrated in the present tense, but the futuristic voice cuts through both parts of the narrative. Stripped of the traditional novel's chronological cohesion, which rests on our concepts of 'community' and of 'meanwhile' (Anderson 1991:24), this text hints at the unknown and unknowable eternities of other people's experience.

Not until the final chapter do we discover who the organising voice (ostensibly) is: a middle-aged man named Verner, who works as a janitor at the community nursing home. His own story is an account of the coalescence of the aged residents' voices, stories and dreams in the rooms and corridors of the home, as he goes about his early cleaning shift. It may or may not be

Verner who acts as a kind of portal for the hi/stories of these institutionalised, silenced geriatrics – or is he, too, a jarring witness?

> Jeg skubber og trækker. Og folk puffer til mig. Stemmerne begynder at ramme mig, først som enlige, små sten, siden som haglbyger. (290)

> (I shove [the machine] back and forth. And people nudge at me. The voices begin to hit me, at first like isolated little stones, then like a hailstorm.)

In any case, the nursing home as organising principle is pleasingly Foucauldian, but it is also an iconic trope of Denmark's Welfare State, that marriage of democracy and totalitarianism that usurped the functions of the matriarchal family. *I dag*, then, I would argue, is a work of mourning for the *folkhem* of the past. But in forming itself as a vortex of silenced stories, it also maps out the relationship between *institutional* centre and periphery in twentieth-century Denmark. And in situating itself in the romantic (but crumbling) rural landscape of Denmark, it deconstructs the imaginings, rooted in the national landscape, of the metropolitan centre.

This, then, is quite a different problematic of silence and silencing, though it is still a matter of power. Any telling of hi/stories is an act of interpretation, and therefore a kind of violence; any appropriation of the spoken word in written, literary language is doomed to itself become a kind of pedagogy, for the perplexity of difference, topographical and linguistic, even – especially – within a peripheral region, can never be encompassed.

References

Anderson, B. (1991): *Imagined Communities. Reflections on the Origin and Spread of Nationalism* (revised edition). London & New York: Verso.

Bakhtín, M. (1981): *The Dialogic Imagination. Four Essays*, ed. Michael Holquist, trans. C. Emerson & M. Holquist. Austin, Texas: University of Texas Press.

Bhabha, H. K. (1994): 'DissemiNation: Time, Narrative and the Margins of the Modern Nation', in Bhabha, H. K. (ed.): *The Location of Culture*. London & New York: Routledge, pp. 139-70.

Borup Jensen, T. (ed.) (1993): *Danskernes identitetshistorie. Antologi til belysning af danskernes selvforståelse*. Copenhagen: C A Reitzels forlag.

Craig, C. (1999): *The Modern Scottish Novel: Narrative and the National Imagination*. Edinburgh: Edinburgh University Press.

Crumley, J. (2001): 'The Key to a Fragile Silence', in Finlay, A. (ed.): *The Way to Cold Mountain. A Scottish Mountains Anthology*. Edinburgh: Pocketbooks, pp. 59-64.

Dutton, G. F. (2001): 'Some Scottish Mountain Activities', in Finlay, A. (ed.): *The Way to Cold Mountain. A Scottish Mountains Anthology*. Edinburgh: Pocketbooks, pp. 153-83.

Fellows, G. & Prentice, T. (2001): 'The Material World Shifting Through Us', in Finlay, A.

(ed.): *The Way to Cold Mountain. A Scottish Mountains Anthology.* Edinburgh: Pocketbooks, pp. 113-20.

Foucault, M. (1978): *The History of Sexuality,* vol. 1: *An Introduction,* trans. R. Hurley. New York: Pantheon.

Greig, A. (1992): *Electric Brae. A Modern Romance.* Edinburgh: Canongate.

Greig, A. (2000): *That Summer.* London: Faber & Faber.

Greig, A. (2001): *Into You.* Northumberland: Bloodaxe Books.

Grønfeldt, V. (1998): *I dag,* Copenhagen: Samleren.

Hart, M. (2002) 'Solvent Abuse: Irvine Welsh and Scotland', in *Postmodern Culture,* 12:2.

Hauge, H. (2000): 'Lad dog verden begynde', in *Politiken,* 28 October.

Holton, R. (1994): *Jarring Witnesses: Modern Fiction and the Representation of History.* New York & London: Harvester Wheatsheaf.

Huang, M. P. (2001): 'Gestures of the Unheard – on Style, Rhetoric and Articulation in Novelistic Prose after Bakhtín: Two Novels of the Danish Author Peer Hultberg', in Bruhn, J. & Lundquist, J. (eds): *The Novelness of Bakhtín. Perspectives and Possibilities.* Copenhagen: Museum Tusculanum Press.

Lynch, M. (1992): *Scotland: A New History.* London: Pimlico.

MacCaig, N. (1990): *Collected Poems.* London: Chatto & Windus.

MacCaig, N. (1997): *Selected Poems.* London: Chatto & Windus.

McCrone, D. (1998): *The Sociology of Nationalism.* London: Routledge.

Middleton, P. & Woods, T. (2000): *Literatures of Memory. History, Time and Space in Postwar Writing.* Manchester: Manchester University Press.

Scavenius, B. (ed.) (1994): *The Golden Age in Denmark. Art and Culture 1800-1850,* trans. B. Haveland. Copenhagen: Gyldendal.

Schmidt, P. *et al.* (eds) (1999): *Læsninger i dansk litteratur,* vol. V: 1970-2000. Odense: Odense Universitetsforlag.

Soila, T. (1998): 'Sweden', in Soila, T. *et al.* (eds): *Nordic National Cinemas.* London & New York: Routledge, pp. 142-232.

Thomson, C. C. (1999): '"My Water of Leith Runs Through a Double City...": Cityscape and Landscape in the Poetry of Norman MacCaig and Klaus Rifbjerg', in *Northern Studies,* vol. 34, pp. 61-88.

Thomson, C. C. (2004): '"Slainte, I goes, and he says his word": Morvern Callar Undergoes the Trial of the Foreign', in *Language and Literature* vol. 14 (1).

Thrane, L. (2002): 'Visual Pleasure and Writerly Delight. On the Longing for Apocalypse in Baggesen's Alpine Journey', in *Scandinavica* vol. 41 (1), pp. 5-20.

Trägårdh, L. (1997): 'Statist Individualism. On the Culturality of the Nordic Welfare State', in Sørensen, Ø. & Stråth, B. (eds): *The Cultural Construction of Norden.* Oslo: Scandinavian University Press, pp. 253-85.

Tägil, S. (ed.) (1995): *Ethnicity and Nation-Building in the Nordic World.* London: Hurst & Co.

Warner, A. (1996 [1995]): *Morvern Callar.* London: Vintage, 1996.

Warner, A. (1997): *These Demented Lands.* London: Vintage.

Wesling, D. (1993): 'Mikhail Bakhtín and the Social Poetics of Dialect', in *Papers on Language and Literature,* vol. 29 (3), pp. 303-22.

Østergård, U. (1992): *Europas ansigter.* Copenhagen: Rosinante.

Østergård, U. (1996): 'Peasants and Danes: The Danish National Identity and Political Culture', in Eley, G. and Suny, G. (eds): *Becoming National. A Reader.* Oxford: Oxford University Press, pp. 170-222.

Østergård, U. (1998): *Europa – Identitet og identitetspolitik.* Copenhagen: Munksgaard Rosinante.

Notes

1. Without eliding the fundamental differences in status between Denmark as a relatively ethnically homogeneous nation-state, and Scotland as a devolved, and yet still 'stateless' nation within the British state, I am assuming (a) that national imagining functions in comparable ways in Scotland and Denmark, and (b) that implicated in both national imaginaries are common non-national dimensions (supra-national, international, global/local) that render 'statehood' increasingly incidental to the discussion of 'nationness'.

2. The debate among parents and acquaintances when I enquired how to spell this word – 'wholly' in standard English – serves to illustrate my point here. I have adopted the spelling suggested by the *Online Scots Dictionary* (www.Scots-online.org).

3. It should be observed here that 'power' is not used by Foucault as a synonym for Force, e.g. military violence.

4. 'Otherside' is a neologism of Morvern Callar's in *These Demented Lands*, an idea interpreted spatially by Cairns Craig (1999:240).

5. See Thrane (2002) for an interesting discussion of what happens when a Danish romantic finds himself face to face with the Alps...

6. Tytti Soila (1998) argues that the business of nostalgia, or even mourning, for the *folkhem* is reflected in recent trends in Swedish cinema, especially the glut of childhood-themed films of the mid-1970s on.

7. From the poem 'Memorial', in *The White Bird*, 1973 (MacCaig 1997:93). I have discussed elsewhere the multiple geometries of cityscape and landscape in MacCaig's poetry (Thomson 1999).

8. The pun on 'roots and routes' is suggested by Anders Öhman. See pp. 61-62.

9. *Electric Brae* contains several references to the '1977 faultline' (Grieg 1992: 16, 43 and *passim*). This year marked a peak in support for the Scottish National Party, the introduction of the second Bill on Scottish devolution (Lynch 1992:446) – as well as the breakthrough of Punk, which also seems pertinent to the novel's generational concerns (Grieg 1992:44)

10. This aspect of *Morvern Callar* is discussed at more length in Thomson (2004).

11. See, for example, his novel of 1889, *Tine*, translated into English as *Tina*, London, 1984; or his contemporary Holger Drachmann's *Derovre fra Grænsen* (1877), both of which deal with the aftermath of the loss of Denmark's southern-most provinces after the Dano-Prussian war of 1864.

12. For a rare analysis that concentrates on language rather than landscape, see Inger-Lise Hjort-Vetlesen's article on Grønfeldt's novel *Den Blanke Sol* in Schmidt (1999:115-30).

The Debatable Lands and Passable Boundaries of Gender and Nation

Aileen Christianson

'Debatable lands' and 'passable boundaries': both concepts are emblematic of the kind of inevitably shifting, multi-dimensional perspectives that are found in any consideration of nation and gender.[1] Homi Bhabha's 'ambivalent margin of the nation-space' (Bhabha 1990:4) is contained in the Scottish metaphor of 'Debatable Lands'. This was first a term for the Scottish/English borders as a whole when Scotland and England were independent nations, pre-1707. Their borders were fought over and consequently neither static nor entirely definable. Its subsequent manifestation is as a metaphor for any borderline state or idea; it has been used in particular to assess women's writing in terms of borders and margins which provide those tropes of liminality which we use to point up the fluidity and ambiguity identified with the position of women in society.[2]

Nation, region, gender, class and sexuality: they all produce their own boundaries and we pass back and forth across them throughout our lives, all of them constructed by our circumstances and our societies' expectations. These multi-dimensional perspectives are in a perpetual state of flux, with oppositions and alliances in constantly shifting relationships, both within ourselves and with others. It is this same kind of plurality, circularity and interconnection that occurs in the conflicting discourses of nation, region, gender, sexuality and class. These discourses also provide the problematic 'contours' in our 'imagined or ideal community' (Said 1994:280). His notion of literature and culture 'as hybrid [...] and encumbered, or entangled and overlapping with what used to be regarded as extraneous elements' (Said 1994:384) also applies to society's conflicting demands on our loyalty, creating particular and, at times, clashing demands on our commitment. The question is how conjunctions and disjunctions between the marginality of our femaleness and of our nation are to be figured.

If nationalism is a post-rationalist or enlightenment substitute for religion, with fake-historical roots to legitimise it, as Benedict Anderson argues (1991:11), then given the patriarchal, male-centred nature of Christianity and most other world religions, and the oppressive nature of their relation to women, it is inevitable that the construction of the idea of the 'nation' should have been equally male-centred and patriarchal, manifesting itself in the traditions of warrior nations, warrior clan systems, with women as bearers of warriors or symbolic female figures of nationhood, the equivalent nationalist muses to the traditionally female poetic muse. The Irish poet Eavan Boland problematises this within the Irish context:

> Within a poetry inflected by its national tradition, women have often been double-exposed, like a flawed photograph, over the image and identity of the nation. The nationalization of the feminine, the feminization of the national, had become a powerful and customary inscription in the poetry of that very nineteenth century Ireland. 'Kathleen ni Houlihan!' exclaimed McNeice. 'Why / must a country like a ship or a car, be always / female?' (Boland 1996:196)

Anderson, despite seeing nationhood as a socio-cultural concept, a given, like gender: 'everyone can, should, will 'have' a nationality, as he or she 'has' a gender' (Anderson 1991:5), nowhere examines the role of gender in nationhood. His national movements are run by men for men; historically accurate perhaps, but his lack of examination is unimaginative in relation to more than half of the populations of his imagined communities.[3] Perhaps we imagine a different community, one in which we are not represented by Britannia, the 'motherland', or Kathleen ni Houlihan. Ellen Galford's cantankerous Pictish Queen, 'Albanna, She Wolf of the North', rising up from Arthur's Seat in our hour of need under Thatcherite rule, described in her novel *Queendom Come* (Galford 1990:7, 11), is much closer to an imagined possible saviour for women than Robert the Bruce or William Wallace.[4]

Problems created by systems of representation for the nation are only one aspect of the issue of identification. Region, gender, nation, sexuality, class (as well as work and family) also produce particular and conflicting demands on our loyalties, creating a shifting sense of priorities and commitment. It is not so much that class, region or gender intersect with nation, as that they interrogate and problematise it. There is no need to be an international Marxist or Catholic or feminist believing that loyalty to class, religion or gender is supra-national, to be conscious that particular group identities can resist a central national identity. It is clear that women have always had different kinds of split demands and pulls of loyalty, stemming in part from the original passing of ownership of the woman's body from fathers to husbands, loyalties split between outside and inside the family, between parents and partner (of whatever sex), between children and husband/father. These kinds of shifting demands ensure that a commitment to monolithic concepts like 'nationality' is problematic, especially if legal nationality is seen as stemming from the father, not the mother. If the national ideal is constructed around primarily male concerns or ideologies, then commitment to those wide general concepts is likely to be difficult, tinged by scepticism, ironic dismissal, or feelings of exclusion or incompletion. 'Scottish' is tempered or altered by 'woman'. And if Scottish is the 'other' to English, with England used as the dominant reference point, and woman the 'other' to man, Scotswomen have felt a double otherness, a double marginality, or 'double democratic deficit' as the political scientists named it (Brown 2001:204). We experience ourselves 'only fragmentarily, in the little-structured margins of a dominant ideology, as waste, or excess' (Irigaray 1985:30), the dominant ideology for us being both Anglocentric and male.

But experiencing ourselves 'fragmentarily, in the [...] margins of the dominant ideology' can be given a positive reading. Janice Galloway, one of the most thoughtful about her craft and radical in style of contemporary Scottish fiction writers, points out that the 'structures and *normal* practices of both politics and the law make it difficult for women to speak as women directly because there's little accommodation for a female way of seeing' (March & Galloway 1999:85). But she sees women's 'traditional attraction to fiction' as having 'a go at reconstructing the structures':

> Simply for a woman to write as a woman, to be as honest about it as possible, is a statement; not falling into the conventions of assuming guy stuff is 'real' stuff and we're a frill, a fuck or a boring bit that does housework or raises your kids round the edge. That stuff is not round the edge! It's the fucking middle of everything. Deliberately pointing up that otherness, where what passes for normal has no bearing on you or ignores you – that fascinates me. (1999:86)

Said's 'complex and uneven topography' and his 'atonal ensemble' (1994:386), like our 'debatable lands', are metaphors for the shifting inclusiveness necessary to encompass the confusing demands on our loyalty of nation, region, gender, sexuality and class. The complexity and unevenness of the topography is fruitful. So there is a lure in fragmentation and the margins for some of us; there are possibilities for ambiguity and for the power of the marginal, the dispossessed, the peripheral, to assert our right to existence, to be heard, to be experienced positively. No one on the margins wants to acknowledge being central and those truly of the centre rarely acknowledge the power of the margins. Our dialogue is not with them but with each other.

If Scotland's sense of nationhood has a civic rather than an ethnic base, with our surviving national institutions such as the law and education, and the mixed ethnic origins of Scots, then it is not surprising that women may feel excluded from a full sense of being part of the imagined nation of

Scotland. Only in the last twenty-five years or less have women been able to participate fully in the civic institutions which constitute our nationness. And there is a persistent maleness in Scottish civic life which is problematic. Even now, there are very few women in top education posts, despite a majority of women in the lower echelons; the first female High Court judge was not appointed until 1996; the first female Solicitor General not until 2001; there have been no women Lord Advocates; the first female Moderator of the General Assembly of the Church of Scotland was not until 2004. There is still an almost overwhelmingly male bias of central government at Westminster and of senior local government officials, leaders and elected MPs (for example, there were only 118 women elected out of 659 MPs in 2001). The higher proportion (39.5% as opposed to 18%) of women MSPs in the Scottish Parliament (and high profile posts for women in the Scottish Executive between 1999 and 2001) might have indicated some kind of positive change in Scotland, but the recent Executive is predominantly male despite the high proportion of women MSPs to draw from (48 out of 129 MSPs were elected in 1999, and 51 in 2001).

As long as this maleness is central to the political/national structures, the acceptance of maleness as 'universal-male', with female categorised as 'particular-female', continues. Nan Shepherd (the modernist North-East Scottish novelist) reverses and undercuts the universal/particular, male/female conflict in her intensely complex novel *The Weatherhouse* (1930), exposing the universal as less important, less truly honest, than the particular. She explores a version of the male-universal, female-particular dichotomy when the central male character, Garry, is shown pursuing 'splendid generalities' ([1930] 1996:84) at the expense of the specific. In his persecution of a particular woman, he denies his motives are personal: 'It was not as a person that he wanted Louie punished, but as the embodiment of a disgrace' (1996:72). But Garry's certainty in 'splendid generalities' is interrogated by the women in the novel, providing a critical opposition to any assumption by the reader of a male-universal connection. Shepherd's fiction has been long neglected by virtue of her specificity in North-East, rural, female subject matter. In contrast to this neglect, there is a view which sees fiction about working class men as having a national (with an implicit universal) application. In an essay interrogating the concept of the 'hard man' ('terminal form of masculinity') as representative of Scottishness or Scottish maleness, Christopher Whyte perceives 'a "hegemonic shift"' where 'urban fiction in Scotland has increasingly and explicitly assumed the burden of national representation [...] Once urban fiction was assigned a central position, its class and gender placements took on national implications' (1999:278):

The task of embodying and transmitting Scottishness is, as it were, devolved to the unemployed, the socially underprivileged, in both actual and representational contexts. Even a writer like James Kelman, despite his libertarian and egalitarian views, can be seen as participating in a 'representational pact' of this kind with consumers of his fiction. (Whyte 1999:275)

This 'representational pact' allows James Kelman's intensely personal and particular explorations of individual working-class West of Scotland men to be seen as both representing Scottishness and containing a 'commitment to celebrating the realities of contemporary and essentially urban Scotland' (Gifford 1992:9). But this same pact means that Elspeth Barker's *O Caledonia* (1991) was explicitly rejected by Gifford (1992:11) as having any national application – because the heroine is middle class and diametrically opposed in her femaleness to anything that Kelman's heroes might represent. A heroine shown growing into 'the dim, blood-boultered altar of womanhood' (1991:130) is too gendered for some. But why should the intensely imagined girlhood in the North East of a heroine who is murdered in a castle, aged sixteen, be any less emblematic of nationhood than a man who wakes up blind in a prison cell in the West of Scotland (Kelman 1995:9)? His essential 'maleness' is not any more intrinsically a comment on the 'Scottish' condition than her femaleness. It has been interpreted into that by the assumptions of his critics/readers. Working class, male, Glaswegian writers are constructed as more 'authentic' than middle class, female writers in exile, cut off from the authenticity of 'folk' roots by their class, their gender, and their exile. But for those of us brought up as women in Scotland, *O Caledonia* contains an authenticity of response to the condition of Scottish womanness that Kelman cannot offer.

Scottish women's twentieth century fiction, whether centred fully on women or equally on women and men, ensures at least that, in reading it, we start from a position of imagined identity with women. It starts from the position that women are central rather than peripheral or marginal, even when social constrictions are being examined and the limitations of gender roles explored. Galloway links women's writing with Scottish writing in this:

And to reprioritise, to speak as though your norms are the ones that matter, is what's happened to Scottish writing as well recently. Scottish writers have started writing as though their language and national priorities signify, whereas for years we took on the fiction they didn't. The Let's Imagine We Matter thing is important. *What if I don't accept that I'm marginal, add-on territory* – it's the same root for me (March & Galloway 1999:86).

Just as previously the male was always seen and used as of central importance in constructions of 'Scotland', now the female can be interpreted in the same extrapolated way to define Scottishness.

But what earlier twentieth-century Scottish women's fiction mapped out were the infinite possibilities of the imagination: through education, through reading, through landscape. Landscape in Scotland incorporates light and infinity. The imagery of light and infinity permeates Shepherd's *The Weatherhouse*, 'the blue sea trembled on the boundaries of space' ([1930] 1996:112), infecting those characters (female and male) who experience it with the sense of invisible edges to the world, of possibilities reaching out into infinity, in contrast to the constrictions of their daily life. It is as though for early twentieth century women writers the constrictions of earthly life are released by the light and landscape into the edge of time and endless uncharted possibilities, possibilities that were more fractured or constrained in life. Shepherd is most explicit about this conjunction of landscape, light, and Scotland in her first novel, *The Quarry Wood* (1928). The protagonist Martha is told of a half-remembered 'bit screed' (piece of writing or recitation) by her father:

> 'On the sooth o' Scotland there's England, on the north the Arory-bory ... fat's east o't?
>
> ... I some think it was the sun – the risin' sun. Ay, fairly. That's fat it was. Noo, the wast. Fat's wast o' Scotland, Matty' ... Geordie could get no further with the boundaries of Scotland ... They stood on Scotland and there was nothing north of them but light. It was Dussie who wondered what bounded Scotland when the Aurora was not there. ... 'Eternity. That's fat's wast o' Scotland. I mind it noo' ... Eternity did not seem to be on any of her maps: but neither was the Aurora. She accepted that negligence of the map-makers as she accepted so much else in life. She had enough to occupy her meanwhile in discovering what life held, without concerning herself with what it lacked. (1996:19-20)

Shepherd shows here the disjunctions between the maps available for women, 'the negligence of map-makers', and the pragmatic capacity of women to get on with the exploration of the reality of 'discovering what life held'. Martha, setting out on her voyage of the intellect, education and love, accepts the oddity of the boundaries of Scotland which are shown as mysteriously and infinitely expansive through light and eternity. Only to the south is travel in the imagination limited by the real border with England.

Janice Galloway, in a novel written sixty-one years later, charts different boundaries from Shepherd in her novel *The Trick is to Keep Breathing* (1989). In its first person portrayal of a breakdown there are internal, conflicting senses of existence and non-existence and absence. Joy, the narrator, scours the written word in a search for self:

> It's important to write things down. The written word is important. The forms of the letters: significances between the loops and dashes. You scour them looking for the truth. [...] I read magazines, newspapers, billboards, government health

warnings, advertising leaflets, saucebottles [sic], cans of beans, Scottish Folk Tales and The Bible. They reveal glimpses of things just beyond the reach of understanding but never the whole truth. I fall into a recurring loop every morning after. (1991:195-96)

This passage provides emblematic juxtapositions which show the extent that our 'selves', written and lived, are constructed from heterogeneous cultural influences, clamouring and clashing discourses found in the cultural artifacts of late twentieth century Scottish women's lives. Galloway's 'glimpses of things just beyond the reach of understanding' are the internal landscape's confused equivalent to the 'far limits of the visible world' of the external landscapes of Scotland in Barker's *O Caledonia* (1991:34).

Contemporary Scottish women writers may now write from an assumption of rights and possibilities for change but they also still write out of the inequalities of women's positions, 'writing to *make visible*' (March & Galloway 1999:92), writing themselves into a culture that has been dominated by male cultural icons. As the poet Kathleen Jamie has said in relation to Robert Burns:

I don't think we need a national bard. I think folk call him that out of laziness, because they can't be bothered to read what's been written since. It's a monolithic attitude, where every era seems to have enshrined one male. A vibrant culture, as we have, is in the hands of many, many people.[5]

Hugh MacDiarmid, the writer who bestrode the Scottish literary renaissance of the 1920s and 1930s (in many ways defining it), had an iconographic function similar to Burns's previous function in post-world war two Scottish intellectual and literary life. The female equivalent to the MacDiarmid monolith seemed to be Muriel Spark in the 1960s and 1970s: prolific, isolated, providing a slippery, elliptical and philosophically cunning counterpart, both of them admired or revered, but neither apparently directly the beginning of a vibrant new tradition. Spark has previously been largely treated as a unique writer, subsumed into the 'English' canon by non-Scottish readers. Her themes and preoccupations with the oral tradition, truth, lies and fiction, however, place her firmly within the Scottish tradition and her inheritors have appeared in the 1990s; Elspeth Barker, Shena Mackay, Candia McWilliam, A. L. Kennedy and Janice Galloway all carry elements of Spark within their themes and style. Spark's writing has a cold, observant eye (a 'people-watcher, a behaviourist', as she describes herself (Spark 1992:25)), detached from the life around her, amused and unengaged, containing both the coldness of the excluded and a cool observation of the masculinised world of Scottish life and culture. It is, perhaps, symptomatic of that Scottish life and culture that the woman writer that has had most obvious influence on contemporary women writers chose exile and that her work should be so open to critical interpretations which ignore or are ignorant of the obvious Scottish dimensions of her work.

The specific social changes of the 1980s and 1990s (both in attitudes and in laws affecting women) were accomplished by women's issue based groups such as Women's Aid and Rape Crisis Centres, by the political campaigning that culminated in the Scottish Parliament's opening in 1999, and the cultural energy represented by Alasdair Gray's and James Kelman's fiction and by the writing of Tom Leonard and of poet and dramatist Liz Lochhead. It is against this background that the newer writers in the 1990s (such as Galloway, A. L. Kennedy, Jackie Kay or Laura Hird) emerge and move in fresh directions. The map has been redrawn so that they write from a confident assumption that being female and being Scottish are culturally positive; writing out of the same kind of natural assumption of place in the culture previously available to male writers. Galloway, with her intensely individualised, West of Scotland women's stories, explicitly draws attention to her feminism and her femaleness. A. L. Kennedy, less overtly political, perhaps, writes that she has 'a problem. I am a woman, I am heterosexual, I am more Scottish than anything else and I write. But I don't know how these things interrelate' (1995:100) and insists that 'the great thing about books' is that they are 'not nation-specific, not race-specific, not religion-specific' but 'about humanity' (March & Kennedy 1999:108). Jackie Kay's works, from the poetic drama of *The Adoption Papers* (1991) to the novel *Trumpet* (1998), centre on complicated questions of gender, sexuality and race in a way new to Scottish writing. Laura Hird represents younger voices, part of a group with those male writers she appeared with in *Children of Albion Rovers* (Williamson 1996) and the writers interviewed in *Repetitive Beat Generation* (Redhead 2000); she draws the harshness of young Edinburgh lives, writing of the complicity of women in our position, and looking on middle age as a foreign country.[6] In Anderson's phrase, their 'fiction seeps quietly and continuously into reality' (Anderson 1991:36). Their writing is essential for the part it plays in contributing to an imagined wholeness in the nation, ensuring that Scotland's 'narrative of "identity"' (Anderson 1991:205) includes women. Their work ensures exploration of shifting allegiances and passable boundaries in counterpoint to the limiting containment of that earlier static male cultural mode which was the stultifying norm.

It used to be said that nineteenth-century fiction looked for closure, and twentieth-century literature resisted it (although when we looked again, post-postmodernism, it was clear that much nineteenth-century fiction carried its own anxieties in the metaphors and subtexts embedded in its apparent order).

But the resistance to, the *impossibility* of closure, is carried into the twenty-first century. So Margaret, at the end of A. L. Kennedy's *Looking for the Possible Dance*, walks out into an urban landscape through a door which is as suggestive of light and infinity as the edges of the North-East world:

> ... from a distance its doorways seem white, more like curtains of white than ways through walls and into light. Margaret walks to one door and sinks into brilliant air, becoming first a moving shadow, then a curve, a dancing line. (Kennedy 1993:250)

This ending (now criticised by Kennedy as 'the illusion of arriving at the end of a story but actually you just arrive at the end of a railway line' (March & Kennedy 1999:100)) shimmers with possibilities. It is in this openness that Scottish women's writing presents its multiple and heterogeneous relation to gender and nation.

There is a constant leap of imagination required of women reading literature by men, with male-centred concerns. As Boland writes:

> ... teenage dreams of action and heroism are filled with exciting and impossible transpositions of sexuality [...] If I wanted to feel the power of nation as well as its defeat, then I would take on the properties of hero (Boland 1996:65)

In twentieth and twenty-first-century writing, the same kind of imaginative travel is necessary to where gender interacts with nation so that nation cannot be narrated as exclusively male or, indeed, exclusively female. Any exploration must be tentative, flexible, non-linear, as the only certainty carried by 'debatable lands' is that of uncertainty, of border crossings, passable boundaries, dispute, debate, contiguity and interaction, equivalent, perhaps, to Bhabha's:

> ... inscription and articulation of culture's *hybridity*. To that end we should remember that it is the 'inter' – the cutting edge of translation and negotiation, the *in-between* space – that carries the burden of meaning of culture (Bhabha 1994:38)

Lands of thought that are interrogated and fought over, our debatable lands that are Said's 'complex and uneven topography' (1994:386), are as much about women's space within the nation as about the boundaries of Scotland.

References

Anderson, B. (1991): *Imagined Communities. Reflections on the Origin and Spread of Nationalism* (revised edition). London & New York: Verso.

Anderson, C. (1992): 'Debateable Land: The Prose Work of Violet Jacob', in C. Gonda (ed.): *Tea and Leg-Irons: New Feminist Readings from Scotland.* London: Open Letters, pp. 31-44.

Anderson, C. & G. Norquay (1984): 'Superiorism', in *Cencrastus*, vol. 15, pp. 8-10.

Barker, E. (1992 [1991]): *O Caledonia.* Harmondsworth: Penguin.

Bhabha, H. K. (1990): 'Introduction: narrating the nation', in H. K. Bhabha (ed.): *Nation and Narration.* London: Routledge, pp. 1-7.

Bhabha, H. K. (1994): *The Location of Culture.* London: Routledge.

Boland, E. (1996): *Object Lessons. The Life of the Woman and the Poet in Our Time.* London: Vintage.

Brown, A. (2001): 'Women and Politics in Scotland', in E. Breitenbach & F. Mackay (eds): *Women and Contemporary Scottish Politics: an Anthology.* Edinburgh: Polygon, pp. 197-212.

Christianson, A. (1993): 'Flyting with "A Drunk Man"', in *Scottish Affairs*, vol. 5, pp. 126-135.

Christianson, A. & A. Lumsden (eds) (2000): *Contemporary Scottish Women's Writing.* Edinburgh: Edinburgh University Press.

Galford, E. (1990): *Queendom Come.* London: Virago.

Galloway, J. (1991 [1989]): *The Trick is to Keep Breathing.* London: Minerva.

Gifford, D. (1992): 'Honour Where It's Due', in *Books in Scotland*, vol. 41, pp. 7-16.

Hird, L. (1997): *Nail and other stories.* Edinburgh: Rebel Inc.

Irigaray, L. (1985 [1977]): 'This Sex Which Is Not One', in C. Porter with C. Burke (trans.): *This Sex Which Is Not One.* Ithaca, New York: Cornell University Press, pp. 23-33.

Kay, J. (1991): *The Adoption Papers.* Newcastle upon Tyne: Bloodaxe Books Ltd.

Kay, J. (1998): *Trumpet.* London: Picador.

Kelman, J. (1995 [1994]): *How Late It Was How Late.* London: Minerva.

Kennedy, A. L. (1993): *Looking for the Possible Dance.* London: Secker and Warburg.

Kennedy, A. L. (1995): 'Not changing the world', in I. A. Bell (ed.): *Peripheral Visions.* Cardiff: University of Cardiff Press, pp. 100-102.

March, C. L. & J. Galloway (1999): 'Interview', in *Edinburgh Review*, 101, pp. 85-98.

March, C. L. & A. L. Kennedy (1999): 'Interview', in *Edinburgh Review*, 101, pp. 99-119.

Redhead, S. (2000): *Repetitive Beat Generation.* Edinburgh: Rebel Inc.

Said, E. (1994 [1993]): *Culture & Imperialism.* London: Vintage.

Shepherd, N. (1996): *The Quarry Wood* [1928] and *The Weatherhouse* [1930], both in R. Watson (ed.): *The Grampian Quartet.* Edinburgh: Canongate Classics.

Spark, M. (1992): *Curriculum Vitae.* London: Constable.

Whyte, C. (1998): 'Masculinities in Contemporary Scottish Fiction', in *Forum for Modern Language Studies*, vol. 34, pp. 274-85.

Williamson, K. (ed.) (1996): *Children of Albion Rovers.* Edinburgh: Rebel Inc.

Notes

1. This essay is a shorter version of Christianson, A. (2002): 'Gender and nation: debatable lands and passable boundaries', in G. Norquay & G. Smyth (eds): *Across the Margins.* Manchester: Manchester University Press, pp. 67-82.

2. See, for example, Anderson 1992:34-35.
3. The nation is '*imagined* because the members of even the smallest nation will never know most of their fellow-members, meet them, or even hear of them, yet in the minds of each lives the image of their communion' (Anderson 1991:6).
4. The historical figures with their acquired heroic and nationalist meanings are intended, rather than their Hollywood manifestations in *Braveheart* (1995), though the two may well interconnect as male symbols, as in the adoption of the face painted with the Saltire by fans of football (that centralising trope not of nationhood but of maleness).
5. Chris Dunkerley, 'Bard for Life', *The Scotsman Week End*, 20 Jan. 1996, p. 8. For some of the problems present in MacDiarmid for women, see Anderson & Norquay (1984) and Christianson (1993).
6. The woman of 'the elderly couple' in Hird's 'Tillicoutry / Anywhere' is in her fifties (1997:143). For further consideration of contemporary Scottish women writers, see individual chapters in Christianson & Lumsden (2000).

'To say "beautiful" in Swedish': The Periphery as Centre in Stephen Greenhorn's *Passing Places*

Bill Findlay

Stephen Greenhorn (b. 1964) is one of the leading middle-generation playwrights in Scotland and creator of BBC Scotland's television soap opera *River City*. *Passing Places* is his best-known work and one of the most significant Scottish plays of the last decade. It proved a sell-out success when premiered in 1997 by the Traverse Theatre in Edinburgh, which led to a revival and Scottish tour in 1998, and a BBC Radio production. It has subsequently become a text taught in Scottish secondary schools.[1] *Passing Places* has also attracted international attention, about which Greenhorn has commented:

> The happy irony is that the most specific and localised piece of theatre I have ever written is beginning to travel all by itself [...] It is enjoying life in Germany, Croatia, Finland and now Denmark.[2] I'm touched by the fact that such a personal truth can have such a wide recognition. (Greenhorn 1999:16)

The nature of that 'personal truth' to which he alludes is illuminated by an introduction he provided specifically for a Danish edition of *Passing Places* in 1999. He offers there a clearly articulated account of the background informing the composition of the play and remarks that 'to a great extent *Passing Places* was written from instinct rather than intellect' and drew on his personal experience (Greenhorn 1999:14). That experience, he reveals, further developed in him a political sensibility. Like the two central characters in the play, Alex and Brian, Greenhorn grew up in a working-class community in Scotland's urban 'Central Belt' – in his case in Fauldhouse, a mining village in West Lothian. He saw at first hand the impact on his community of the free-market ideology of what we have come to term 'Thatcherism', and the eighteen years of Conservative rule between 1979 and 1997; a period when Scotland, at each of the General Elections that successively brought the Conservatives to power in Westminster in those years, voted in a different direction in rejection of Thatcherism. 'My view is that these are the eighteen years,' he writes, 'in which the infrastructures of the country were attacked so ferociously that the people were forced to redefine themselves politically, socially, and culturally [...] [which] contributed to a growing politicisation of people in Scotland', because, he goes on, 'Thatcherism was destroying people's lives and condemning whole communities to the status of 'underclass' – typically without jobs and without hope' (Greenhorn 1999:9-10).

The two young protagonists in the play, Alex and Brian, are members of this marginalized underclass. The play opens with them introducing their hometown:

ALEX: Motherwell!
BRIAN: West central Scotland. Population 27,000.
ALEX: Work base...
BRIAN: Traditionally... heavy industry... predominantly steel...
ALEX: And now...
    BRIAN shrugs.
(Greenhorn 1998:3)

That non-verbal gesture, the shrug, speaks volumes about the decimation of their community and the hopelessness that has followed. As Alex says later in the play: 'Where I come from, they took all the jobs away then called it a special development area' (Greenhorn 1998:56). Greenhorn's choice of Motherwell is not without special significance as it was home to the Ravenscraig steelworks, the last symbol (or 'icon' as he calls it (Greenhorn 1999:12)) of Scotland's pre-Thatcher economy of heavy industry. The public library in the town, as described by Alex, seems symptomatic of the community's decline once Ravenscraig had been, in Greenhorn's phrase, 'put to the sword' in the early 1990s (Greenhorn 1999:12)[3]: 'The library! Hang out for pensioners who can't pay their gas bills. Ex-steelworkers who can't bring themselves to watch Australian soap-operas. Jakeys [down and outs] who fall asleep over *The Independent*' (Greenhorn 1998:4).[4] In his Danish essay, Greenhorn writes:

After more than a decade of political brutality, a generation of young people had emerged into a world which had little to offer. They watched their parents' sense of security be eroded to the point where redundancy might mean never working again. They discovered what jobs there were tended to be short-term, low-paid and unskilled. [...] They learned that life on the dole was a series of petty bureaucratic humiliations and meaningless compulsory training schemes. They decided that the government had abandoned them and that politicians could not be trusted. They were left with nothing to rely on but themselves. This is the world of Alex and Brian. This is where the journey starts. (Greenhorn 1999:12)

Passing Places has the sub-title 'A Road Movie for the Stage', hence that reference to the two protagonists' 'journey'; but the journey is, as we shall see, both real and metaphorical.

Brian is unemployed and frequents the public library with the aforementioned unemployed steelworkers, impoverished pensioners and assorted no-hopers. His friend Alex has one of those 'short-term, low-paid and unskilled jobs' Greenhorn just referred to – in a sports shop owned by a psychopathic would-be gangster called Binks. Alex says: 'It's not even a real sports shop. All it sells are trainers and baseball caps. And bloody shells-suits' (Greenhorn 1998:6). This leads one to suspect that the shop is a cover for drug-dealing. After a violent robbery Alex is fired without pay. Later, in drunken revenge, he smashes in the shop window and steals a surfboard. This is no ordinary surfboard but the shop owner Binks's pride and joy, and in which, unbeknown to Alex, he has stashed South African krugerrands. Once sober, to get rid of the evidence and escape Binks's wrath, Alex and Brian set off for Thurso with the surfboard strapped to the roof of a clapped-out Lada they have borrowed without permission. Of their destination, Thurso, Brian asks, 'Do you know where that is?', to which Alex replies, 'North. On the coast, I presume.' Brian is aghast: 'North is right. Next stop Iceland.' (Greenhorn 1998:13). Alex has read in a magazine that Thurso is a magnet for surfers, hence he thinks he can sell the surfboard and 'use the money to lie low for a while'. Thus begins their journey north, in flight, departing from Scotland's aptly named *Central* Belt – the lowland region straddling the centre of the country where the majority of the country's population live, mostly in urban communities – and travelling progressively deeper into the sparsely populated and largely mountainous Highlands (what we can term for our purposes here, the northern 'periphery').

Given the nature of their lives and that of their demoralized community, and given the larger political consciousness on Greenhorn's part informing the play, Alex and Brian can also for our purposes here be read as representative of the marginalized young, in social, occupational and identity terms. Assisting this interpretation is, again, Greenhorn's introduction for the Danish edition of *Passing Places* and his discussion of the dire contemporary reality he drew on in writing the play:

In this situation, the question of identity ceases to be simply a psychological concept, it becomes a basic survival issue. A sense of identity was no longer conferred by a nurturing society. It was something which had to be struggled for, fought over. Something which had to be won. The base line from which I – and many others I suspect – started from in this struggle was a sense (however vague) of 'Scottishness'. The difficulty came with the realisation that the exact nature of 'Scottishness' was so ill-defined and cluttered with cultural debris that it provided little in the way of answers. Instead, it simply propelled the search for identity down two closely connected avenues – 'Who are you? And what exactly is a Scot?'. These parallel lines of investigation are at the heart of *Passing Places*. They are also I think at the heart of more recent changes in Scotland. (Greenhorn 1999:12-13)

Greenhorn is explicitly flagging up here that *Passing Places* was conceived in part as a kind of state-of-the-nation play, in reflecting a larger examination of Scottish identity in the 1990s in response to what he saw as 'the years of isolation and oppression under a distant government'; a situation in which Scotland as a whole was, politically, at the periphery, which in turn, he says 'contributed to a growing politicisation of people' and 'seemed to foster a growing sense of "Scottishness"' (Greenhorn 1999:13,10,13). This, along with the nature of the boys' journey north, illustrates how there can be multiplicities of centre/periphery relationships: Scotland seen as politically peripheral within the British state, and geographically peripheral in distance from London as the seat of political power and as the capital of the United Kingdom; 'a growing sense of "Scottishness"' as a 'centre' to turn to because of that experience of being 'peripheralised'; the Central Belt as the centre within Scotland, in terms of population, major cities, industry, national institutions, and so on, and the Highlands seen as the periphery in relation to that Scottish centre.[5] Tellingly, the journey that the boys embark on in the play, into the periphery, and in flight not just from Binks but from the failures of the centre (defined both in British political terms and in Scottish social ones), proves empowering, both to them and to the periphery, in the sense of demonstrating the latter's positive, regenerative qualities. It should be said, too, that in providing answers to the parallel lines of investigation, 'Who are you?' and 'What is a Scot?', the play also allows us to see that the centre/periphery model can be applied to personal identity, in that the boys are troubled by 'dislocation' (Greenhorn's word[6]) on different levels, including emotionally and psychologically, and their journey is as much about their unknowing quest as individuals to achieve a sense of self and self-worth, defined, one could say, as 'centredness'. For example, when they are travelling through Assynt in north-west Scotland, with its curious mountain formations like Suilven, Canisp and Ben More, they learn from a guidebook that the mountains 'seem as if they have tumbled down from the clouds, having nothing to do with the country or each other in shape, material, position or character, and look very much as if they were wondering how they got there'. In response to this, Alex comments to Brian: 'Nothing to do with anything and wondering how we got here. That's us.' (Greenhorn 1998:55).

The bulk of the play comprises the journey that the boys undertake through the Highlands, via Loch Lomond, Inverary, Mallaig, and Skye, then through Sutherland and Caithness to their destination of Thurso on the northern coast of the mainland. They have never been to the Highlands before. Brian, the more intellectually curious of the two, is a reader, and, just as this has expanded his horizons, he is more naturally open to being influenced by his experiences on their journey. Alex, in contrast, is surly and snarling, closed-minded and reductive in his attitudes. Early on in their journey they have to pull into a lay-by in a mountain pass because steam is pouring from the engine of the ailing Lada:

> BRIAN: They're designed for Murmansk not Milngavie. It's meant to be traversing the icy wastes of Siberia. It's out of its natural environment. Give it a chance.
> ALEX: Brian, how are we going to get to Thurso if this thing won't do more than forty-five and can't even get us over a fucking hill?
> BRIAN: It's not a hill. It's a mountain. Three thousand three hundred and eighteen feet. That makes it a munro.
> ALEX: I don't give a fuck.
> (Greenhorn 1998:17)

That 'I don't give a fuck' just about sums up Alex's attitude. Brian, though, as we see here, is interested in the wider world and has brought along a guidebook, from which he provides a running commentary, at different points on the journey, to Alex's exasperation:

> BRIAN: Inverary. A picturesque township on the shores of Loch Fyne. Notable for its carefully planned layout, its church tower and its historic court-house, now an award-winning museum.
> ALEX: White-washed tourist hell-hole.
> BRIAN: Excellent sea-fishing opportunities. In season.
> ALEX: We're not stopping.
> BRIAN: Hard right on to the B819 up and through Glen Aray.
> ALEX: More hills.
> BRIAN: Then down to the shore of Loch Awe.
> ALEX: More water.
> BRIAN: Loch Awe is the longest inland loch in Britain if you include the bit that goes off at right-angles. If you don't then Loch Ness is longest.
> ALEX: More useless shite. [...] For fuck's sake! It's like being on the road with Norris McWhirter!
> BRIAN: I was just saying...
> ALEX: We're not tourists, Brian.
> BRIAN: I've not been here before.
> ALEX: We live here.
> BRIAN: Not here.
> ALEX: We're only a hundred miles from Glasgow.
> BRIAN: Yeah? Look though. See anything familiar?
> ALEX: Only you talking shite.
> (Greenhorn 1998:18-19)

That 'we're not tourists [...] we live here', said by Alex, is of course ironic, because they know so little about their country that they are the equivalent of tourists within it (even down to the guidebook). And, contrary to Alex's protestation, it is the uncomfortable sensation of being just that that is one source of his expletive-ridden discomfiture.

As their journey progresses the boys encounter people, and have experiences, sometimes bizarre, that challenge their perceptions of the Highlands: new age travellers from England, a Gaelic-singing Canadian geologist, Ukrainian sailors who can recite and are 'big fans' of the poetry of Robert Burns, an eccentric French sculptor-cum-car-mechanic, a refugee from the Central Belt who works on his 'electric croft' designing software for a Californian company from his supposedly remote Highland base, a 'mystic surf guru' who quotes Walt Whitman and builds surfboards. The encounters with such people are particularly challenging for Alex, the play's principal protagonist. For that reason, and in view of the limited space at my disposal, I will concentrate on the impact on him.

As just indicated, one of the people they meet is a Canadian geologist living on Skye. Through her they go to a ceilidh. Alex is amazed at the mix of people there, which includes the aforesaid Ukrainian sailors whose factory ship has been anchored in the loch for months because they have been abandoned without fuel or money by their government.[7] Like the mix of people, the mix of music at the ceilidh Alex finds 'mad... really weird', commenting: 'It seems strange coming to a ceilidh and hearing some highlander belt out "Folsom Prison Blues" [...] I thought people up here would be less... confused'[8] (Greenhorn 1998:45). Again, the irony is that it is Alex who is confused. He knows little about life in the Highlands, yet holds a naive and stereotypical view of what he expects to find. It is a view challenged by the Canadian, Iona, who has a more clear-eyed appreciation of the reality:

> IONA: You think we should be like a big Braveheart theme park? Pickled in tradition? C'mon Alex. Loosen up. You can have it all.
> ALEX: How?
> IONA: Choose your influences...
> ALEX: I'm not sure you get to choose...
> *Pause.*
> IONA: What are you looking for?
> ALEX: Just... somewhere that doesn't make me feel like an outsider.
> (Greenhorn 1998:46)

It is even more ironic that he, a Scot, should feel this way, but the outsiders from other countries do not; they just take the Highlands as they find them and fit in.

That outsider perception he expresses has implications for Alex's sense of national identity. A key character he meets is a young woman called Mirren, with whom he tentatively embarks on a relationship that eventually works a positive change in him. She is a Highlander (or, at least, migrated to the Highlands at a young age[9]), and seems to him to possess a self-assuredness that he envies:

> ALEX: You just fitted in [...] Looked like you belonged. I feel... out of place. A misfit.
> MIRREN: It's still Scotland. You're Scottish.
> ALEX: I'm a foreigner here. Even the midges know that. Look, my face is like a page of braille. They don't bother you at all.
> (Greenhorn 1998:57)

Alex is Scottish but feels a 'foreigner' in the Highlands; he is, he says, 'confused', 'a misfit', 'an outsider'. 'I'm the wrong person. In the wrong place', as he also puts it (Greenhorn 1998:39). Alex's condition encapsulates that search for identity in the play that, as noted earlier, Greenhorn expressed in terms of a nation-self duality: 'What is a Scot?' and 'Who are you?' Part of the problem for Alex is that he expects to find the Highlands as fulfilling a received and unexamined image he has of it as uncomplicated and traditional. What he sees in the reality as 'confusion' is what Greenhorn in his Danish essay terms, more positively, 'diversity'. He sees contemporary Scotland as 'striving for a broader, more inclusive, definition' of Scottish identity which acknowledges and celebrates that diversity (Greenhorn 1999:13). By the end of the journey Alex has had his mind opened to this in a way that has been educative and liberating both for his sense of Scotland and being Scottish, and, most keenly, for his sense of self.

That liberation of self extends to his emotional life. Part of Alex's problem is that his narrowness of view has bred a narrowness of spirit and feeling (or vice versa, in a vicious circle). To grow he must also mature emotionally and expressively. Instrumental in the change brought about in him by the end of the play are the landscape and the young woman Mirren. When he is in Skye, the Canadian geologist, Iona, asks him about his response to the island and the Highlands:

> IONA: Wouldn't you say it's beautiful?
> ALEX: I suppose it's alright.
> IONA: Alright!
> ALEX: It's very nice.
> IONA: Nice! It's beautiful. Why don't you admit it?
> ALEX: I just did.
> IONA: You said it was 'nice'.
> ALEX: Same thing.

> IONA: No way. It's beautiful.
> ALEX: Fine. It is.
> IONA: So why not say so?
> ALEX: Because...
> IONA: Because?
> ALEX: I can't.
> IONA: Can't what?
> ALEX: Can't say it. Okay?
> (Greenhorn 1998:35-6)

This exchange continues, with her pressing him till he says: 'I can think it but I can't say it. It's just... It's not part of my language, alright?' There are other instances where he thinks but cannot bring himself to utter that word 'beautiful', whether of the landscape or of Mirren. It is indicative of how far his journey through the Highlands has taken him as a person that by the end of the play he stands with Mirren at destination's end – the surfing beach outside Thurso – and in response to her question, 'What now?', he answers:

> ALEX: Don't know. Maybe I'll just keep going north. [...] Orkney. Shetland. Scandinavia.
> MIRREN: I'm going that way.
> ALEX: Yeah? Maybe we could...
> MIRREN: Maybe.
> ALEX: I'd like that. I'd like to be able to say 'beautiful' in Swedish.[10]
> (Greenhorn 1998:83)

That Alex by play's end not only has changed to the extent that he can openly use the word 'beautiful' but can express an ambition to say it in Swedish and to keep travelling north to Scandinavia, demonstrates how marked an attitudinal transformation has been brought about in him through journeying through the periphery since leaving his Central-Belt hometown Motherwell and its post-industrial depredations. The instrumental objective of the journey – to sell the surfboard – has been replaced by a larger attainment for Alex (and for Brian, who embraces the periphery by deciding to make a new life in Thurso): he has acquired a more informed knowledge of his country, a more defined sense of self, and a new-found ability to express a sentiment and ambition that was inconceivable at his journey's start. At the end of the play, as he stands on the northernmost shore on the Scottish mainland – at the edge of his country's periphery, as it were – Scandinavia beckons as a promising horizon: the northern European peripheries seen as a new kind of gravitational centre, one could say.

It was suggested at the outset that the boys' journey of discovery of nation and self was presented by the author in both real and metaphorical terms. As regards the latter, one can detect on occasion the playwright's artistry at work in his employment of patterning that carries a metaphoric intent. Alex's wish to say 'beautiful' in Swedish, for example, is echoed in Brian's delight at having learnt the Ukrainian word for 'beautiful', *chudovyj*, from one of the sailors at the multi-national ceilidh. 'Doesn't it sound good?', he enthuses, to the gradually thawing Alex (Greenhorn 1998:51). It would therefore be wrong to read the Scandinavian references in the play in too literal a light. The urge that Alex feels to expand his world by continuing his northwards trajectory does not necessarily betoken an awakening sense of affinity with Scandinavian countries per se; rather, Scandinavia represents a destination whose promise is metaphorical in terms of the further flowering it will come to mean for Alex's metamorphosis from the unhappy and emotionally and psychologically repressed person he was at journey's beginning. As Scotland's own northern periphery, the Highlands, has done, but will now be taken a stage further, the northern European periphery that is Scandinavia will provide enabling challenges for Alex that will nurture in him a previously missing sense of 'centredness'.

There is also, it can be argued, another dimension to the significance of Scandinavia in *Passing Places*. It is bound up with the way in which imaginative writing can prove a barometer of subterranean shifts in a nation's 'climate', as it were. In the play, Mirren explains to Alex why the Highlands are so deserted: 'Clearances. Whole families packed off to Canada and Australia. Driven out to make room for sheep' (Greenhorn 1998:56). The mostly nineteenth-century enforced emigration of Highlanders to Canada and Australia, brought about by a mixture of landlord greed and indifference, and economic imperative, has become emblematic of a long tradition of Scottish emigration to the English-speaking countries of the New World (as well as to England).[11] It is a reflection of this that not only has the Highland Clearances proved a potent subject for one of the key works of modern Scottish drama (McGrath 1981),[12] but emigration – from the Highlands and from Scotland generally, and from the period of the early nineteenth century through to the late twentieth century – has had recurring mention in many modern Scottish plays. Those references are predominantly to emigration to Canada, the USA, Australia and England. Whilst examples of this can continue to be found in plays produced, in recent-time terms, either side of *Passing Places*,[13] that Greenhorn's play has its central protagonist embark on a Scandinavian 'migration' of a kind, albeit we assume temporary, can be read as signifying an as yet tentative shift of sorts taking place within Scottish society.[14] As the boys find, Scotland is becoming more multi-national in the migrants it is attracting, particularly from within Europe; concomitantly, Scottish horizons, too, are broadening in employment and travel terms in the direction of Europe rather than, as traditionally and predominantly, the New World.[15] It is in this context that the significance of Stephen Greenhorn's choice of Scandinavia as an alluring prospect for Alex to experience can also be placed.

Bound up with this, too, is the implicit rejection that it represents, in the world of the play, of what Greenhorn refers to as 'the central belt's love affair with American culture' (Greenhorn 1998:Playwright's Note [n.p.]) and 'the comic implausibility' of that fixation (Greenhorn 1999:99). He notes, too, 'the penchant many Scots have of finding an empathy with the most specifically American idioms [...] and situations [...] in a way that they often fail to do with Scottish culture' (Greenhorn 1999:110). From the employment of incongruous Americanisms in language, such as 'chill man' and 'cool the beans, pal', to the wearing of baseball caps and Air Jordan trainers, the wielding of baseball bats and adoption of pseudo-gangster behaviour modelled on 'Al Pacino. Scarface [...and] Michael Corleone', and police behaving as if in an episode of the television series *Miami Vice*, who 'Rush around going "freeze". And, "make my day"' – not to mention the Hawaii-aspiring Binks thinking he is, in Alex's dismissive words, 'the Don-fucking-Jonson of Meikle Earnock!'[16] – the Motherwell the boys have turned their backs on is, to borrow Greenhorn's words from before, 'cluttered with cultural debris' of a kind which contributed to the 'dislocation' that Alex felt before embarking on his journey to the clearer air, literally and metaphorically, of the Scottish and European peripheries; peripheries not without their own complexity, but which are not deleteriously affected by the centre's 'cultural debris' as symbolised by Americanisation. Towards the play's end, Alex asks why surfers make the pilgrimage to Thurso to surf in 'cold and dangerous' conditions when they could 'go to California'. The resonant answer he is given is: 'It's a key spot. Best waves in Europe on a good day' (Greenhorn 1998:73).

References

Brown, I. (ed.) (1999): *Antologija suvremene skotske drame*, trans. K. Horvat. Zagreb: Hrvatski centar ITI-UNESCO.

Devine, T. (ed.) (1992): *Scottish Emigration and Scottish Society.* Edinburgh: John Donald.

Fisher, S. (2004): 'Continental drift hooks Scots keen to leave domestic troubles behind', in *Sunday Herald Sport*, 25 July, p. 7.

Gallacher, T. (n.d. [1999]): *Of Time and Loss.* Self-published. [The title was changed for the stage production to *The Summertime is Come*.]

Glover, S. (1997) *Bondagers & The Straw Chair.* London: Methuen.

Glover, S. (2000): *Shetland Saga.* London: Nick Hern Books.

Greenhorn, S. (1998): *Passing Places.* London: Nick Hern Books.

Greenhorn, S. (1999): *Passing Places*, ed. M. Høxbro & A. Kristensen. Århus: Forlaget Systime.

Greenhorn, S. (2001): 'Lugares de Passagem' [*Passing Places*], trans. F. Frazao, in *Artistas Unidos Revista*, no. 6, pp. 2-29.

Greig, D. (1996): *The Architect.* London: Methuen.

Greig, D. (2000): *Victoria.* London: Methuen.

Harrower, D. (2003): *Dark Earth.* London: Faber & Faber.

Heggie, I. (1989): *American Bagpipes.* London: Penguin.

Hunter, J. (1994): *A Dance Called America: The Scottish Highlands, the United States and Canada.* Edinburgh: Mainstream.

Lochhead, L. (1998): *Perfect Days.* London: Nick Hern Books.

Lochhead, L. (2003): *Britannia Rules.* [No place]: Learning and Teaching Scotland.

McGrath, J. (1981, with subsequent reprints): *The Cheviot, the Stag and the Black, Black Oil.* London: Methuen.

Roper, T. (1990): *The Steamie*, in *Scot-Free: New Scottish Plays*, selected and introduced by A. Cameron. London: Nick Hern Books, pp. 201-75.

'Trends and Issues in Contemporary Scottish Theatre', [no author or date], pp. 55-92, at: *http://www.ltscotland.org.uk/nq/files/contemporary_scottish_theatre.pdf* (accessed 31 July 2004).

Notes

1 Although a critical literature on *Passing Places* has not yet developed, a teaching resource for use in Scottish secondary schools is available for downloading online: [no author], 'Trends and Issues in Contemporary Scottish Theatre', pp. 55-92, at *http://www.ltscotland.org.uk/nq/files/contemporary_scottish_theatre.pdf* (no date; accessed 31 July 2004). Also, work questions in English for school use can be found at the website of the publisher of the Danish edition of the play (Greenhorn 1999): *http://www.systime.dk/titel.asp?udgivelseid=2699* (click there on 'Arbejds-spørgsmål') (1999; accessed 31 July 2004).

2. *Passing Places* has subsequently been staged by a youth theatre in Switzerland in the German translation. (The play was adapted, with the stolen surfboard becoming a snowboard and the two youths heading into the mountains to surf a glacier!) Also, it has been translated into Portuguese and given a public reading in Lisbon; and, at time of writing, it is being translated into Québécois for a performed reading in Montreal. The Portuguese translation has been published (Greenhorn 2001), as has the Croatian translation (Brown 1999). (Stephen Greenhorn kindly supplied these performance and publication details.) The published Danish edition (Greenhorn 1999) reprints the original Scottish version, not a Danish translation.

3. He writes, too, of 'Ravenscraig's execution' (Greenhorn 1999:10).

4. Of his choice of *The Independent* here, Greenhorn (1999:99) wrote in the notes he furnished for the Danish edition: '*The Independent* is a paper which was still relatively new on the scene when *PP* was written. It's an English based broadsheet and seemed to be favoured by a certain kind of image-conscious young professional type for whom the tabloids were too tacky, the Scottish broadsheets were too parochial, *The Guardian* was too liberal and *The Times* or *The Telegraph* were too reactionary. The choice was not about making a political point with the title but simply undermining the pretensions of the readers.'

5. The existence of a Scottish Parliament may be thought to problematise the point being made here; however, the devolved Scottish Parliament opened in 1999, subsequent to the writing and first performance of *Passing Places* in 1997. Greenhorn's introduction to the

Danish edition of the play, it should be mentioned, was written in 1999, in the immediate wake of the opening of the Scottish Parliament that year, to which he makes reference in explaining the social and political factors informing the work.

6. He speaks of 'my story of dislocation' in the 'Playwright's Note' prefaced to Greenhorn 1998:[n.p.].

7. This is based on the reality of the crews of 'klondykers' (factory ships for processing fish), from former Soviet satellite countries, suffering hardship and being anchored indefinitely in West Highland ports – Ullapool particularly – as a consequence of being starved of funds by their governments. A similar story, involving a crew of Bulgarian sailors being abandoned in Shetland, is the subject of a Scottish play premiered three years after *Passing Places*, Sue Glover's *Shetland Saga* (Glover 2000).

8. Greenhorn supplies a note on the reference to 'Folsom Prison Blues' in the Danish edition of *Passing Places*: '"Folsom Prison Blues" is used as an example of the penchant many Scots have of finding an empathy with the most specifically American idioms (country music) and situations (Folsom Prison) in a way that they often fail to do with Scottish culture. It is also my favourite Johnny Cash song' (Greenhorn 1999:110).

9. Mirren's father is from Paisley in the Central Belt. Following the death of his wife, he moved to the Highlands with Mirren when she was thirteen (Greenhorn 1998:22,64). An irony, then, in Alex's sense of Mirren being self-assured because of her rootedness, is that she, too, is an incomer.

10. Mirren's reference to 'going that way', to Scandinavia, is because her father corresponds with an academic at Stockholm University whom she can contact to help her find a job.

11. Greenhorn provides an explanatory note on the Highland Clearances (Greenhorn 1999:110-11). There are a number of books on both the Clearances and Scottish emigration: see, for example, Hunter 1994 and Devine 1992.

12. This play, *The Cheviot, the Stag and the Black, Black Oil*, was first staged in 1973 and became a landmark work in Scottish theatre. It launched the best-known of Scottish touring companies, 7:84 Scotland. Greenhorn provides an explanatory note on the company and its significance (Greenhorn 1999:97-98).

13. Heggie 1989:5-122 *passim* (USA, present); Roper 1990:213, 231 (England, 1960s); Glover 1997:22 (Canada, 1860s); Lochhead 1998:20 (Australia, present); Lochhead 2003:82, 90-91 (USA, 1950s); Gallacher 1999 (Canada, present).

14. The shift of focus to Europe as a place of opportunity and potential for growth is, it must be said, in terms of its contemporary expression in drama, still inchoate. But, arguably, there are little signs of it detectable in, for example, Greig 1996:80 (Greece, Spain, Italy, Amsterdam), Greig 2000:179 (Spain), Harrower 2003:71-72 (Rome).

15 This is partly because of the exponential growth in low-cost air travel within Europe, facilitating much greater interchange. One sees it at work, too, in the increased flow of Scandinavian students into Scottish universities and in the two-way exchange of footballers. Not only have Swedish, Danish, Norwegian and Finnish football players become ubiquitous in Scotland's Premier League, but Scottish players are in demand in the Scandinavian (and Dutch) leagues: see Fisher 2004

16 These American references can be found at Greenhorn 1998:3-8 *passim*. Greenhorn explains that Meikle Earnock is 'an outlying area of the town of Hamilton which adjoins Motherwell and is essentially part of the same conurbation', and that Don Jonson [an American actor] was 'the icon of eighties American cool' (Greenhorn 1999:98-99). It is of interest to note in this context that Greenhorn says of the American television series *The Waltons* that it is 'exactly the kind of American sentimentality which would make Alex bristle' with revulsion (Greenhorn 1999:108).

Origins, Centres and Peripheries:
The Case of Early Scottish Literature

R. D. S. Jack

In the 1950s, when I was studying at senior secondary school and University Scottish writers were studied within English Literature and evaluated against English literary criteria. I was brought up almost entirely on a diet of English writers. Only Burns and Scott won their way on to the Glasgow University curriculum in those days and even they were evaluated against the Leavisite norms of the great English tradition.

In these circumstances, it was a major relief to read Kurt Wittig's 1958 monograph, *The Scottish Tradition in Literature*, which proposed the opposite paradigm. Having designated the ways in which Scottish society differed from English, he openly admitted the synchronic eclecticism of his methodology: 'In expounding these values I have picked out the ones which seem to me specifically Scottish and have largely ignored the rest' (Wittig 1958:3). This was only intended as a kind of interim canonical counterbalance. But, for a number of reasons, including the arguments of extreme cultural materialists and the Anglophobic, nationalist and communistic programme of Hugh MacDiarmid, Wittig's criteria of one race (Scottish), one language (Scots), one theme (Scottish) and one focus (left wing political realism) has outlasted even the intentions of its own creator.

In the space at my disposal, I shall not deny the validity of this approach within its own, defined, premises. I shall however argue that in the Scottish case an alternative, multi-racial, polymathic, decorous and allegoric model had been presented from the Middle Ages onwards. It is because of this that I am superimposing a diachronic line (Origins) upon the synchronic circle (Centre and Peripheries) evoked by the title of this volume.

There is, admittedly, a pragmatic angle to my own approach, for what have been the canonical results of this reluctance to widen Wittig's paradigm? Obviously, if one looks for left wing realism in Scots about Scotland, some writers are going to come out of the process better than others. At the highest level of popularity, the radical nationalism of Burns will be preferred to the Toryism of Walter Scott. Poor Muriel Spark survives for *The Prime of Miss Jean Brodie* (1961) because it is the only one of her novels set in Scotland while William Drummond and his fellow anglicising mannerists of the seventeenth century pass ingloriously below the hermeneutic salt entirely. And how would we Scots feel if a similarly Anglo-obsessive canon were derived south of the border? 'Ah, Shakespeare – *Henry IV*, lovely! *Othello*? A bit foreign. Oh and certainly not the Scottish play!'

And where does this competitive canon begin? Where are the MacBeowulfs? The answer to this is, 'nowhere'. The first major text preserved in Scots is Barbour's *Bruce* and that was probably composed in the mid-1370s (Duncan 1999). Almost 800 years of comparative canonical competition disappears! As the period from about 1585 until the end of the seventeenth century is also rejected on the grounds of linguistic treachery, another century and more drops out. Little wonder, Scottish literature's success in broadcasting its existence across the free world is actually confined to small enclaves of enthusiasm, centred on individual scholars. The central curricular place enjoyed by Irish studies has not been attained.

If it seems rather odd to announce literary rivalry with England by opting out of more than half the chronological range available for comparison, the facts of language and history suggest that there is another definition of Scottishness, which renders the half-truths of Wittig unnecessary now that the first essential victory of gaining disciplinary status has been won. Historically, of course the inhabitants of modern Scotland come from a variety of strains – Celtic, Saxon, Pictish and Norman to name but a few.

This multi-racial definition historically and geographically, was accepted by the erudite Scottish 'makars' of the medieval period. Most of these were masters of many tongues, well-educated and given to commentating on their own poetic practice. They were well aware that Scots was a branch of Northumbrian English and so, like William Dunbar, usually derive their literary origins from Chaucer.

> O reverend Chaucere, rose of rethoris all
> (As in oure tong ane flour imperiall)
> That raise in Britane evir, quho redis rycht,
> Thou beris of makaris the tryumph riall;
> Thy fresch anamalit termes celicall
> This mater coud illumynit have full brycht.
> Was thou noucht of oure Inglisch all the lycht,
> Surmounting eviry tong terrestriall,
> Alls fer as Mayes morow dois mydnycht?
> *The Goldyn Targe* (Jack and Rozendaal 2000:134)

If Dunbar uses his rhetorical training to argue the decorous case for breadth, subtlety and an alliance with the English tongue, his brother-makar, Gavin

Douglas, already suggests the alternative, patriotically distinct, view of language.

> And yit forsuyth I set my bissy pane
> As that I couth to mak it braid and plane,
> Kepand na sudron bot our awyn langage,
> And spekis as I lernyt quhen I was page.
> Nor yit sa cleyn all sudron I refus,
> Bot sum word I pronunce as nyghtbouris doys:
> Lyke as in Latyn beyn Grew termys sum,
> Some behufyt quhilum (or than be dum)
> Sum bastard Latyn, French or Inglys oyss,
> Quhar scant was Scottis – I had nane other choys.
>
> (*Eneados*: Prologue, 109-118) (Jack and Rozendaal 2000:286)

Characteristically, he does so only in his translation of Virgil's *Aeneid* for, as Matthiessen notes, translation was viewed as 'an act of patriotism', colonising words as adventurers colonised lands (Matthiessen 1931:3). The medieval and renaissance translator colonises words from other languages to increase the subtlety of the national vernacular. Within the comprehensive dialectic of the period, these two models were not seen as mutually exclusive; the decorous and nationalist models co-existed within a modally and persuasively differentiated agenda.

These distinctions were inherited by the even more erudite later makars writing under the patronage of King James VI at the Edinburgh court in the 1580s. At this time various anglicising forces threatened the subtlety-in-distinctiveness of Scots. In his own critical treatise the *Reulis and Cautelis* (1585), the king defensively highlights the nationalist model, urging his poets to make their Scots as different as possible from English and encouraging translation. At this time, he condemned the 'harsh Inglis vearsis' of his friend, William Alexander, Earl of Stirling (Jack and Rozendaal 2000:354).

When James became King of Britain, however, the Earl became the proper model for imitation. His predominantly decorous approach to language now became official court policy, replacing the nationalistic perspective of the early Edinburgh movement. In Alexander's rhetorical treatise, *Anacrisis* (1630c), he clearly spelt out the subsidiary position of language in a developed conceit. Language is only the conduit watering the garden of poetry, whose plants and paths are tended by decorum (Jack and Rozendaal 2000:475).

The patriotic consistency of this change was justified on two grounds – (1) A Scottish king now leads Britain and the nationalist focus broadens accordingly. (2) Scots is not distinct from English. To anglicise while retaining some distinctive Scotticisms – not to mention Scottish pronunciations – more accurately mirrors the shared historical origins of the two dialects.

Once it is accepted that earlier Scottish writers worked on a flexible linguistic model allowing them to claim both decorous and nationalistic grounds for composition, the inadequacy of a number of critical clichés is revealed. In the eighteenth century, for example, Ramsay, Fergusson and Burns are credited with leading 'the vernacular revival', as if all Scots were writing in English alone. This is because, as Jacques Roubaud argued, 'If you are a nationalist there is a nation and it has one language' (Roubaud 1997:12) – in this case, a constantly weakening Scots. Yet, arguing from the decorous angle, Burns and his predecessors see the linguistic situation much more optimistically. Yes, the Scots element in the vernacular needs strengthening and thick Scots may be used when patriotic interests are being directly expressed. But decorously the Scottish writer in the 18th century believes his inheritance of both Scots and English gives him an advantage when covering the various stylistic levels outlined in classical rhetorical treatises. A carefully graded decorous league table in which the lowest topics are handled in thick Scots, the middle style becomes Anglo-Scots and high middle becomes English governs the poet's thinking in this area. As the most elevated style of all is Latinate or artificial English, Burns can properly echo the high style of Sidney and Spenser when describing the Bard of Scottish Poetry in his allegorical poem, 'The Vision' (*Poems 1884-5*):

> Her Mantle large, of greenish hue,
> My gazing wonder chiefly drew;
> Deep lights and shades, bold-mingling, threw
> A lustre grand;
> And seem'd, to my astonish'd view,
> A well-known Land.

> (Kinsley 1968:82)

This is also why Allan Ramsay demands two literary pen-names adding the English neo-classical name of Isaac Bickerstaff to that of the Scots makar Gavin Douglas[1] while fictively Walter Scott, from the microcosmic *Lay of the Last Minstrel* (1805) onwards, provides the imaginative multiracial counter-balance to set beside Burns' more stridently post-colonial vision.

These two visions of language and nation were still being advocated from an essentially classical base by the Scottish Rhetoricians of the eighteenth and nineteenth centuries. They were advocated by David Masson, from the chair of Rhetoric and English Literature at the University of Edinburgh in the 1880s, and were in my own time perpetuated by a steadfast refusal to split the Scottish Higher Grade of secondary school qualification into Literature and

Language papers on the English 'A' level model. In this way, the distinctive and enduring 'rhetorical' case made by the makars was confirmed for Scottish writing across the centuries.

With this in mind, I propose to use the alternative diachronically decorous, multi-racial and polymathic model of Scottishness to examine the years of apparent silence. Clearly, it is better equipped to cope with the Scots dialect's mongrel history as spelt out by the enlightenment grammarian Alexander Geddes:

> On analysing the Scoto-Saxon dialect, I find it composed; first and chiefly of pure Saxon; secondly of Saxonised Celtic, whether Welsh, Pictish or Erse; thirdly of Saxonised Norman or Old French; fourthly of more modern French Scoticized; fifthly of Danish, Dutch and Flemish occasionally incorporated; sixthly of words, borrowed from the learned dead languages. (Geddes 1792:415)

As the term Scoto-Saxon reminds us, in the sixth century, the modern map of Scotland was the home of warring tribes led by warlord-kings. To the north of the Forth and Clyde were the Picts; the Scots (i.e. Irish) were striving to establish themselves in modern Argyll, while Strathclyde was mainly the homeland of the Britons, although Anglo-Saxon forces were infiltrating more and more into their southern territories. Norse influence in the northern mainland and islands further complicated this ever-changing map of motliness. While trading links and political alliances with Scandinavia lay behind this, the Norse heritage of Scots-English was largely derived from the Anglo-Scandinavians of Northumbria whose dialect found its way into Scotland in the later Middle Ages. And crucially – from the eleventh century onwards, Anglo-Norman as well as English influence extended in the south-east especially.

I shall look at five representative texts, written about Scotland by poets resident in Scotland, three from the earlier period – the seventh century; and two from the later, thirteenth century with these considerations of medium and message uppermost in mind. Unfortunately, it is necessary to add a third 'm': mode for this is a diachronic enquiry embracing the different dialectic and evaluative structures of the Middle Ages. As Alastair Fowler notes, we forget at our peril that this period exists at the 'edge of our historical reach [and] opens a strange, ceremonious world – hierarchically ordered, comprehensively meaningful' whose ideals differ from our own (Fowler 1987:28).

Around AD 600 we find a bard based in the Lothian region following his king south to Catterick to fight the Saxons and then composing a heroic epic celebrating their heroism in defeat. So what's the problem? Why do long analyses of this poem not figure in most histories of Scottish Literature?

Gwÿr a aeth Gatraeth gan wawr
Trafodynt eu hedd eu hofnawr,
Milcant a thrychant a ymdaflawdd.
Gwyarllyd gwynoddyd waywawr,
Ef gorsaf wriaf tng ngwriawr,
Rhag gosgordd Mynyddog Mwynfawr

(*Gododdin* St 11)

(Warriors went to Catraeth with the dawn,
Their fears departed from their dwelling place,
A hundred thousand and three hundred charged against each other.
He stains his spear with blood,
The most valiant resister in battle,
Before the retinue of Mynyddog Mwynfawr) (Jarman 1990:8-9)

Linguistically, the first authentic poetic voice of Scotland speaks to us not in Scots but the Welsh of *Y Gododdin*. Racially and geographically, it describes alliances among the Britons (in modern geographic terms between Scotland and Wales). And it does so aurally, in the panegyric mode of classical, oratorical practice. More precisely, it celebrates the heroic defeat at Catterick of a king based in this region of Scotland – the Lothians. While that king's bard, Neurin, had come south with his troops, and (St 49) composed this formulaic lament on the night of the battle, the opening as shown stresses that this version of it is now performed in adapted form, at the Welsh court by the Welsh bard Taliesin, who remembers with honour (St 1) 'the gentle one', his fellow bard in Scotland – now 'earth-covered'.

By way of contrast, the second authentic voice of Scotland I have chosen is in the shared language of medieval learning, Latin. It belongs to the end of the seventh century; stresses our *Irish* links and exists in written form (Anderson 1991). Nonetheless, as the chosen extract shows, it still relies on aural sources.

While converting the Picts, Columba saw a man, who had just been consumed by a water-beast ('aquatilis [...] bestia'), being buried on the banks of the river Ness. Later, the beast re-surfaces but the holy man drives it off and orders it never to return:

Vir tum beatus videns [...] cum salutare sancta elevata manu in vacuo aere crucis pincxisset signum invocato dei nomine feroci imperavit bestia, dicens: 'Noles ultra progredi, nec hominem tangas. Retro citius revertere'.

(The blessed man, who was then watching, raised his holy hand and drew the saving sign of the cross in the empty air; and then invoking the name of God, he commanded the savage beast, and said 'You will go no further. Do not touch the man; turn backward speedily') (Anderson 1991:132-33)

Here, then is the first known story of the Loch Ness Monster along with an early Christian explanation of the creature's reluctance to break the surface again!

As the *Vita Columbae* is a legend, its national and geographic focus also differs from *Y Goddodin*. Columba's teaching centred domestically on the Islands and the Highlands but is seen miraculously to expand across Europe as well. This divine history also reminds us that Aristotle had reserved the total allegorical range for imaginative writers while the early Christian church had determined that politics stood low within that range at the level of practical tropology. The structure signs this clearly. To proclaim Columba as Christ's messenger, a three-in-one division of material is announced in the second preface. Three books celebrate his miracles under differentiated headings – prophetic miracles giving way to miracles of power in Book Two and to angelic visions in Book Three. Allegorically, the bias of emphasis also moves upwards accretively from a shared basis in history. Political concerns dominate the first book, philosophical and spiritual concerns the second and the mysteries of anagogy the third.

For nationalist critics, of course, Gaelic and Latin origins are much less threatening than English ones. Yet students of Old English will recognize the lower extract (B) cited below. It is from the tenth Century Vercelli MS version of the *Dream of the Rood*, regarded by many as the finest of all Old English religious poems. The upper version (A) of the same lines may not be so well known but they are almost certainly much earlier – late seventh century – and are a transliteration from the Northumbrian runes of Scotland's oldest concrete poem as preserved on the Ruthwell Cross near Dumfries.

A: krist waes on rodi
    Hweþræ þer fusæ farran kwomu
    Æþþilæ til anum ic þæt al biheald
    Sar[æ] ic wæs mi[þ] sorgum gidræ[fi]d [...]

    (Christ was on the cross.
    But hurrying thither came
    noble ones to the
    One; I beheld all that.
    Grievously was I afflicted with sorrow)

                                                      (Swanton 1992:90, 92)

B: Crist þæs on rode.
    Hþæðere þær fuse   feorran cþoman
    to þam Æðelinge.   Ic þæt eall beheold.
    Sare ic þæs mid sorgum gedrefed [...]

(Christ was on the cross.
Yet eagerly some hurried from afar
to him there came noble men from afar
To him who was their Prince. I beheld all that.
Ah, then I was deeply afflicted with sorrow to him. I who beheld it all, was sorely
affected by pains).

(Dickins 1934:28)

These Northumbrian runes first remind us that there were more sign-systems
then, than are usually remembered now. The ancient language of the Picts, for
example, is only preserved epigraphically. The runes also remind us that this
was the zenith of Northumbrian power and the realm ruled by the Barons of
Northumbria included much of what is, today, Southern Scotland. To
understand their meaning, however, it is important to see them within the
cross as a whole. Without 'reading' the scenes and icons on the north and
south faces, the ornaments and the runes on the east and west faces lose their
wider hermeneutic context.

Five hundred years later, the multi-racial and multi-linguistic origins of
the Scottish nation change to take into account the time of Anglo-Norman
influence politically and culturally. French chivalric literature enjoyed
unchallenged superiority at this time. In looking at this evidence, I shall
change discursive tack here to highlight the vacuous literary history left by the
unitary national and linguistic paradigm. With no acknowledged Scottish
sources prior to Barbour, does the lively and varied, witty and serious,
Romance tradition of fifteenth century Scotland not only *deal* with the matters
of England and France but arise from them alone?

There is indirect proof that Scottish bards were recounting Romances at
court well before that time as this excerpt from the *Karlamagnússaga*
illustrates:

> Saga þessi, er hér byrjast, er eigi af lokleysu þeirri, er menn gera sér til gamans,
> heldur er hún sögð med sannindum, sem síðar mun birtast. Fann þessa sögu herra
> Bjarni Erlingsson úr Bjarkey, ritaða og sagða í ensku máli, í Skotlandi, þá er hann
> sat þar um veturinn eftir fráfall Alexandri konungs. (Vilhjálmsson 1961:101)

> (The saga which starts here is not the sort of pointless nonsense which men devise
> to amuse themselves – rather, it tells the truth, as will be apparent later. Lord
> Bjarni Erlingsson of Bjarkey found this saga written and told in the English
> language, in Scotland, when he stayed there during the winter after the death of
> King Alexander). (Hieatt 1975:178)

Inserted as Part II of Book 1 of the *Karlamagnússaga* is the 'Romance of Olif
and Landres'. As the quotation reveals, it was recited aloud at the court of the
King of Scotland in the winter of 1286, and heard by Bjarni Erlingsson, the

chief ambassador sent by King Eirik to negotiate the succession of the Maid of Norway after the death of Alexander III. Erlingsson had the tale translated and in that form the earliest written proof of aural Scottish 'Romanticism' remains.

Given more time, I could have dwelt on my fifth language and fifth racial grouping more fully. Regretfully, however, I can only suggest that those who wish to study the first example of Scottish Romance's strange balancing of comedy and heroism, courtly privilege and democratic aspiration, might do worse than read the D'Artagnan-like tale of the rough Galloway farmer cum knight errant, Fergus, who, as the following extract shows, lays down his plough to follow the knights of King Arthur:

> Quant li fius au vilain le voit
> La karue que il tenoit
> Laisse estraiere enmi la placeÉ
> Si saissit au frain l'escuier
> Molt sagement et se li dist:
> 'Biaus dols frere, se Dius t'ait,
> Ne me celer, di moi qui sont
> Cil chevalier qui par chi vont'

(Fergus, ll. 381-83;392-96)

> (When the peasant's son saw them (Arthur and his knights) he abandoned where it lay the plough he was holding... [and] very politely took hold of the squire's bridle and said to him 'My dear good brother, in God's name tell me without hiding who those knights are, who are passing this way') (Frescolin 1983:42-43)

Although the major sources for *Le Roman de Fergus* are French, its author Guillaume le Clerc lived in Scotland and sets Fergus's quests and tests against a mainly Scottish backdrop, which includes Galloway, Ayrshire, the Forest of Glasgow, the Lothians and Fife.

Why are these works not listed proudly as Scottish rivals to the English legends and Romances of the Old and Early Middle English periods? Well, a critic will only see what his chosen methodology allows. Modern concentration on one language, one nation and one political text within an antithetical dialectics which sets Scots against English is at odds with the many languages, races and levels of interpretation favoured originally and with the comprehensive, ultimately spiritual dialectics used to discuss them. The definition of Scottish literature thus defined has endured from the sixth century until this one. In drawing attention to it, I hope that I have justified my temerity in adding 'Scottish Origins' to 'Centres and Peripheries'.

References

Anderson, A. & Anderson, M. (1991, 2nd ed.): *Adomnán's Life of Columba*. Oxford: Oxford University Press.

Dickins, B. & Ross, A. (1934): *The Dream of the Rood*. London: Methuen.

Duncan, A. (1999): *John Barbour: The Bruce*. Edinburgh: Canongate.

Fowler, A. (1987): *History of English Literature*. Oxford: Blackwell.

Geddes, A. (1792): 'Three Scottish Poems with a previous dissertation on the Scoto-Saxon dialect', in *Transactions of the Society of Antiquaries of Scotland*. Edinburgh.

Frescolin, W. (ed.) (1983): *Guillaume le Clerc, The Romance of Fergus*. Philadelphia: William H. Allen.

Hieatt, C. (trans.) (1975): *Karlamagnússaga*, vols I-III. Toronto: Pontifical Institute.

Jack, R. & Rozendaal P. (eds) (2000, 2nd edn): *The Mercat Anthology of Early Scottish Literature 1357-1707*. Edinburgh: Mercat Press .

Jarman, A (ed.) (1990): *Aneirin, Y Gododdin*. Llandysul: Gomer Press.

Kinghorn, A. & Law, A. (eds) (1970): *The Works of Allan Ramsay*, vol. 4. Edinburgh: Blackwell.

Kinsley, J. (ed.) (1968): *The Poems of Robert Burns*. Oxford: Clarendon.

Matthiessen, F. (1931): *Translation an Elizabethan Art*. Cambridge, Mass.: Harvard University Press.

Roubaud, J. (1997): 'Pursuing the Voice of Poetry in the Conversation of Mankind', in *Translation and Literature*, vol. 6, pp. 8-22.

Swanton M. (ed.) (1992, 2nd ed.): *The Dream of the Rood*. Exeter: Exeter University Press.

Vilhjálmsson, Bjarni (ed.) (1961): *Karlamagnœs Saga og Kappa Hans*. Rejkjavik: Björnsonnar H. F.

Witttig, K. (1958): *The Scottish Tradition in Literature*. Edinburgh: Oliver and Boyd.

Note

1. As the editors of the Scottish Text Society edition of Ramsay's poems explain (Kinghorn 1970:10-17), Ramsay later added Douglas to mirror the Middle Scots tradition, having first been satisfied with an English neoclassical *nom de plume* alone.

'It follows me, that black island...': Portraying and Positioning the Hebridean 'Fringe' in Twentieth-Century Gaelic Literature

Donald E. Meek

Peripheries and centres are very much a matter of perception. For those of us brought up in the Hebrides, as I was in the 1950s and 1960s, the idea that we were somehow peripheral was hardly worth a second thought. We would not have known then, of course, what the word 'periphery' meant, and if we had heard its Gaelic equivalent, 'iomall', we would have thought of something else – the edge of a garment or the edge of a plate of porridge. Many a morning, when I was confronted with that delightful substance before going to school, I would plunge into it with the wild abandon typical of young people. Then, having scalded myself, I would spit it out, and my aggrieved old relatives would say, 'Ith e on iomall' (Eat it from the outer edge). Sometimes 'iomall' could mean the 'remaining scrap', which was left when the centre of a cake was eaten out by an earlier enthusiast. The vocabulary which is now the special property of those advanced thinkers on Gaelic economics (usually based in Inverness) was very personal and domestic to me in those far-off days. I still cannot conceive of 'edges' and 'peripheries' in geographical terms when I think of the Hebrides. If there was a 'periphery' at all, it was the land mass of the Scottish mainland, which seemed mysterious and remote. I remember how sorry I felt for those distant members of my family who had the misfortune to live off the edge of things in smog-filled Glasgow, and could not share the delights of my island paradise at the centre of the universe. I had everything that I could have wished for, including an abundance of food, almost all of it home-grown. It was only later in life, when I myself had migrated to the aforesaid smog-filled metropolis, that I began to realise that there was another view of the islands which tended to see them as peripheral. That was in the late 1960s and early 1970s. By the end of the twentieth century, however, the concept of 'marginalisation' had become endemic among those who planned the destiny of the Hebrides. The term 'The Celtic

Fringe' had been invented by Michael Hechter in 1975 (Hechter 1975), and it began to pop up everywhere, accompanied by a haze of popular misconception and Celtic romanticism. By 1970, too, the islands were being opened up to so-called 'incomers' and 'white settlers', and a new vocabulary of remoteness and inaccessibility was finding its way into the area.

As I prepared this chapter, I was comforted to find that I was not alone in my perspectives. Poets down the centuries, far from feeling isolated and remote, affirmed the centrality of the Gaelic world in its own terms, and even those who had left the area lived with a very real awareness of their former island homes. The nineteenth century, in particular, witnessed a great deal of migration and emigration from the Highlands and Islands, but the migrants did not suddenly lose touch with their native heath. They retained their links through their families, and formed associations in the cities to maintain their territorial loyalties – the Islay Association, the Tiree Association, the Lewis and Harris Association. There was, admittedly, a romantic dimension in such recollection and reconstruction. It is evident in the work of many poets and songsters, as they idealised, and idolised, the homeland that they had forsaken. But, however difficult and decisive the physical separation may have been, the original homeland travelled with them, and they were compelled to explore their relationship to it (Meek 2003).

The same is true of the twentieth century. Twentieth-century Gaelic writers and composers who have left the Hebrides have a very strong sense of belonging to the area, and they are in no doubt about its symbolic significance. Admittedly, the styles of composition have been diversified, and the themes likewise, since the nineteenth century. The relationship to the homeland has come to be explored in a much more analytical manner, particularly by the more 'academic' poets, who have been influenced by English literature and its philosophies, and have turned from song and quatrain to free verse. For those who remain in the Hebrides, however, the islands have continued to be the centre of a self-sustaining world, which they have been pleased to describe and affirm in song and verse, formal and informal, light and profound. We will look at specimens of twentieth-century Gaelic verse, traditional and more modern, in a moment, but before doing so, it is essential that we consider Gaelic prose.

Prose writing

It is a significant fact that there is very little Gaelic prose, from the twentieth century or any other, which describes the Hebrides, either in whole or in part, as a geographical unit. I can think of only one book which describes a Hebridean island, and is actually written in Gaelic. It is *Hiort: far na laigh a' ghrian* (St Kilda: where the sun went down), by Calum MacFhearghuis (Calum Ferguson), a native of Portnangiuran in the Point district of Lewis. It was published as recently as 1995 (MacFhearghuis 1995). It is noteworthy that this book should be about St Kilda, an archipelago which lies west of Harris, and which was evacuated in 1930. The sad fate of St Kilda has given this remarkable outcrop of small islands a particular resonance, and the number of books about it in English is legion. Memorialisation is common, but the later twentieth-century volumes often have their own agendas, portraying the archipelago as either a utopia or a dystopia. Such writing is not new, however. St Kilda has had a special niche in literary consciousness from the time of Martin Martin in the seventeenth century, as it was the Ultima Thule of the traveller seeking remoteness and the 'Other' (MacDonald 2001). Ossianic romanticism gave it an indelible place as the uttermost and grandest expression of the Sublime on the very edge of the Hebridean 'fringe', with its massive cliffs towering out of the surging Atlantic billows, and offering a home to clouds of fulmars which became food for the St Kildans. Its inhabitants were sometimes compared to seabirds, or portrayed as animal-like, living in a primitive zoo. In keeping with the travellers' cultural identity, writing about St Kilda, as about the Hebrides, has been almost wholly in English.

It is perhaps an indication of the penetration into Gaelic of that wider fascination with desolate and formerly inhabited islands that we now have a Gaelic book about St Kilda, and none about any of the other islands. This is not, however, a traveller's account, nor that of the sociologist researching for a Ph.D. about the 'natives'. MacFhearghuis is no cultural or intellectual tourist. He writes with the eye of a skilled film-maker, producing a documentary history of the archipelago. The scenes shift from the earliest inhabitants to the last, from folk belief to austere Christianity, from emigration to evacuation. The book is interspersed with songs and tunes, accompanied with relevant photographs, and sketches. In this splendid 'docu-book', it seems to me that what MacFhearghuis does superbly is to repossess the 'St Kilda experience' from a Gaelic perspective, and to reclaim the island for the Gaelic world, to which it properly belongs. The island becomes surprisingly normal in the process. The island that we see is not the human zoo that titillated the romantic travellers of the nineteenth century (Cooper 2002). It is an island that once throbbed with Gaelic life, a paradigm of the Hebrides, raising profound questions for other Hebrideans about the sustainability of their own cultural units.

MacFhearghuis's work is remarkable because it is in Gaelic. I have a very large shelf of 'island books' in my study, but only one of these, MacFhearghuis's, is in Gaelic.

Even when the writer is fluent in Gaelic, he or she may well opt for English as the language of Hebridean description. There are various reasons for this code-switch. Volumes of this kind – like their nineteenth-century predecessors – are evidently aimed at enlightening an English readership in the first instance. We may cite Finlay J. MacDonald's trilogy *Crowdie and Cream*, *Crotal and White*, and *The Corncrake and the Lysander* on his boyhood in Scarista, Harris, as a particularly good example of work in English by a fully fledged Gaelic writer who evidently chose not to use Gaelic (MacDonald 2001). Finlay J., as we call him, was a pioneering radio and television producer based in Glasgow, and he was at the forefront of the development of twentieth-century Gaelic literature. He frequently wrote Gaelic short stories which were set in the islands, but he evidently did not see the need to describe his own island in Gaelic for the benefit of other Gaels. His upbringing would not have been unusual in the Gaelic context, and therefore he may have assumed that it was hardly worth his while writing about it in Gaelic. Finlay J. may also have reasoned that what he had to say would be more interesting for the non-Gaelic reader. So English was chosen. Perhaps the contract from the publisher determined the choice of language, but it is nevertheless true that this is part of a general pattern.

By writing in English about the Hebrides, it appears that Gaelic authors gain certain advantages which are denied to them in a Gaelic context. They gain, for instance, some critical distance, but perhaps the most important thing that they gain is the opportunity to cash in on a more appreciative and, of course, larger readership, gasping for the 'Castaway' experience which has thrust the depopulated island of Taransay into recent general awareness. The 'Other' and the 'peripheral' tend to go together for mainstream Scottish and British readerships, and this external perspective lends itself more readily to being conveyed in English. I have to confess that Finlay J.'s English writing makes me very uneasy, as it seems to me to be in a quite different league from his Gaelic writing, since it makes a pitch for the attention of non-Gaels, and has a touch of caricature, occasionally reminiscent of Lilian Beckwith, whose supposedly 'funny' books (of the 1960s and 1970s) about islanders ridiculed their naivety and simplicity, and made 'Tonald' speak in a mock Highland dialect. Finlay J. is very far from being a second Beckwith (thank goodness!), but he occasionally touches this exploitable vein of insular simplicity, as he shows islanders who gradually emerge from the evasive shadows of tilley lamps into the full glare of electric light. Sometimes, particularly in its frankly crude descriptions of sexual encounters, *Crowdie and Cream* reminds me of Laurie Lee's *Cider with Rosie* (Lee 1962). The Laurie-Leeification of the Hebrides does less than justice to the area or the author. MacDonald is a highly sophisticated and immensely skillful writer, but he is perhaps too deferential to external models, and prone to blotting his indigenous canvases with imported fiction.

In short, when writing about their own islands in English prose, the more self-conscious authors who are aware of expectations are inclined to adopt external perspectives and styles. This immediately positions their islands in a different mental map. It is one which exploits, often for the benefit of the publisher, the implied distinction between 'centre' and 'periphery'. The Hebridean 'Fringe' inevitably appears to be quaint, remote and in a time-warp. 'Fringe' can all too easily produce cringe.

There is, however, another kind of less popular, less polished, writing in English which describes Hebridean islands, and sits on a rather sharp bilingual cusp. This is not because 'The Writer' is eyeing the big world out there; it is because the writer lacks the confidence and the ability to write in Gaelic – a telling comment on the educational system which prevailed for all too long in the region. An example of this is Angus Edward MacInnes's account of *Eriskay Where I Was Born* (MacInnes 1997). MacInnes's book lacks the stylistic smoothness of Finlay J.'s work. Instead, it has a ruggedness which is convincing, both in its somewhat chaotic structure and in its wonderful portraits of Eriskay people. It is plain, unvarnished stuff, filled with rough and tumble, all hugely readable. It is sometimes grim, sometimes angry, sometimes very funny. Eriskay, like St Kilda, has frequently been romanticised, but MacInnes, a retired Caledonian MacBrayne Captain who travelled the world as a sailor, has turned his back on the romantic recipe of 'Otherness' which sells so well. His adventures in different ports put islanders in a global perspective, rather than a cul-de-sac. MacInnes is a marvellous storyteller, and he writes exactly as he speaks, with Gaelic idioms woven effortlessly into his gloriously Hebridean English (and the publishers had the good sense to let the book stand as it was). Eriskay is at the centre of his mental map, despite his many global travels. MacInnes is writing about community, and not really about himself as 'self' in any consciously autobiographical way; he writes about himself in the context of various communities, including that of Eriskay, that of the Merchant Navy and that of other sailors from different cultures. This is a voyage of self-discovery in which the writer collides with others who are travelling round their own global islands.

It is important to note that we do have prose writers in Gaelic who describe, or portray, different aspects of island life through their native language. The perspective which is gained thereby is a much more immediate one, and it is directed at the Gaels themselves. Gaelic, the mother tongue, is the language of intimate connection between the writer and the native island. It is the language of personal analysis within the island frame, and more specifically the analysis of the relationship between the writer and the community. When Angus Campbell, from Ness, Lewis, wrote his autobiography, *Suathadh ri Iomadh Rudha* (Rubbing against Many Headlands) (Caimbeul 1973), he did not offer the standard writer-centred autobiography that one might expect. The 'self' for him (as indeed for Angus Edward MacInnes) is a vehicle for engaging with the community on the one hand, and with you, the reader, on the other. It is clear from his preface that Campbell battled with an inadequate grasp of the finer points of Gaelic literacy to produce this remarkable book, which is an insider's critique of a Hebridean community across a range of events and experiences, from social engineering to spiritual remaking through the power of the church. An essential degree of critical distance is achieved largely by making the 'self' ambiguous and non-central. This is the biography of a community rather than an individual, and stands largely alone in its self-effacing power and honest observation.

The Campbells of Ness – the northern tip of Lewis, and of the Hebridean archipelago, as it happens – have been remarkable for their literary skills. Angus's relatives, Norman and Alasdair Campbell, have written very effectively about Lewis life, through Gaelic novels, essays and short stories. Their concern is to provide snapshots of island life, as in Norman Campbell's black comedy, *Deireadh an Fhoghair* (The End of Autumn) (Caimbeul 1979), in which he portrays a very small and isolated Lewis community in its death-throes, sustaining and entertaining itself by living on recycled materials of all sorts, including memories of basic, and sometimes very trivial, events. Poems and songs to things such as washed-up casks figure in the narrative. The cask is admired for its technical excellence and heroic qualities, and for the memories of the worthy ancestor who rescued it from the shore and hauled it home. A good meal of chicken with the neighbours provides ritual power, and reconstructs fleetingly the dynamics of the dying community. This evinces stories, genealogies, and reminiscences. The mental map represented in this kind of writing is much more detailed in terms of local observation, and may contain a considerable amount of local Gaelic dialect. Satire and humour intermingle too, and these function at a level which a non-Gaelic reader could not grasp readily, if at all. The book is thus beyond adequate translation into any other language. At times even the Gaelic reader, and especially the reader from another dialect area, feels almost overwhelmed, if not excluded, by the relentlessly local perspectives. The critical nuancing of such books is sewn into the language in such a way that one is not conscious of external evaluation; it is 'friendly fire' from the inside.

Gaelic verse

Prose, then, has not been fully exploited as a medium for describing or analysing island life in the Gaelic context, but there have been very significant contributions from the Campbells of Ness. Verse has been the main medium for exploring the relationship between Gaelic people and their native islands. We can distinguish two types of verse. First, there is what may be loosely term 'traditional' verse, employing quatrains and commonly intended for singing. This is the form which the resident islander will normally use. The traditionally-minded exile will also employ song. Then, there is modern free verse, employed mainly by exiles who have been educated at mainland universities, and are often academics themselves – poets such as Donald MacAulay, formerly Reader in Celtic at Aberdeen and latterly Professor of Celtic at Glasgow, and Derick Thomson, his predecessor as Professor of Celtic at Glasgow, and a very important figure in the revitalisation of Gaelic literature in the twentieth century. Iain Crichton Smith is also in this category. All three men come from Lewis, two (Smith and Thomson) from Point in the east, and one (MacAulay) from Great Bernera on the west side.

As might be expected, there is a considerable difference between the approaches of the two types of poet, though there is a certain amount of common ground. If I were to put it in a nutshell, I would say that the traditional Gaelic poet affirms the islands, using a well recognised and time-honoured rhetorical code, while the more modern poet raises questions about his relationship to the islands, using codes which belong to a wider stream of contemporary verse in English and other languages, but which nevertheless have a close connection with Gaelic rhetoric of various kinds. As Iain Crichton Smith put it in the English poem, 'Lewis', which gives this paper its title (Stephen 1993:44-45):

> It follows me, that black island without ornament,
> which I am always questioning.

For the traditional poet, affirmation, rather than interrogation, of the islands is of the essence, and there is often a focus on individual islands. The rhetoric of affirmation stresses fecundity, beauty, flower-covered machairs, abundance of wild life, and pre-eminently self-sufficiency. 'Uibhist mu Thuath' (North Uist) by Dòmhnall Ruadh Chorùna (Donald MacDonald) of North Uist represents this genre (MacAmhlaidh 1995:92-93). A theme touched on in this song is loyalty to the island, and it is only when loyalty is affirmed that there is any reference to the location of the island within Scotland. The poet claims (v. 4) that North Uist is preferable to the whole of

Scotland. The poet does not want to be an exile, however attractive the prospects. The extent to which this affirmative rhetoric can be used of other islands is well illustrated by 'Uibhist nan Sguaban Eòrna' (Uist of the Barley Sheaves), composed by the South Uist poet, Dòmhnall Iain Dhonnchaidh (Donald John MacDonald) (Innes 1998:80-81). There again you will see that Scotland is mentioned only to affirm the qualities of the native island (v. 2). Scotland serves for both poets as a 'value additive', reinforcing a sense of identity which has little to do with physical geography, and everything to do with the qualities of the homeland. Scotland is the periphery, and the periphery is invoked to validate the superiority of the insular centre.

The focus in such verse, as I have said, is usually on individual islands, but occasionally it can be broader. Donald John MacDonald of South Uist composed a long 'epic' poem in praise of the Hebrides (Innes 1998:86-93). This is a fine example of poetic positioning which allows us to see South Uist as part of a wider Hebridean panorama. The poet's concept of the Hebrides is very much a northern one, taking in the Outer Isles, from Barra to Lewis, but excluding the Inner Hebrides. (We may say in passing that poets from the Inner Hebrides worked in the same way, positioning their particular island in terms of their immediate neighbours. To Inner Hebrideans, St Kilda was, and is, utterly remote – a place to send naughty children!) The poet takes pride in what the Hebrides have done for the wider world, and his vista extends far beyond Scotland (which is not mentioned once in the entire song). There is no sense of inferiority; rather, the message is the opposite, as the poet claims that the defence of the wider world was dependent on the contribution of the brave men from the isles. He is thinking particularly of the First and Second World Wars. He himself was a prisoner of war, and has left us a fascinating account, in fine Gaelic prose, of his incarceration in a German concentration camp (MacDhòmhnaill 1998).

Donald John's poem is a proud celebration of the Outer Hebrides, but it is far from insular. The Hebrides are mapped globally. Scotland is missed out as a point of reference, as it is irrelevant and not necessary for the argument. Like the rest of the world, it is dependent on the islands, and not vice versa. In such poets' minds, then, the islands are self-contained, self-sustaining units, whose riches sustain other areas. The poets have no place for the language of economic subservience which has become so much the hallmark of modern discourse about the islands. The islands are enduring and powerful, independent and proud.

When we turn to the academic poets, such as MacAulay, Thomson and Smith, affirmation is more muted, but the themes of enduring, powerful islands are still very evident. Their power and influence are, however, portrayed very differently. The islands endure in the sense that they are ever-present in the poets' minds, in their mental geographies, so to speak, and they are powerful in wielding an ongoing influence in shaping their outlooks. Donald MacAulay's poem, 'Comharra Stiùiridh' (Landmark) (MacAulay 1995:210-1), is a particularly poignant and incisive examination of the exile's relationship to the island, which he revisits and leaves year after year. The picture is shot through with irony. The poet leaves the island in sorrow, but renounces the conventional remedies for sadness, such as drinking and singing sentimental songs on the MacBrayne steamer. The normal palliatives will not suffice for him. Each time he goes back, he returns to an island that has changed, but he departs from an island that refuses to leave him, and sails his mental ocean like an iceberg. There is a hint of 'Titanic' imagery here, as the island is also threatening. The poet has lost the island, but it is still there nevertheless, submerged in himself and acting as a kind of magnetic menace in his soul. MacAulay makes it clear that for him the island is certainly not peripheral; rather, it is very much central to his experience, and to his self-awareness. It has, however, been inferiorised and marginalized by others. The position is a mosaic of paradoxes, which cut across one another in a splendid medley of conflicting emotions which those of us who have shared MacAulay's experience know only too well. The mapping is a personal one, which is drawn by the pencil of inner self-analysis. Thomson's 'An Uilebheist' (The Monster) likewise explores this theme (Thomson 1982:126-7).

In verse, as in prose, there is a bilingual tension at the heart of the poets' presentations of their island experiences, and this reveals itself particularly clearly in anthologies, which often provide the poets' own translations into English. All the poetry that I have mentioned is available in translation in readily accessible texts, and this makes a concession to external readers who are interested in Gaelic verse but cannot read it for themselves. The periphery, it seems, needs to ensure that the centre knows that it is there, and that it is aware of the quality of the local production!

Only one writer – Iain Crichton Smith – wrote comfortably in Gaelic and in English about his native island, namely Lewis. The poem which gives this paper its title was written originally in English, and has no Gaelic equivalent, though Smith frequently has Gaelic and English versions of the same poem or short story. What is fascinating is that when Smith presents a word picture of Lewis in English rather than in Gaelic, the choice of language and artwork is rather different. In English, his pictures of Lewis tend to be more romantic and less gaunt than his Gaelic ones. In 'Lewis' (Stephen 1993:44-45), the picture is one that is much closer to traditional Gaelic verse when celebrating the homeland, and in this way we encounter another paradox, which reminds us of the problems which I identified in Finlay J. MacDonald's English prose. When writing in Gaelic about Lewis, however, Smith tends to eschew the romantic palliatives of the exile, and he goes out of his way to confront the insularity of the islands by referring to the crises of the wider world, such as the nuclear threat (MacAulay 1995:174-75).

Conclusion

For most writers who describe the Hebrides and who belong to the area, the islands are central, rather than peripheral, to their experience. Yet there are considerable differences in presentation and approach. The more traditional composers of Gaelic verse are firmly rooted in their own communities. They do not ask questions; they affirm certainties, at least rhetorically. Their concern is to keep the morale of their communities high within these communities themselves. Their rhetorical codes, handed down through the centuries, bind the islands into their own physical and cultural archipelagos, with their own centres and peripheries (the Inner Hebrides versus the Outer Hebrides, St Kilda versus the rest of the world). Scotland is a remote concept, which, when occasionally invoked, usually serves only to strengthen (by contrast) the value of the islands concerned. The writers of Gaelic prose, on the other hand, are prepared to be more critical than the traditional poets, and to offer critiques of their own areas, while affirming community values. The liberated power of prose, however, has not been fully exploited in Gaelic, as there is a general tendency to turn to English when describing localities in detail.

The frame of reference for 'non-traditional' writers is much more complex and ambivalent. We can see the tensions fairly clearly, in both prose and verse. Gaelic writers who operate between cultures are commonly exiles, functioning in an adopted culture beyond the islands. This means that they have to face up to the demands of a variety of maps before they begin to compose. The geographical map is submerged in a range of other drawings, imposed from the inside and the outside. The creative tension in this complex fusion nullifies any meaningful distinction between core and periphery.

As a result of their position outside their own communities, such writers face considerable challenges when presenting their native islands to themselves and to their readers. They have to confront the issue of which language(s) they will use – Gaelic, English, or both? This in turn helps to determine the positioning of the islands on the creative map (or maps). Which readership should they address? Gaelic intellectuals like themselves? The Gaels back in the islands? The general Scottish readership? Or can they address all communities at once? Should they pander to romantic external interest, and titillate the palates of the Home Counties in the hope of selling their work? How they travel according to their linguistic and rhetorical charts will determine who sails with them; who is on the outside of the experience, and who is on the inside.

To sum things up, one might say that, while the islands are never presented as a remote Hebridean 'fringe' in the work of the modern exile poets, any more than in the work of the traditional poets, the centre in which the exiles operate is much broader, much more ambiguous, and much less secure than that which sustains the traditional composers. The centre, like the periphery, is also infinitely portable and easily expandable. For any Gaelic writer, at home or abroad, there may be no periphery which is not central to his or her experience.

References

Caimbeul, Aonghas (1973): *Suathadh ri Iomadh Rubha*. Glaschu: Gairm.

Caimbeul, Tormod (1979): *Deireadh an Fhoghair*. Edinburgh: Chambers.

Cooper, Derek (2002): *Road to the Isles: Travellers in the Hebrides 1770-1914*. London: Macmillan.

Hechter, Michael (1975): *Internal Colonialism: The Celtic Fringe in British National Development*. Los Angeles: The University of California Press.

Innes, Bill (ed.) (1998): *Chì Mi: The Gaelic Poetry of Donald John MacDonald*. Edinburgh: Birlinn.

Lee, Laurie (1962): *Cider with Rosie*. Harmondsworth: Penguin Books.

MacAmhlaidh, Fred (deas.) (1995): *Dòmhnall Ruadh Chorùna: Òrain is Dàin le Dòmhnall Dòmhnallach*. Loch nam Madadh: Comann Eachdraidh Uibhist a Tuath.

MacAulay, Donald (ed.) (1995): *Nua-Bhàrdachd Ghàidhlig: Modern Scottish Gaelic Poems*. Edinburgh: Canongate.

MacDhòmhnaill, Dòmhnall Iain (1998): *Fo Sgàil a' Swastika*. Stornoway: Acair.

MacDonald, Finlay J. (2001): *The Finlay J. MacDonald Omnibus*. London: Warner Books.

MacDonald, Fraser (2001): 'St Kilda and the Sublime', in *Ecumene: A Journal of Cultural Geographies*, 8 (2) (April 2001), pp. 151-74.

MacFhearghuis, Calum (1995): *Hiort: far na laigh a' ghrian*. Steòrnabhagh: Acair.

MacInnes, Angus Edward (1997): *Eriskay Where I Was Born*. Edinburgh: Mercat Press.

Meek, Donald E. (ed.) (2003): *Caran an t-Saoghail: The Wiles of the World*. Edinburgh: Birlinn.

Stephen, Ian (ed.) (1993): *Siud an t-Eilean: There Goes the Island*. Stornoway: Acair.

Thomson, Derick (1982): *Creachadh na Clàrsaich: Plundering the Harp: Collected Poems 1940-1980*. Edinburgh: MacDonald Publishers.

Questioning the Idea of the Marginal: Aspects of the Poetry of Christian Matras

Anne-Kari Skarðhamar

The Faroe Islands as periphery and centre (according to William Heinesen)

'Far out in an ocean that gleams and glitters like quicksilver may be found a small leaden-coloured land. In proportion to the immense ocean the size of the tiny mountainous land is like a grain of sand to a ballroom floor'. This frequently quoted opening passage from William Heinesen's novel *De fortabte spillemænd* (1950) (*The Lost Musicians*, 1971) describes the position and the size of the smallest of the Nordic countries, the Faroe Islands. Heinesen's poetic prose description also underlines the reader's impression that the country itself is peripheral: far out in the Atlantic ocean, and far from what we may regard as geographical or cultural centres like Copenhagen or Edinburgh.

However, the oppsite point of view is expressed in Heinesen's short story 'Småstad og Babel' (Village and Babel) from *Kur mod onde Ånder* (1967) (Cure Against Evil Spirits). Heinesen claims that the mini capital of his Lilliputian country is nevertheless the centre of the universe: 'Men denne flække er ikke blot et helt lille ølands hovedstad og den største by i mange hundrede kilometers omkreds; den kan tillige, som ethvert sted på kloden, hvor mennesker er født og vokset op, gøre krav på at være selve verdens navle' (Heinesen 1967:105) (But this spot is not only the capital of a whole little island country and the biggest town for several hundred kilometres around; it can also, like any place on the globe where people have been born and grown up, claim to be the very navel of the universe).[1]

This country, which is small and seemingly peripheral but also the navel of the universe, is the background of the poetry of William Heinesen's friend and fellow poet Christian Matras.

The marginality of the language

Christian Matras (1900-1988), who was professor of Faroese language and literature at the University of Copenhagen, wrote his poetry in Faroese. This fact may be sufficient to classify him as an exclusively regional or marginal poet, as few people or even few scholars in the Nordic field read Faroese. In a letter to the Norwegian poet Aslaug Vaa in the 1950s Matras reveals that a dream from his young days was to be appreciated in his original language by Norwegian readers, a dream which is rather unlikely ever to come true. A few of Christian Matras' poems have been translated into Danish, Norwegian, Swedish, Icelandic and English (Skarðhamar 2002:314).

If the marginality of a language is measured according to the number of native speakers, Faroese is definitely more marginal than the other Nordic languages. However, Faroese literature is worth attention for its literary qualities and not for its marginality. Besides, may not all the Nordic languages be regarded as marginal compared to a world language like English?

The ambition of Christian Matras in his scientific as well as in his poetic work was to cultivate and develop the Faroese language and give it an acknowledged status among the other Nordic languages. The Danish authorities in the nineteenth century tended to argue that Danish was a superior language to what they regarded as the barbarian mountain dialect of the Faroes. To Christian Matras Faroese was a language in its own right and with a high literary value through orally transferred literature, above all through the poetical tradition of the Medieval ballads, among them the *Sjurðarkvæði*, a heroic ballad of more than six hundred stanzas about the Nibelungs. The Faroese ballads are a unique literary heritage, though the texts are not very well known outside the Faroes.

Christian Matras describes the continuity of the Faroese language and reveals his devotion to it in the poem 'Moðurmálið' (1940) (My Mother Tongue): 'Eg fann teg í kvæðum, sum fólksins varrar / lyftu úr øld í øld' (I found you in the ballads that were lifted from age to age by the lips of the people). This language pleaded and called him to release it through poetry from the chains that had subdued and hampered its futher development: '...nú andi tín/ teg loysa úr fjøtrum bað' (now your spirit begged me to set you free).

And the poet Christian Matras responded to the call. His lyrical production covers sixty-six years and includes six collections of poems. His first book of poems was published in 1926 and the last one in 1978. Besides, he translated several European poets into Faroese, among them Robert Burns, whom he related strongly to. A Faroese version of some of Burns' poems was published in 1945. One may easily conclude that Matras' feeling of kinship with Burns might have to do with the regional background of the two poets as regards the language of the people, their assumed marginality by geographical distance to cultural centres and the fact that Burns as well as Matras had been influenced by the ballad tradition of his country. Even if these points are of a certain relevance, the kinship is also of a more spiritual kind. The title of a Matras poem from 1939 is simply 'Robert Burns'. The poem expresses a feeling of identification with Burns: 'Eg havi livað lívið títt [...] Eg havi sungið songin tín' (I have lived your life [...] I have sung your song). It probably refers to Matras' work with translating Burns' poems, but also to a kind of spiritual kinship expressed by the words 'uggi' (comfort) and 'eldur' (fire):

> Og alla tíð var lagið tað
> ið skalv í tíni sál
> ein uggi og ein eldur sum
> av nýggjum gav sær mál.

> (And all the time there was a tune
> shivering in your soul
> a comfort and a fire that
> once more were given a voice.) (Skarðhamar 2002)

In the poetry of Burns as well as in the poetry of Matras there is a tension between extremes: joy and despair, delight and fear, calm and turbulence. While Robert Burns' experiences of storm and calm are connected to being in love, Christian Matras hardly wrote love poetry at all. He describes and interprets how his experience of storm and quiet in nature is reflected in his mind and urges him to write. I shall develop this point of view and give a few examples in the following.

The marginality of motifs?

Nature, descriptions of experiences of huge landscapes and minute nature details, are the main motifs in the majority of Christian Matras' poems. The nature he describes borrows features from the nature of the island where he grew up, and sometimes even place names are mentioned. I will argue through text examples that identifiable nature motifs do not restrict or reduce the value of Matras's poems to a local, regional or marginal level. The Faroese scenery, and more specifically cliffs, rocks, sea, sky, grass and plains of the island Viðoy where the poet was born, is very often the point of departure of his poems, but he extends his perspective. Early childhood impressions made Christian Matras a poet, as he recounts in his poem 'Songurin í mær' (1978) (What Sang In Me):

Songurin í mær
er slíkt eg ungur sá
Tey syngja enn sum áður í mær:
Bakkin líðin fjallið
og hitt sjónvíða hav.

Og so Múlalandið
sum eg var góður við
alla mína ævi
sum við eina væna moyggj.

(What have sung in me
are what I saw as a child:
bank, grass cliff, fell
and the eye-wide sea.

And the Mulaland too
that has been dear to me
all my life
as a dearly-loved girl.) (Matras 1986)

Whereas this poem explains the poet's urge to write and give voice to his experiences of a landscape, the poem 'Viðoy' more clearly places his home island in a wider context.

Christian Matras wrote in an autobiographical essay that his childhood mountains and the stars in the sky gave him a feeling of space and endlessness. The sense of life that is expressed in 'Viðoy' is not local nor nostalgic, but cosmic. The poem describes the island Viðoy by the metaphor of a ship sailing out into the world or into the universe. The word 'heimur' in Faroese has a double meaning of 'home' as well as the extended meaning of 'the world' or 'the universe'. The local landscape, the familiar home, is surrounded by a wider conception of home: sky, sea and space beyond the limitations of time. Christian Matras second collection of poems from 1933 played with this ambiguity in its title *Heimur og heima*.

In the poem 'Viðoy' a number of metaphors create an allegorical pattern. Ridges and peaks are masts, and people, sheep and birds are the precious cargo on board the ship. The perspective opens from the local and familiar towards the world and infinity. The poem shows a dynamic movement forwards through breakers and currents, and the island of Viðoy becomes part of the great world in the widest possible sense:

Viðoy

Sigl, oyggj, fram úr mjørka, nú ert tú eitt skip
og tindarnir siglutrø,
tú stevnir í veldiga heimin út
við høgum og fjallarøð.

Nú brýtur frá stevni vid Enniberg,
og við Nánestanga er hvítt.
Enn liggur tú fremst í skipaheri,
har streymurin rennur strítt.

Og líta vit upp at mastrartræ
har lýsir við tind og rød.
Nú tekur at lætta við helluna
og um brekkur og fjálggrønan bø.

Og fuglaringar um stavn og bógv
teir lívga upp urð og skor.
Og fólk og fæ og spógvamál
er hin dýra farmur um borð.

(Vithoy

Sail, island, forth from the fog, you are a ship now
with peaks for masts;
you set your course into the great world
with your pastures and mountain crests.

Your prow breaks water at Enniberg,
white water at Nanestang.
Always you sail foremost of the fleet
where currents are running strong.

We look up to the masthead,
ridges and peaks show bright.
Now it clears down to the rock strand
and homely fields take light.

And circling birds fore and aft
they liven up scree and sward.
And folk and flocks and curlew cries
are the dear freight on board.) (Johnston 1981)

The fact that the literary landscape may be fairly easily identified has led, or perhaps rather misled, some Faroese critics to denegrate Matras as a local or a regional poet.

Matras does not describe nature photographically or exactly, nor does he admire a certain landscape from a distance. Most often the poet or the first person narrator in the poem is positioned in the middle of the landscape, and the poem shows the impact nature makes on him. Above all, the poet interprets nature. He interprets the actions of the forces of nature and the interaction between nature and man.

One may ask then: what kind of experience does the poet describe? What impact does this nature have on the poet, or what is the content of this 'song' that has sounded in the poet?

The first of the two poems we have read contributes to Matras' poetics as it shows that his devotion to the landscape made him a poet. The other poem emphasises the dynamic movement outwards from the periphery to the universe. Most of Christian Matras' poems describe action in nature, dynamic and dramatic elements, and constant shifts.

The marginality of experience

Nature in Matras' poems is wild and uncultivated with storm, wind, breakers, mountains, cliffs, waterfalls, clefts, abysses – all of these may induce awe, fear and the feeling of being small, overwhelmed by the uncontrollable forces of nature as in the opening stanza of the poem 'Undir hesum øgis-eggjum' (1933) (Beneath the Terrifying Cliff-tops):

> Undir hesum øgis-eggjum
> stendur land við meitilveggjum
> skapandi úr tómum lofti
> ørsku-rúmd.
> Streymbrátt hav í viðum fløtum
> Andar undir mannagøtum
> – sum ein fyrndar-jøtuns ond.

> (Beneath the terrifying cliff-tops
> lies a land whose walls are steep
> and where the vast nothingness
> creates dizzying depths.
> The boundless stormy ocean
> heaves below ancient man-made paths
> – like a giant from the past.) (Skarðhamar 1996)

The other type of experience in his poems is of harmony, light, flowers, grass, joy and peace, as shown in a few lines from 'Sælar løtur í barnalund' (1933) (A Child's Moments of Joy):

> Her skygdu hyljar í sóljugrøv –

> (The glinting pools of water in the buttercup-covered verges –)

or:

> Ein hagasólja vid neytarveg
> tað var sum ein sól, ið signdi meg.

(A dandelion by a cattle track
was like a blessing sun.) (Skarðhamar 1996)

Still, even the frightening experiences include an element of fascination. They
are ambiguous in the sense that man is terrified and attracted at the same time.
Joy and awe are coexistent.

In his book *A philosophical Enquiry into the Origin of our Ideas of the
Sublime and Beautiful* from 1757, the philosopher Edmund Burke
distinguishes between the beautiful and the sublime. The sublime according
to Burke is 'a state of the soul, in which all its motions are suspended' (Burke
1990:53). The sublime is ambiguous because it has its origin in pain, while
the beautiful is unambiguously connected with pleasure. The sublime is
boundless and magnificent, but also awesome because it is threatening. It is
not an aesthetic experience, but a question of life and death. The sublime
arises on the brink of the abyss and is a mental ascent when one is faced with
the grandeur of nature. It implies a tension between fear and fascination. The
sublime is connected with pain caused by the feeling of threat. It is not the
awe in itself that characterises the sublime effect, but the delight one feels
when the danger is over.

Matras seems to have a similar notion of delight in several poems. The
description of a sublime experience is based on the rhythmic shifts between
storm and calm. The storm and the idyll unite to become an entity, and man's
joy of light and harmony is intensified by the awareness of the threat of
sudden turbulence.

The poem 'Fjarlagt hvesti hann sjogvin' (1933) (Far Off the Sea Whets
His Roar) may illustrate this point. It describes a summer night where sense
impressions, softly fading light, a dusk field, sounds of a barn door, smell of
hay form an atmoshere of peaceful harmony:

Mjúkliga myrkrið seig.
Og børn um hógv undir gørðum.
Mál teirra gomul hoyggjhúshurð
har gisnaður viður lak
út søtan anga í kvøldið.

Fjarlagt hvesti hann sjógvin
á undurnátt millum fjalla.

(Softly falls the night
and children arc in the field below the fences.
They run for the haybarn door
whose shrunk boards leak
sweetness into the dusk.

Far off the sea whets his roar
in the hushed night between the hills.) (Johnston 1981)

The poem conveys a tension between a hushed night between the mountains and the possibility of a sudden change. The fear of the violent forces of nature is present in the background. This is underlined by the title of the poem: 'Far off the sea whets his roar'.

The danger is not overhanging, but its presence is latent. That makes the poet's delight sublime. These shifts in nature are reflected in the mind of man. Nature is not sublime in itself, but the changes in nature from violent destructive storms or breakers to calm, sunshine and tranquility are overwhelming and produce the sublime. In Matras' poetry the awesome feeling is not a product of man's imagination, not a construction, but real and experienced in practical life. Matras writes in his autobiographical essay:

> Tidlig lærte man at erkende den stærke virkelighed, der skabes af højde og hav og af elementernes lunefulde spil, en erkendelse, som ikke blev uden indflydelse på ens livssyn senere hen, men også forudsætningen for, at man kom til at opfatte idyllen som en kraft i højeste plan (Matras 1953:114)

> (Early on, you learned to acknowledge the stark reality of the cliffs and the sea and the fickle actions of the elements, a realisation which could not fail to influence your view on life at a later stage, but which also meant that you saw moments of extreme happiness as something granted by a higher power.)

Is such a conception of the sublime experience and dependence on nature marginal in the sense of provincial or peripheral? Is it more 'central' or more cultivated to regard nature as controllable and awe as a feeling to be overcome by being conscious of its origin?

The marginality of a sense of life?

So far I have called the experiences of nature in Matras' poems sublime. Several of these experiences could just as well be called religious. Matras' poetry conveys a sense of non-confessional religiosity. The dependence on an omnipotent force of nature is of a religious kind as in the poem 'Fátækt er mansins hjarta' (1972) (Poor is the Heart of Man):

> Kennir tú tó í løtum
> máttin ið heimin ber,
> Kemur sum glottar av ljósi
> ið óvart nema við jørð.

(But still you sometimes feel
the power that carries the world.
It comes in a flash of light
which briefly touches the ground.) (Skarðhamar 1996)

These flashes of light may have the character of a vision. The Danish professor Klaus P. Mortensen sketches a typology of the sublime experience in his book *The Time of Unrememberable Being. Wordsworth og det sublime* (1996). The shift from one extreme to the other in nature causes a similar movement in man from joyful tranquility to fear of destruction and back to calm and bliss. The third stanza of Matras' poem 'Barnsligt minni' (1933) (Childhood Memory) illustrates the relief one feels after the storm:

Men rak burtur myrkur, og makaði hválv,
og tók hann úr sjónum ilsku og gjálv,
tá lýsti ein heimur við dýrasti logn,
og aftur var sæla í mínari ogn.

(But darkness was dispelled and the skies settled down,
and the sea became calm as the waves levelled out,
the world glowed with precious silence
and happiness was mine once again.) (Skarðhamar 1996)

The relief may also release a new recognition of continuity in space and time. According to Mortensen the sublime experience may cause the senses to widen to a visionary new insight. In Christian Matras' poetry the movement goes from the experience of contrasts to glimpses of a vision of entity in the world. This is what happens in the poem 'Hitt blinda liðið' (1926) (The Blind Flock), where people are walking in the dark without aim or intention. In rare sudden glimpses their eyes are opened and they are able to see and understand:

So í sælum stundum
hendir lívsins undur,
blindir fáa megi
at lata eygu sundur,
liva ríkar løtur,
ið leingi minnast,
síggja allar gøtur
saman finnast.

(Then in some blessed time
what's wonderful
opens the blind eye,
gives life and will,

173

moments remembered
of bright weather
that bring long and sundered
paths together.) (Johnston 1981).

Then night falls over them again and the blind flock goes on rambling aimlessly in darkness.

The vision of harmony is not something which man discovers by himself; instead, it appears as the power which is given to the blind. The insight is a gift, not an achievement caused by their own effort. This feeling of receiving insight from the power of the world or the universe is one aspect of what I would call religious aspects of Matras' poetry.

Now and then the description of experiences of nature or of visionary insight approaches mysticism. In Matras' poems, however, there is no *unio mystica*, but man is touched by a creative force which is perceived as the most profound source of life. In one short poem from 1978 the creative force is called 'meginmáttur í heimi', a great power in the world:

Og ein meginmáttur í heimi
nam onkuntíð við meg
Eitt nú eitt kvøldið
undir Múla bø
Tá var mál hansara
livandi kyrra
og skapandi friður
á tarastrond.

(And a great power in the world
sometimes touched me
As one evening
under Mula field
Then his voice was
a living stillness
and creating peace
on the seaweed shore.) (Skarðhamar 1996)

The situation described is similar to a religious experience, and even approaches a mystic experience. The narrator of the poem is touched by the omnipotent power in nature. He senses a voice and reaches a point of insight into the character of this power, which is living stillness and creating peace. The word 'then' implies that the great power will not always expose this side. The sudden shifts from storm to calm will continue, but the glimpses of a creating peace will give hope and encouragement to the poet who is able to sense and interpret his experience. In this poem Matras most clearly exposes what the Swiss professor Oskar Bandle calls his inclination towards mysticism (Bandle 1982:102) and Matras himself, in a letter to William Heinesen, describes as a touch of a mystic (Matras 1936-37, 13.08.36). The Norwegians Kværne and Vogt give a wide definition of mysticism as 'an intuitive sense of entity and harmony' (Kværne & Vogt 1992:228). According to their definition, Matras' poem 'And a Great Power in the World' describes a mystic experience.

Matras' poems also frequently express a sense of eternity. This sense is conveyed by the description of light and of the unconquerable forces of nature. William Heinesen's poems – written in Danish – share some similar features. Christian Matras complains in a letter to Heinesen that Heinesen's poems had not obtained the attention they deserved and had been overshadowed by Danish poets in the 1930s. Matras refers to Norwegian authors who were also ignored, misunderstood or not appreciated in Denmark, and he explains it by a metaphor of surgery. The Danes had had their sense of eternity cut away (Matras 1936-37, 01.02.37). Is it provincial or marginal to have kept a sense of eternity alive? Is this feeling of dependence and eternity in descriptions of the relationship between man and nature a marginal phenomenon which hardly can be found except in peripheral areas?

Conclusion

Matras creates a specific Faroese combination of local realism and cosmic perspective which transcends the local and redefines the idea of the marginal or peripheral. Matras writes about life and death, joy and fear. He recognises man's dependence on the great creative and awesome forces of nature, of the world or in cosmos, and he responds to nature by astonishment, wonder and delight. Besides, he follows the challenge from nature by giving the shifts between the violent and the mild a voice in his poetry. In one sense he may be called a metaphysical poet as his poetry reveals religious experiences and even a touch of the mystic.

His poetry is deeply human and universal and by no means marginal or peripheral, even though he wrote in a small language. In my opinion Christian Matras deserves attention as one of the great Nordic and European poets, not only because he deals with the relationship between man and an overwhelming nature, but also because of his poetics and the aesthetic qualities of his poetry (cf. Skarðhamar 2002:151-176).

References

Bandle, Oskar (1982): 'Modern färöisk litteratur', in *Kung.Vitterhets Historie og Antikvitets Akademiens årsbok*. Stockholm, pp. 96-109.

Burke, Edmund (1990 [1757]): *A Philosophical Enquiry into the Origin of our Ideas of the Sublime and Beautiful*. Oxford, New York: Oxford University Press.

Heinesen, William (1950): *De fortabte spillemænd*. Copenhagen: Gyldendals Tranebøger.

Heinesen, William (1967): *Kur mod onde Ånder*. Copenhagen: Gyldendal.

Heinesen, William (1971): *The Lost Musicians* (trans. Erik J. Friis). New York.

Johnston, George (ed. & trans.) (1981): *Rocky Shores. An Anthology of Faroese Poetry*. Paisley: Wilfion Books.

Jones, W. Glyn (1980): 'Nature and Man in Christian Matras's poetry', in *Scandinavica* vol. 19 (no. 2), pp.181-197.

Kværne, Per & Vogt, Kari (1992): *Religionsleksikon. Religion og religiøsitet i vår tid*. Oslo: Kunnskapsforlaget.

Matras, Christian (1936-37): Unpublished letters in Det Kongelige bibliotek, Copenhagen.

Matras, Christian (1953): 'Et færøsk bygdehjem. Handelen i Viðareiði', in *Danske hjem ved århundredskiftet*, Fjerde samling. Edited by Tove Clemmensen. Copenhagen: H. Hirschsprungs forlag, pp. 114-125.

Matras, Christian (1975): *Leikur og loynd*. Tórshavn: Bókagarður.

Matras, Christian (1978): *Úr sjón og úr minni*. Tórshavn: útgáva yrkjarans.

Matras, Christian (1986): *Úr sjón og úr minni. Seeing and Remembering* (trans. George Johnston). Tórshavn: Føroya Fróðskaparsetur.

Mortensen, Klaus P. (1996): *The Time of Unrememberable Being. Wordsworth og det sublime 1787-1805*. Copenhagen: Litteraturkritikstudier.

Dikt fra Færøyene. Et utvalg dikt av Christian Matras (1993). Presentert og oversatt av Anne-Kari Skarðhamar. Oslo: Norsk-Færøysk Lag.

Skarðhamar, Anne-Kari (1996): '"Growing up on the edge of the abyss": Childhood impressions in the poetry of Christian Matras', in *Scandinavica* vol. 35 (no. 1), pp. 71-104.

Skardhamar, Anne-Kari (1998): "Drinking my eyes full of sea. – Faroese nature and interpretation of life in the poetry of Christian Matras", in *Laboratorio di Geografia e letteratura*. Anno III, n.1. Padova, pp. 67-77.

Skarðhamar, Anne-Kari (2002): *Poetikk og livstolkning i Christian Matras' lyrikk med et tillegg om Matras og færøysk lyrikk*. Oslo: Unipub forlag.

Note

1. All translations are by the author unless otherwise stated.

Beyond the Periphery: Icelandic Literature in a Scandinavian Context

Baldur Hafstað

Njal's Saga and the *Götterdämmerung*

Every year Icelanders witness 'the Christmas flood of books': the publication of a number of new literary works and translations, as well as the reprinting of works, such as the Icelandic Family Sagas or the novels of Halldór Laxness, who passed away in 1998 at the age of 96. Also, conferences are held on various themes and authors. In the past decade, for instance, three conferences have been held, two in Reykjavík and one in Canada, on the Icelandic-Canadian poet Stephan G. Stephansson (1853-1927), who literally lived on the periphery of the Icelandic cultural domain, by the Rocky Mountains in Alberta, Canada.

In this chapter, I will briefly discuss the following topics: a Family Saga, a novel by Laxness and the poetry of Stephansson. All three are interrelated, and they are all the fruit of a Scandinavian heritage. At the same time, they have to be examined in a global context. My goal is to describe, to some extent, the technique used in their composition.

Njal's Saga is available in the brilliant translation of Hermann Pálsson[1] and Magnus Magnusson. In an interview, Halldór Laxness once said of this saga: 'Ich las zum Beispiel die *Njálssaga* als Kind, und ich hatte eine große Freude daran. Es war erregend und spannend wie ein Roman. Als Kind mit sieben bis acht Jahren habe ich das zu meinem Vergnügen gelesen. Als junger Mensch, als Erwachsener las ich dieses Buch viel wegen seiner großen Kunst, und als älterer Mann lese ich diese *Njála* wegen der Weisheit darin' (Sauter 1986:188) (I read, for instance, *Njal's Saga* as a child with great delight. It was as stimulating and exciting as a novel. As a child of seven or eight, I read it for pleasure. As a young man, as an adult, I read this book because of its great art, and now, as an elderly man, I read it because of the wisdom in it).

Hermann Pálsson pointed out in his book on *Njal's Saga* (1984) that the history of the Icelandic nation can be divided into two periods: The period before *Njal's Saga* and the period after it. He added, in his humorous way, that the author of the saga was brought up in a country without *Njal's Saga*; he thereby stressed his opinion that the saga is first and foremost a literary creation. The events it describes are to have taken place around the year 1000, in Southern Iceland, Norway, Scotland, in the Hebrides, in Ireland and elsewhere, almost 300 years before the work was written. It may be added that, in an interesting way, the saga is based on, or reflects, the old *Landnáma[bók]* (*Book of Settlements*) which has some information on the ancestors of Njal and other characters of the saga. A close look at the two works reveals that the descendants, that is, the partly fictional characters of the saga, carry the same names as their ancestors in the *Book of Settlements*. Furthermore, similar events occur in both works, even at the same places (Hafstað 2001). *Njal's Saga* also makes use of Norse mythology. Mörður gígja, the wicked person, resembles Loki, 'the mischiefmonger of the gods'. The killing of the innocent Höskuld reminds us of the killing of the god Baldur. The wise Njal tries without success to prevent catastrophy, namely, the burning of his farm. In that sense, he is like Odin before *ragnarök*, the *Götterdämmerung*. Furthermore, the reconciliation that follows the burning of Njal has something in common with the rise of the new and good world at Gimlé after *ragnarök*.

Moreover, *Njal's Saga* seems to make use of contemporary events: The fall of the brave Gunnar of the saga resembles the actual fall of a chieftain in Northern Iceland in 1255 (Jóhannesson *et al.* 1946:516). In other words, the saga can possibly be interpreted as a critical or satirical text on the political situation in Iceland during the thirteenth century, the turbulent 'Age of the Sturlungs', which culminated in the fall of the Icelandic Commonwealth between 1262 and 1264, some twenty years before the saga was written.

Njal's Saga, however, is also inspired by ideas and events of foreign places, known to its thirteenth-century author, such as chivalric literature and Christian legends. Hermann Pálsson (1984) has, for instance, pointed out that, if you run into a *proverb* in the saga *without alliteration*, it may as well originate in classical Latin works.

In light of the analysis above, one can conclude that *Njal's Saga* has many roots. Given our emphasis on Iceland and Norse mythology, we must bear in mind that the characters, as well as the author, have an obvious desire to return 'from the exile' to the places of their forefathers. They need to be in touch with their Norse and Celtic origin, the heritage of Odin and spirit of Christ, so to speak.[2]

Njal's Saga is a constant source of investigation. The latest contribution is the opinion of the Icelandic scholar Ármann Jakobsson (2000) that Njal, his sons and their good friend Gunnar were all homosexuals!

Laxness and his *Independent People*

Let us now return to Laxness, Iceland's most controversial man of letters, admired by many – and despised by others. In Laxness' works we see reflected the feelings and the state of our nation in the twentieth century. Laxness was a critical person; he did not hesitate to tell his countrymen 'the truth' about themselves. In *Alþýðubókin* (1929) (*Book of the Common People*), after having spent a couple of years in America, he told Icelanders they were dirty, that they should wash and brush their teeth. In some of his later articles, he advised them to drink less hard liquor. He claimed that beer was a good beverage which should be available in Icelandic stores. (At that time, beer could only be bought in the duty-free store at the airport).

In that sense, Laxness wanted to pull us towards the centre, move us away from the margin, make us part of Western civilisation. He wanted to 'elevate the discussion to a higher level', to quote a famous remark he made in a televised debate around 1970. At the same time, he wanted us to be left alone: In *Atómstöðin* (1948) (*The Atom Station*, Eng. tr. 1961) he criticised those who wanted a foreign army to be based on Icelandic soil. It is worth noting that Hermann Pálsson (1975) wrote an article on the novel, in which he put it into a mythical context.

Laxness introduced Icelanders to new and old foreign ideas in literature. He translated Hemingway, and even Voltaire, and, as a young man, he wrote poetry in the spirit of those who were experimenting with new forms and ideas on the Continent. He had many faces. He respected his country, his nation, (in his critical way), its history and myth, its language, folklore and literature. In fact, he was a specialist in the nation's old literature and its history, as, for example, can be seen in his works *Gerpla* (1952) (*The Happy Warriors*, Eng. tr. 1952) and *Íslandsklukkan* (1943-46) (*Iceland's Bell*, Eng. tr. 2003). *Happy Warriors* is, in fact, a parody of one of the Icelandic Family Sagas, and among the characters in *Iceland's Bell* is the collector of old manuscripts, the learned Árni Magnússon, who lived around 1700. Simultaneously, *Iceland's Bell* is a challenge to the Icelandic nation during World War II, when tremendous changes took place in society.

Laxness brings us to the question of marginal literature. His books are available in many languages, his novel *Sjálfstætt fólk* (1934-35) (*Independent People*, Eng. tr. 1946) was the book of the month in the United States in 1946, he won the Nobel Prize for literature in 1955, and a number of films are based on his works. *Independent People* is the story of a lonely and stubborn Icelandic peasant on a remote croft by the inland moor, during the first two decades of the twentieth century. Having read the novel, a literary person from America visited Laxness and remarked that, in New York City alone, there were millions of people who lived in just about the same way as the peasant Bjartur and his family; not only were they in the same financial circumstances as he, but also similar to him in thought and moral attitudes.

That statement did not surprise Laxness himself, but his countrymen may have been puzzled, because to them, Bjartur is the traditional poor Icelandic peasant and poet who is occupied with only two things: his sheep and the old sagas and poetry. He would never say the Lord's prayer, because it has neither rhyme nor alliteration. The traditional ballad that rhymes, on the other hand, or, let us say, the spirit of Odin, prevented him from falling asleep and perishing in a snowstorm, during which he stayed overnight under a heap of snow, soaked to the skin, after an unexpected bath in a glacial river. Bjartur had left his small house and his pregnant wife, Rosa, in order to look for one of his sheep. (That sheep would never have been found, though, because his wife had slaughtered it in her desperate desire for meat). He was away for four days, and when he got back, his wife lay dead on the floor after having given birth to her child, who was only Bjartur's officially! The dog Bjartur had left with his wife kept the child alive with its warm body.

Readers have also seen in Bjartur the Norwegian farmer Isak in Knut Hamsun's *Markens grøde* (1917) (*Growth of the Soil*, Eng. tr. 1920). Of course, Laxness knew Hamsun's work quite well. He said of his own novel: 'The same questions are being asked here as in *Markens grøde*. But the answer is exactly the opposite to Hamsun's answer.' Isak became a well-off farmer. The 'independent' Bjartur moves at the end of the novel from his hopelessly isolated farm to another, even more isolated one, oppressed by the inclement forces of nature and society – and cursed, as it seems, by the ill spirits who had shadowed his croft for centuries. His constant 'World War' is reminiscent of the everlasting war of Odin's warriors in Valhalla, or the battle of Hedin and his men in the Orkney Islands, described in the *Prose Edda* (see Young's translation 1973:65, 121).

It may be added that Laxness' visit to the Soviet Union in 1932 helped him focus on the structure of the novel concerning the three levels of farmers with respect to their financial situation and their attitude towards the workers' union and their struggle against 'capitalism'.

Bjartur's youngest son left the country for America; we are told that the sounds of the moor and his sorrowful longing for his homeland made him a great singer in the big world. Another young man left the country somewhat earlier. He had never gone to school, and he never did. He moved to America (via Scotland) in 1873, with his parents and sister and his small bookcase, in one of the first groups of Icelanders to leave for America. He was to become one of the greatest poets of his nation. His name was Stephan G. Stephansson.

Stephansson and his *Sleepless Nights*

Stephansson had already tasted the mead of Odin: he had read the old sagas and lays of the gods, he was familiar with Germanic and Scandinavian legendary heroes, the kings of Scandinavia and the Icelandic chieftains, such as Njal the Wise. It is remarkable that, at the age of nineteen, Stephansson had had time for all this and much more. One winter in Iceland, he read the Bible three times, because there was nothing else to read. The case of books he brought with him from Iceland was destroyed on the way to America and he did not have a chance to access these texts after he settled there, first among Norwegian immigrants in Wisconsin, then in North Dakota, later in Alberta, Canada, where he built his farm and cultivated a new land. He died in 1927, at the age of 74. He seems to have kept the old tales and poetry in mind all his life. Much of this material he later used in his poetry. From it, he created new works, a new thought. Still, instead of retelling an old myth or saga he reflects on them and uses them as an occasion for presenting his ideas on various matters: politics and religion, war and peace. He was, in fact, an atheist and a passionate pacifist, and because of his resolute opinion, especially on Canada's participation in World War I, there was for a while a strong feeling of animosity towards him among a number of Icelandic Canadians.

In his poem on Völund (Weland) the Smith, Stephansson does not mention the cruelty depicted in the old Eddic *Lay on Völund* (see Larrington's translation 1996:102-8). On the contrary, he is only occupied with the ring, the one ring out of seven hundred which is worth something. In Stephansson's poem, the ring becomes a symbol of poetry and wisdom (Hafstað 1998). Poetry, in his opinion, is a decisive factor in the fate of a nation, cf. the following statement in the poem *Bragamál* (The Lay of Bragi, the god of poetry):

> Sporlaust hverfur þú og þjóð þín,
> skilirðu ei framtíð skáldi að gjöf.
>
> (Without a trace you and your nation vanish
> If poetry is not your gift to the future) (my translation).

These words can be taken as Stephansson's motto, or challenge, in the opening poem of his six-volume poetry collection, *Andvökur* (1909-38) (Sleepless Nights).

Stephansson was also inspired by his contemporaries: He corresponded with people of letters in the old country and also with his friends in Dakota, as well as many other Icelanders on the prairies, most of whom were centered in Winnipeg, Canada, some 1,100 miles from Stephansson's tiny

Icelandic settlement far to the west. These letters fill seven volumes. Fortunately, Stephansson managed to return to the old country for a visit. The Icelandic Youth Organisation and other fans of his poetry invited him to Iceland in 1917. He travelled all over the country and was received as well as the king of Denmark, who had been there a decade earlier. People would travel a long way, even on a good day for hay-making, in order to see the poet of the Rocky Mountains.

Stephansson was a poet in exile: He wrote all his poetry in Icelandic. Through his acquaintance with English-American literature and philosophy, however, he brought new metric forms, new vocabulary, a new thought into Icelandic literature and society. As I have mentioned already, conferences were held on Stephansson's poetry, first in Alberta, Canada, in 1995, then in Reykjavík in 1996 and 2003. There, his work was analysed not only by professors of literature, but also by those of philosophy. It may be added that his home in Alberta is now a museum.

Laxness and Stephansson left their country young and stayed abroad for years, Stephansson for the rest of his life. They gathered experience which enriched the literature of their homeland. They criticised their countrymen, but were, at the same time, very dependent on them. Laxness was a bestseller; Stephansson was received as a king. Both of them were loyal to the poetical heritage of Odin.

Books are still a constant subject of discussion in Iceland and that is important. For instance, it was front-page news that one of our authors had taken the liberty of taking a sentence or two from an American novel and putting them into his own without mentioning the source. Of course, he was only doing what the authors of *Njal's Saga* or *Independent People* did all the time.

The examples of Laxness and Stephansson show the main difference between Icelandic and, say, Norwegian, Swedish and Danish literature. Icelanders are more occupied with tradition; the old texts and ideas remain somewhere in the background. The spirit of Njal and Odin hovers over the waters.

References

Bessason, Haraldur (1990): 'Halldór Laxness', in George Stade (ed.): *European Writers. The Twentieth Century* (12). New York: Charles Scribner's Sons, pp. 2457-78.

Hafstað, Baldur (1998): 'Út í heim frá vinum. Um nokkur ljóð Stephans G. Stephanssonar, byggð á fornum arfi', in *Greinar af sama meiði helgaðar Indriða Gíslasyni sjötugum*. Reykjavik: Rannsóknarstofnun Kennaraháskóla Íslands, pp. 17-25.

Hafstað, Baldur (2001): '*Egils saga*, *Njáls saga*, and the Shadow of *Landnáma*. The work methods of the saga writers', in Ásdís Egilsdóttir & Rudolf Simek (eds): *Sagnaheimur. Studies in Honour of Hermann Pálsson*. Wien: Fassbaender, pp. 21-37.

Hreinsson, Viðar (2002 & 2003): *Landneminn mikli* and *Andvökuskáldið* (The biography of Stephan G. Stephansson). Reykjavik: Bjartur.

Jakobsson, Ármann (2000): 'Ekki kosta munur. Kynjasaga frá 13. öld', in *Skírnir*, 174 (1), pp. 21-48.

Jóhannesson, Jón, Finnbogason, Magnús & Eldjárn, Kristján (eds) (1946): *Sturlunga saga*, I. Reykjavik: Sturlunguútgáfan.

Larrington, Carolyne (trans. & ed.) (1996): *The Poetic Edda*. Oxford: Oxford University Press.

Laxness, Halldór (1946): *Independent People* (trans. J .A. Thompson). (*Sjálfstætt fólk* 1934-35). New York: Alfred A. Knopf.

Pálsson, Hermann (1975): 'Beyond the Atom Station', in Sveinn Skorri Höskuldsson (ed.): *Ideas and Ideologies in Scandinavian Literature since the First World War*. Reykjavik: University of Iceland, pp. 317-29.

Pálsson, Hermann (1984): *Uppruni Njálu og hugmyndir*. Reykjavík: Menningarsjóður.

Pálsson, Hermann & Magnusson, Magnus (trans. & eds) (1960): *Njal's saga*. Harmondsworth: Penguin Classics.

Sauter, Josef-Hermann (1986): *Interviews mit Schriftstellern – Texte und Selbstaussagen*. Leipzig: Gustav Kiepenheuer Bücherei.

Stephan G. Stephansson (1909-38). *Andvökur*, I-VI. Reykjavik and Winnipeg: Friends of the author.

Young, Jean (trans.) (seventh printing 1973): *The Prose Edda. Tales from Norse Mythology*. Berkeley: University of California Press.

Notes

1. I dedicate this short essay to the memory of the great scholar Hermann Pálsson, who passed away in August, 2002.

2. A general comment could be made in this connection: The poets of medieval Iceland learned the details of Odin's heritage: poetry, meter and myth, and also a great deal about the kings of the neighbouring countries. They were driven by the desire to go abroad and recite their poetry at the courts of kings and earls. In this way, they seem to have laid the foundation for the sagas of the kings of Norway. The isolation the poets grew up in seems to have helped them concentrate on important issues concerning myth and heroic legacy, history, law and poetry. Snorri Sturluson is a good example: a man of an influential family in Iceland, brought up by a learned chieftain, he became a poet, and through poetry befriended the rulers of foreign places. In the end, however, it did not help Snorri to have written the history of Norwegian kings: King Hákon of Norway had him executed on a gloomy day in the autumn of 1241, for having left Norway without leave. This tragic event did not hinder Snorri's nephew, Sturla Þórðarson, from writing the history of king Hákon (*Hákonar saga Hákonarsonar*) and his son, Magnús (*Magnúss saga lagabætis*).

'New' Icelandic Literature: Icelandic-Canadian Challenges to Icelandic National Identity

Daisy Neijmann

'The fiction makes us real' is how the Canadian writer and critic Robert Kroetsch (1970:63) once summed up the importance of narrative literature for the transformation of cultural identity in immigrant cultures. This certainly seems true for the Icelanders who left Iceland during the years 1870-1918. Their immigrant experience was rather unique in North American immigrant history in that immigration largely occurred during this period only, and permanent settlement took place mostly in western Canada. There was virtually no influx of new arrivals from Iceland after 1918, and the larger cultural context for the immigrants and their descendants was the same for most settlements. As a result, the immigrants were able to develop a unique minority culture of their own.

The first immigrants arrived in Canada in the early 1870s. It is very clear from the documented history of these early years that their leaders were well versed in the Romantic nationalist rhetoric that dominated Iceland at the time, and that their actions and intentions for the future of Icelanders in the New World were, importantly, guided by nationalist politics. The tract of land the leaders eventually chose along Lake Winnipeg, in what is now Manitoba, was turned into an exclusively Icelandic colony called New Iceland, with its own newspaper, schools, and community pastor.

The colony newspaper, called *Framfari* (Progress), provides some valuable insight into the nationalist idealism that motivated the immigrant leaders. At a time when Iceland was still fighting for independence and the struggle appeared to be stagnating, settlement in the New World was seen as an alternative means to create an independent Iceland. The early settlers regarded themselves as pioneers of a transplanted Iceland, where Icelandic culture could thrive in an environment that fed rather than starved its inhabitants. Indeed, early poems submitted to the newspaper use the Romantic *fjallkona* or 'Mother Iceland' trope to posit Iceland as the 'bad' mother who starves her children, and New Iceland or Canada as the 'good' mother who feeds them. As pioneers, they romantically likened themselves to the Settlement Age heroes of early Iceland, creating a new golden age.

In reality, however, nationalist fervour and cultural politics created factionalism, which kept the leaders busy while the immigrants starved in their isolation and ignorance of how to survive in the new environment. Gradually, as it became clear that survival in the new environment and cultural exclusivity did not go together, the immigrants began to disperse and the leaders had to admit defeat as far as the ideal of a single, exclusive Icelandic colony was concerned. This was reinforced in practical terms when New Iceland was annexed by the province of Manitoba in 1881. Ukrainian and Polish settlers were allowed into the area and quickly outnumbered the Icelandic immigrants who had remained, while most of the Icelanders sold their land and entered other occupations and/or moved to Winnipeg.

Living among other cultural groups in rural or urban areas created very different conditions for cultural adaptation and survival, but it did not spell the death of the Icelandic cultural heritage in the New World, as the leaders had feared. It merely meant the end of the ideal of cultural purity and of recreating an independent version of the motherland. At the very same time, immigration from Iceland was reaching its peak and large numbers arrived every year, while in Iceland frustration was growing at the stagnation of the political ideal of independence and seeing such large numbers of its people leaving. A vicious campaign against emigrants and emigration agents resulted, abuse was heaped on everyone who had left or was thinking of leaving, and letters from immigrants often did not reach their final destination. The Icelandic immigrants in Canada were well aware of these events, as the immigrant newspapers regularly carried news from Iceland, and relations between the two communities cooled significantly. The result of these developments was twofold: on the one hand, some immigrants now felt less obligation to remain obsessively loyal to Iceland and its nationalist ideals, which created some room for experimentation and flexibility in the area of cultural adaptation and preservation. On the other hand, a defensiveness on the part of many immigrants ensued, which expressed itself in rather forced efforts to prove their cultural loyalty.

Within this context, it should not be forgotten that the immigrant experience is one of profound duality, and that the immigrants were in a sense fighting a war on two fronts. Not only were they engaged in efforts to prove their continuing 'Icelandicness', as it were, but they also had to counter prejudice and accusations on the part of a Canadian establishment that, in the face of increasing numbers of so-called 'foreign' immigrants, considered everyone not of white, Anglo-Saxon, Protestant stock inherently inferior and suspect, and demanded that all immigrants were assimilated into their dominant culture as quickly as possible.

It is against this background that Icelandic immigrant literature develops. Poetry and fiction became the main vehicle for the expression and negotiation of the issues of acculturation, cultural preservation and identity construction, and provides an insight into the process of how Icelanders in Canada began to, and continued to, imagine themselves as a separate community, and wrote themselves into existence (Mandel 1977). However, as a cultural minority group, this process was of course never independent from developments in and influences exercised by the two main majority cultures that produced it, Iceland and Canada.

The first immigrant literature was written almost as soon as the Icelanders arrived in the New World, and was published by the immigrant papers or circulated. Within a short span of time, poets and writers proliferated in the immigrant community, as *Vesturheimsprent*, a compilation of all Icelandic works published in Icelandic in the New World until 1900, bears witness to. The narrative impulse has been shown to be common to almost every immigrant group, but it was particularly strong among the Icelanders, who brought with them a strong popular tradition of literature which constituted a natural creative outlet in the midst of profound cultural shock and change. This context was neither understood nor appreciated in Iceland, where this initial proliferation of poetry quickly earned the Icelandic immigrant community the name *Eldórado leirskáldanna* (the El Dorado of bad poets; Guttormsson 1966:159). It effectively sent out the message that any literary efforts overseas would be viewed exclusively on Icelandic terms, interpreted in an Icelandic rather than a Canadian immigrant context.

The earliest literature expresses either deep sorrow and loss, nostalgia for the old country and the past, or tries to deal with the immediate effects of the immigrant experience: either celebrating the achievements of the settlers as brave pioneering heroes of old, or, in a very few cases, lamenting the fates of those who failed or fell victim to physical or social hardship. Failure and sorrow, however, quickly became a taboo – originally perhaps as a means of survival, later on as a significant gap or silence in community memory (Hreinsson 1993). Instead, cultural defensiveness created an obsession with achievement, the ambition to be both 'the best Icelanders' and 'the best Canadians'. At this early stage, it is not yet possible to speak of what Homi Bhabha (1994) has termed the manifestation of transformational change, a 'hybrid moment', as yet made impossible by the notion of cultural purity that was such an important part of Icelandic nationalism and that still dominated Icelandic immigrant culture. Any definition of 'Icelandicness' was still on national Icelandic terms. As in the ideal of New Iceland, the expression of transplantation was through the articulation in literary terms of a different natural and social landscape: the introduction of the wide-open prairie, the Rocky Mountains, agricultural crops, thunderstorms, cultural diversity and urban frontier life. The immigrants found these easier to embrace in their literature, and they had the added advantage of finding a relatively easy and interested reception among Icelanders at home.

We find this perhaps most clearly exemplified in the fiction of Jóhann Magnús Bjarnason and the poetry of Stephan G. Stephansson. Bjarnason wrote short stories and adventure novels, but has become best known for his autobiographical novel *Eiríkur Hansson* (1899-1903), which relates the adventures of a young boy who emigrates to Canada with his grandparents. Although his prose style was subject to criticism by Icelanders, who found it too verbose and sentimental, his new world recreations of Icelandic heroes, fighting and conquering against all odds in their pioneer struggles, all the while staying true to their Icelandic heritage even if it meant living in the contempt of the English, became extremely popular, also in Iceland, where his collected works were eventually published. Bjarnason occasionally experimented within this nationalist framework, describing the less glorious lives of the culturally and socially disenfranchised in the slums of the multicultural boom-and-bust frontier cities, and attempting to create an Icelandic-Canadian literature by transplanting Icelandic folklore into a Canadian setting. The ultimate message of these experimental New Icelandic folk tales remains, however, that of confirming the possibility of being an Icelander in Canada, without changing the definition of 'Icelander'. The aim is still transplantation, not transformation, of cultural identity.

In Stephansson's poetry, we find this combination of Old World culture and New World landscape perfected. A self-taught man who left Iceland at seventeen and settled land three times over, Stephansson achieved a mastery of the long-standing Icelandic popular poetic tradition, in language and form, and skilfully used it in completely new ways to describe his new environment as a pioneer farmer in the Albertan foothills of the Rocky Mountains. Stephansson, like his friend Bjarnason, inevitably shows in his works the change in outlook that his transplantation has effected: his concerns are international, his social criticism largely based in Canadian situations, and there is evidence of the cultural diversity within which he lived. His poems about Icelandic history focus mainly on pioneers, in the broadest sense of the word, celebrating their vision and achievement. However, there is, in the end, no real cultural transformation that occurs in his works, only a sensibility of cultural displacement: 'ég á orðið einhvern veginn ekkert föðurland' (I have acquired somehow no fatherland; 'The Exile', 1988:75) and 'Þó þú víðförull legðir sérhvert land undir fót, bera hugur og hjarta samt þitt heimalands mót' (Though you wide-journeying place every country underfoot, your mind and heart bear your homeland's resemblance; 'From an Islendingadagur address', 1988:53) are lines from two of his most celebrated poems. Stephansson acknowledged that culturally, he would always remain an Icelander living abroad.

I do not think it is at all coincidental that exactly these two writers were so well received in Iceland. Their works constitute the realisation of a nationalist ideal, the transplantation of a national Icelandic culture, its preservation in a different place, widening the scope of Icelandic literature, yet fully recognisable as Icelandic, and uncontaminated at its core. The peak of this ideal was realised in the work of the poet and playwright Guttormur J. Guttormsson, who was born to Icelandic immigrants and lived in New Iceland all his life. He never saw Iceland until he was invited by the Icelandic government in recognition of his cultural achievements in 1938. These 'cultural achievements' were constituted by his poetry and plays, which were written exclusively in Icelandic. Guttormsson frequently described phenomena unknown in Iceland and Icelandic, but succeeded in doing so without admitting English or native Canadian language influences in his poetic language. Instead, he modelled himself largely on traditional Icelandic poetic language and imagery, coining new words where necessary, as had his predecessor Stephansson. Unlike him, however, Guttormur used more international influences in his choice of form; his most famous poem 'Sandy Bar' (1920), a tribute to the hardships and achievements of the Icelandic immigrants, bases itself on the form of Poe's 'The Raven', and his polemic poem 'Indíána hátíð' (Indian Festival, 1930), a scathing critique of the white man's treatment of the North American native peoples, is modelled on Longfellow's 'Song of Hiawatha'. Significantly, I think, he only really felt free to experiment in the ten plays he wrote, a genre where his Icelandic literary heritage could not excercise a dominating influence. They are really pieces of literature rather than drama, and are highly abstract and symbolic in nature and style.

The excitement and recognition Guttormsson's writing generated in Iceland had, in fact, very little to do with his actual poetry (his plays received no attention at all). As Arnór Sigurjónsson admits in his introduction to the collection of Guttormsson's poetry:

> In Guttormursson's poetry there is a wide variety of aspects that are little known or unknown to us here in Iceland. These concern both the subject matter itself and the understanding and opinions of the writer which appear unfamiliar to us, as well as the atmosphere which is enveloped in the subject matter and its treatment. (1947:32, my translation)

Despite all nationalist efforts, a certain alienation had inevitably set in at this stage. Guttormsson's work never made it into the Icelandic literary canon in the way that Stephansson's did. Guttormsson had exceeded all expectations of cultural survival in the new world, and as such his achievement was mostly a symbolic one which was not to last but rather spelled the end of this kind of 'pickled-in-amber' Icelandic immigrant literature, as Bill Holm once called it (1990:2).

During the *interbellum* period, Iceland had received home rule, and the attitude in Iceland towards their emigrant cousins and their descendants had changed significantly. There was celebration of what had been achieved, and optimism and hope for Iceland's future. Icelandic immigrants who had been successful in North America financially supported Icelandic initiatives. Nationalist scholars like Sigurður Nordal and Guðmundur Finnbogason promoted the idea of the organic community, and, consequently, they took great interest in the state and fate of Icelandic culture in North America, which they embraced, or appropriated, as part of a larger Icelandic family and culture, witnessed by the Icelandic name for the immigrants, *Vestur Íslendingar* (Western Icelanders). They acknowledged that certain changes in outlook and custom, resulting from life in a different country, were inevitable, but they tirelessly supported the ideal of cultural preservation, the continuation of the Icelandic language as it was spoken in Iceland, and culture, particularly literature. Newspapers published in the New World had subscribers in Iceland, and in turn carried news from Iceland, and the exchange of literature was promoted and financially supported. This, however, made experimentation and transformation difficult, as reactions from Iceland frequently showed intolerance of change. As George Bisztray, a Hungarian-Canadian scholar once put it: 'Let us face one fact: what we call acculturation, mutual understanding, and good citizenship in this multicultural country, may appear to the cultural chauvinists overseas as bastardization of our ancestral tradition, language and heritage' (1987:112).

The poet K. N. (Kristján Níels Júlíus) was one of the first immigrant writers who defied the colonial influence exercised by Iceland over its Canadian immigrant community. His poetry celebrates the Icelandic-Canadian immigrant language, and often uses it to good effect to create double-voicing, ambiguity and irony. He chastises the cultural purists no less than those who would deny their Icelandic background, focuses on those areas of immigrant culture that the nationalists considered a 'blemish' and preferred to deny, delights in taking the gloss off the glorified image of the mother country, relishes cultural diversity and indeed hybridity, and generally creates poetic glimpses of immigrant culture as it was lived rather than imagined and idealised. K. N.'s immense popularity bears testimony to the extent to which the immigrant community recognised itself in the mirror his poetry held up to them, and his poetry circulated by word of mouth as much as in written form across the scattered Icelandic settlements.

The literary scholar Stefán Einarsson once called K. N. 'the only humorous poet in Icelandic literary history' (1961:460), and perhaps it was, again, the fact that he felt less burdened by the weight of literary tradition within his genre that made him feel free to experiment. His mastery of the traditional Icelandic *ferskeytla*, the quatrain with a sting in its tail, is witnessed by the fact that he reached a certain popularity among the general public in Iceland as well, although he was never officially acknowledged by the literary establishment, which measured everything against purely Icelandic standards. K. N.'s works are in truth a most wonderful bastardisation of the ancestral language and culture, and to some extent point ahead to the changes, or 'bastardisation', Icelandic culture at home would experience in the wake of the American airbase set up near Keflavík in 1946.

The real break, Bhabha's 'hybrid moment', in literature could be said to start with K. N., where we see the first indications of the 'transformational value of change', the creation of something truly new, beyond, or besides, the one or the other – a transformation that transcends mere changes in subject-matter and environment. How difficult and slow this process of transformation could be, however, under the colonising influences of two national cultures, is clearly demonstrated by the oeuvre of Laura Goodman Salverson. Born in Canada to immigrant parents, like Guttormsson, but in the more complex and culturally diverse urban landscape of Winnipeg, Salverson grew up bilingual and had lived in many of North America's urban immigrant slums before she reached adulthood. She was brought up a fierce Icelandic nationalist by her father, but was also immensely proud of being Canadian. She became the first to try to translate the Icelandic immigrant experience into English-Canadian fiction. Her debut novel, *The Viking Heart* (1923), broke new ground in its sympathetic depiction of a non-English immigrant group's experiences settling in Canada and its reception by the dominant Anglo-Canadian minority. The novel was an overnight success in Canada, but not in the Icelandic community. Salverson was harshly criticised for her 'inaccurate' description of Icelandic geography in the opening chapter, and for her portrayal of Icelandic customs and characters.

The reception by the immigrant community constitutes a fascinating lesson in the dangers inherent in 'translating' culture. Salverson had meant the initial chapter to be symbolic, condensing the various, complex and profoundly emotional experiences of leaving the native country into one apocalyptic image of a volcanic eruption which literally drives people into boats and into the ocean. The Icelandic community did not recognise the symbolism and accused Laura of ignorance of Icelandic geography and of having 'shrunk' Iceland. Similarly, criticisms were levelled at her for ascribing personality traits and actions to Icelandic characters which were considered unrealistic, and which have since been discovered to be highly relevant and symbolic in a community context (Guðsteins 2001). In reality, what it appears we have here is a combination of alienation on the part of the immigrant community as a result of reading and seeing itself in the 'other's language, and a clash between 'transformed memory' and historicism (Gunnars 2001).

Gradually, the immigrant community had come to distance itself particularly from the more painful and difficult aspects, the 'ugly part' of its migration history, through a communal denial of that part. Instead, it had begun to create its own community myths, of which the re-enactment of Iceland's own immigrant/settlement past and the ambition to be the 'best of both worlds' explained earlier were the most prominent ones. These myths were an effective cultural binding agent, but they also created problems when faced with individual consciousness and memory, or with historical thinking, which tends to reject the validity of both. And perhaps most importantly, these myths were regarded as an exclusive to the community, a cultural boundary. Salverson was in the awkward position of both 'insider' and 'outsider' to the community (Canadian-born in an Icelandic community, writing in English as an Icelandic Canadian). As 'cultural translator' with her fiction she had appropriated her memory and interpretation of that community, and had tried to find commonalities to make the inevitable untranslatabilities in Icelandic culture understandable in a foreign context, thus changing the accepted definition of Icelandic cultural identity in Canada, and exposing part of the community's innermost sanctum to an outside readership. As Trinh Minh-ha has aptly described it:

> Not quite the same, not quite the Other, she stands in that undetermined threshold place where she constantly drifts in and out. Undercutting the inside/outside opposition, her intervention is necessarily that of both a deceptive insider and a deceptive outsider. She is this Inappropriate Other/Same who moves about with always at least two/four gestures: that of affirming 'I am like you' while persisting in her difference; and that of reminding 'I am different' while unsettling every definition of otherness arrived at. (1991:74)

The community never forgave Salverson for this transgression.[1] And, tellingly, the novel received hardly any attention in Iceland, nor was it ever translated into Icelandic.

Salverson continued to write, and her autobiography, *Confessions of an Immigrant's Daughter*, remains in print. It is also, to date, Salverson's only work to have been translated into Icelandic, published as recently as 1994.

Guðrún Guðsteins (1997) analysed the translation and uncovered some remarkable features, notably the silent 'corrections' on the part of the translator. The corrections in question concern the grammar and spelling of Icelandic names and words, and historical and geographical 'errors'. Yet these 'errors', as Guðsteins rightly point out, are in fact in most instances only perceived as such because they do not conform to the accepted national Icelandic rules and interpretations governing its written language and historiography. The Icelandic we find in Salverson's work is a written representation of the Icelandic spoken in the immigrant community, where the language survived largely as an oral rather than a written language, in a dominant English-speaking context, with the spelling clarifying pronunciation for an English-speaking audience. The correction of the perceived historical errors not only damages the internal structure of the work, as Guðsteins has shown, but also rejects as invalid a community and individual memory of Iceland and Icelandic history as it has survived among the Icelandic immigrants and their descendents, again a traditionally oral way of remembering history, by simply erasing it. These corrections appear to be the result of a misguided and rather patronising attempt to 'save' the author from an expected reaction of alienation and condemnation on the part of Icelandic readers for bastardising 'their' culture.

After 1940 and until the 1970s there is very little evidence of literary activity among the Icelandic immigrant descendents, otherwise known as Icelandic Canadians, other than on a very local, grass-roots level. In Canada, this was a period of rising Canadian nationalism largely based in the Anglo-cultural establishment in Ontario, under the pressure of which third- and fourth-generation Icelandic Canadians now largely grew up unilingually, i.e. English-speaking.

In the course of time, as Icelandic Canadians continued to accumulate and develop their own community history, memory and myths, and supported by this context of Canadian nationalism, Icelandic-Canadian culture has gradually been transformed into a culture that is increasingly hybrid, and where the Icelandic element is increasingly symbolic.[2] Minority cultures in a culturally diverse context often survive through symbolic ethnic acts and rituals, particularly so when the language as a means of daily communication is lost, which allow them to confirm, act out and celebrate their cultural heritage without inhibiting them in their daily lives as Americans or Canadians. The elements of the linguistic heritage and customs that are retained are signs, tokens, icons of identity that carry a symbolic message often not (fully) recognisable to outsiders, thus also creating cultural boundaries. They constitute an ethnic language of their own.

Icelandic Canadians developed several such symbols, which culminate at the *Íslendingadagurinn*, the three-day Icelandic Festival held in Gimli, the old capital of New Iceland and now the cultural centre of everything Icelandic-Canadian. Here, 'Icelandic-Canadian' is put on show for the rest of the continent, while, behind the scenes, community bonds are re-affirmed and celebrated through memory and stories. The ritual food consumed on such occasions consists primarily of *vínarterta*, a cake brought to Canada with the immigrants, which in itself embodies the hybrid nature of Icelandic-Canadian culture as it exits today. There is nothing particularly Icelandic about *vínarterta*: it is a Viennese cake which was very popular across Scandinavia earlier in the twentieth century. It fell out of fashion again in Iceland, but in Canada it has evolved into a community marker, something of which the mention and consumption in certain contexts says 'I am Icelandic Canadian', and which has made it into the Oxford Canadian English Dictionary.

During these decades, literature, too, became important as a token of identity, as the language had made it inaccessible to many. Yet it was considered an important source of cultural pride and also of inspiration, particularly as there were so many works written by Icelandic immigrants about Icelandic immigrants, thereby validating their community culture, history and experiences. And writers and poets continued to be viewed with respect, almost as community scribes, in contrast to Canadian society at large, where writing was never regarded very highly by the larger community unless perhaps it came from England or the U.S.

In Iceland during this same period, interest in Icelandic Canadians decreased significantly. While Icelandic-Canadian culture was being transformed, Iceland itself underwent considerable changes as well. The optimism leading up to complete independence in 1944 was replaced by a period of cultural pessimism in the wake of the occupation first by the British and then the Americans, followed by Iceland's entrance into NATO and the establishment of an American base. Icelandic post-war literature is dominated by a sense of cultural identity crisis, largely resulting from the migration from country to city and the rootlessness that followed it, as well as from the perceived threat posed by the American presence to Icelandic culture. Seen from this angle, it is perhaps not so surprising that the increasingly large differences between Icelandic national and Icelandic immigrant culture, in particular the increasingly 'English/American' appearance of the latter, did not particularly inspire much interest. Icelanders were less and less able to recognise their overseas cousins as 'Icelandic' by the traditional definition based on country, language and history. All that had remained was genealogy.

In the 1970s, however, things began to change, at least overseas, when Canada officially became a multiculturalist country. The multiculturalist policy encouraged the preservation and expression of cultural diversity, imagining Canada as a cultural mosaic. In the wake of this change, whether as a direct result or not, writers of Icelandic descent begin to make themselves heard again, and explore in different ways the issues of immigrant heritage and cultural identity from a minority perspective. They experiment with ways in which to express minority identity, and often question the concept of culture as defined and promoted by official government policy: as something 'authentic', reified and separate, rather than something that is lived, adaptable to circumstances and in constant flux.

W. D. Valgardson, a writer who was born and grew up in the area that used to be New Iceland and has since been known as the Interlake, has been particularly concerned with the question of how to define ethnic identity within a majority cultural context. He has explored the effects of cultural diversity and cultural interaction, and has been particularly instrumental in challenging the ruling monolithic ideas of culture, when for many in Canada intermarriage and multiple origins have become the norm rather than the exception. How Icelandic does one have to be in order to be considered 'Icelandic' in Canada and find acceptance in the community? What does it mean to be considered an 'Icelandic-Canadian writer' when five-eighths of you are in fact something else, as in the case of Valgardson himself? The expectations, both in Canada and in Iceland, can become highly oppressive and an external interference with the creative writing process.

In his short story 'The Man from Snaefellsness, Part I' (1990), Valgardson describes the cultural exclusion of the narrator as a child from both the minority and the majority cultures he grew up in because, being of mixed origins, he was not considered to belong fully to either (Neijmann 1997:238, 241). For Valgardson, what informs his sense of identity and his creative imagination as a writer is the experience of growing up in a culturally diverse community, fraught with tensions but also connected through a shared immigrant background and Canadian present, and the stuff literature is made of; as he himself says: 'This was a world filled with conflict... Drama and fiction are driven by conflict' (2001:212).

Initially, Valgardson remained largely unknown in Iceland. Although he visited a number of times and gave a few interviews, he generated little interest. In the course of the 1980s, however, a gradual change also began to occur in Iceland. In Icelandic literature, a new generation of writers shook off the yoke of post-war pessimism and began to celebrate contemporary Icelandic society, growing up in the city and enjoying a global popular culture: Icelandic cultural identity was being redefined. Younger scholars started a critical examination of Icelandic nationalism and opened up new ways of viewing and interpreting Icelandic history, literature and society. The question of how to redefine Icelandic identity in a global context without loss of language and culture became acute, and undoubtedly had a role to play in the renewed interest Icelanders took in Icelandic Canadians. As Icelandic Canadians began to travel to Iceland again in greater numbers to visit their ancestral country and culture, it may have become clear to Icelanders that perhaps they could learn something from the way in which Icelandic Canadians had managed to retain a sense of 'Icelandicness', however un-Icelandic it might seem to Icelanders on the surface, in an English-speaking environment for over a century.

Perhaps because he grew up so much more secure in his identity, the writing of David Arnason, a 100% Icelandic Canadian with his roots firmly in Gimli, has been less concerned with his Icelandic background. However, his works often contain an ethnic 'subtext', as Guðsteins has shown (1997). For instance, in his novel *The Pagan Wall* (1992), there is one chapter set in Iceland where Arnason deliberately plays fast and loose with Icelandic geography, echoing Laura Salverson's infamous opening chapter, while emphasising the importance of Iceland as passed-down memory and symbol for Icelandic Canadians, irrespective of geographical science and 'reality'. In his collage *The New Icelanders* (1994) Arnason has included a chapter which he calls the 'myth of beginnings', his individual version of the foundation myth of his community, which mythically locates Icelandic Canadians as a new world community in both place and time, rather than as a colony or branch of Icelandic culture.

In Canada, probably the most widely known Icelandic-Canadian author is Kristjana Gunnars. Her situation is rather different from that of Valgardson and Arnason, however, as her cultural identity is a diasporic one. She was born in Iceland to an Icelandic father and a Danish mother and moved to Denmark in her early teens, and to North America in her late teens. As such, she does not really belong to the Icelandic-Canadian community, nor is she recognised as Icelandic in Iceland. In fact, while her literary experimentation with expressions of a diasporic imagination, based largely, though not exclusively, on Icelandic and North American experiences, has been highly acclaimed by Canadian critics, she has received a much harsher reception in Iceland than either Valgardson or Arnason. The inclusion of her short story 'The Song of the Reindeer' (1982), in a collection called *Icelandic Writing Today* (1982), was harshly criticised, as it demonstrated that the author was more Canadian than Icelandic and did not know enough about Icelandic circumstances; indeed, the story was 'too far removed from Icelandic reality' to ever appear in Icelandic as an Icelandic story (Kress 1983:68). As in the case of Salverson's *Confessions* (1939), this assessment is in fact based both on too literal a reading of the story and too narrow and traditional a definition of what constitutes 'Icelandic reality'.

Gunnars' most acclaimed novel, *The Prowler* (1989), was severely criticised by the Icelandic-Canadian community, who objected to the 'negative' portrayal of Iceland they found there. The Icelandic translation of the novel was refused by Icelandic publishers on the grounds that 'it did not reflect Icelandic reality' (Guðsteins 1997:6). The alienating effect of the Icelandic context, words and allusions which Canadian critics found so appropriate to the novel's expression of a diasporic experience and ethnic identity, was equally felt but not at all appreciated in Iceland. This may be partly due to Canada's much longer and more extensive experience with expressions of cultural diversity and re-interpretation of identity. In Iceland, however, cultural interaction has been much more limited and also more traumatic. Traditionally, the expression of Icelandic reality, however supernatural or surreal in other respects, has been firmly demarcated and rooted in time and place, and has largely occurred in Icelandic. As Gunnars herself has since explained it:

> ... since I reside in Canada, all [my] writing has occurred in English. That is a central issue in my experience. It is impossible for the Icelandic reader to see herself in the other's language. What has happened to me in reader response, in Iceland itself, is a form of 'foreignization' of my work. Many have argued the ways in which my own childhood, which is the subject of my book *The Prowler*, is contaminated by foreign influence. This is a thought-version of the idea of exile, and [...] a tool communities use when what is being remembered is inappropriate. (2001:61)

She concludes:

> When you consider the sanctity of 'memory' in [...] creative terms, it seems ludicrous to challenge an imaginative text, and its author, with history. It is ridiculous in a poetic context to criticize on the basis of a 'faulty' memory. There is another memory at work: the memory of passion, of language, of emotion. (2001:67)

Although much of the rediscovery of Icelandic-Canadian history and culture in Iceland has occurred through the intermediary influence of Icelanders themselves such as Böðvar Guðmundsson's novels and recent compilation of Icelandic emigrant letters, the collage *Nýja Ísland* by Guðjón Arngrímsson (1997) and Jón Karl Helgason's radio series ('The Mystery of the Vinarterta', Ríkisútvarpið 1996), Icelandic-Canadian voices are gradually becoming heard on their own terms. Although their reception may not always be sympathetic, yet, it seems obvious that Icelanders are slowly becoming aware of the fact that Icelandic-Canadian experiences and experiments in the area of cultural survival, based in a more flexible interpretation of culture and identity in the midst of cultural diversity, rather than constituting an alien bastardisation, contain some valuable lessons on how to preserve cultural identity in a way relevant to life in the global village.

References

Arnason, David (1992): *The Pagan Wall*. Vancouver: Talonbooks.

Arnason, David with Vincent Arnason (1994): *The New Icelanders*. Winnipeg: Turnstone Press.

Arngrímsson, Guðjón (1997): *Nýja Ísland*. Reykjavík: Mál og menning.

Bhabha, Homi (1994): *The Location of Culture*. London: Routledge.

Bisztray, George (1987): 'Comments', in J. M. Bumsted (ed.): 'A/PART: Papers from the 1984 Ottawa Conference on Language, Culture and Literary Identity in Canada', in *Canadian Literature*, Supplement 1, pp. 111-13.

Bjarnason, Jóhann Magnús (1973): *Eiríkur Hansson: Saga frá Nýja Skotlandi*, in *Ritsafn*, vol. 4. Akureyri: Edda.

Einarsson, Stefán (1961): *Íslensk Bókmenntasaga 874-1960*. Reykjavík: Snæbjörn Jónsson.

Framfari 1877-1880 (1986; translated by George Houser). Gimli: Icelandic National League.

Gans, Herbert J. (1979): 'Symbolic Ethnicity: The Future of Ethnic Groups and Cultures in America', in *Ethnic and Racial Studies*, vol. 2 (1), pp. 1-20.

Guðmundsson, Böðvar (1996-97): *Híbýli vindanna* and *Lifsins tré*. Reykjavík: Mál og menning.

Guðmundsson, Böðvar (2001): *Bréf Vestur-Íslendinga*, 2 vols. Reykjavík: Mál og menning.

Guðsteins, Guðrún (1997): '"Kalda stríðið" í þýðingum á íslensk-kanadískum bókmenntum 1923-1994', in *Jón á Bægisá*, vol. 1, pp. 5-19.

Guðsteins, Guðrún (2001): 'Rediscovering Icelandic Canadian Pacifism', in Guðsteins (ed.): *Rediscovering Canadian Difference*. Reykjavík: University of Iceland Press, pp. 50-60.

Gunnars, Kristjana (2001): 'Translation as Appropriation', in Guðsteins (ed.): *Rediscovering Canadian Difference*. Reykjavík: University of Iceland Press, pp. 61-67.

Guttormsson, Guttormur J. (1966): 'Sigurður Júl. Jóhannesson og íslenzka hagyrðingafélagið', in *Eimreiðin*, vol. 72, pp. 152-60.

Guttormsson, Guttormur J. (1947): 'Sandy Bar' and 'Indíánahátíð', in Sigurjónsson (ed.): *Kvæðasafn*. Reykjavík: Iðunn.

Hjartar, Ólafur F (ed.) (1986): *Vesturheimsprent. A Bibliography of Publications in Icelandic Printed in North America or Elsewhere by or Related to the Icelandic Settlers in the West*. Reykjavík: Landsbókasafn Íslands.

Holm, Bill (1990): 'Kristján Níels Júlíus (K. N.): A Four-Part Project', in *Lögberg-Heimskringla*, 7 December 1990, p. 2.

Hreinsson, Viðar (1993): 'Western Icelandic Literature, 1870-1900', in *Scandinavian Canadian Studies*, vol. 6, pp. 1-14.

Júlíus, Kristján Niels (1945): *Kviðlingar og kvæði* (ed. Richard Beck). Reykjavík: Bókfellsútgáfan.

Kress, Helga (1983): 'Að kynna íslenskar bókmenntir erlendis', in *Tímarit máls og menningar*, vol. 44 (1), pp. 65-79.

Kroetsch, Robert, *et al.* (1970): *Creation*. Toronto: New Press.

Magnússon, Sigurður A. (ed.) (1982): *Icelandic Writing Today*. Reykjavík: Icelandic Writing Today.

Mandel, Eli (1977): 'Ethnic Voice in Canadian Writing', in Wsevolod Isajiw (ed.): *Identities: The Impact of Ethnicity on Canadian Society.* Toronto: Peter Martin, pp. 57-68.

Neijmann, Daisy L. (1997): *The Icelandic Voice in Canadian Letters*. Ottawa: Carleton University Press.

Neijmann, Daisy L. (2000): 'Damned with Faint Praise: The Reception of Laura Goodman Salverson's Works by the Icelandic-Canadian Community', in *Scandinavian Canadian Studies*, vol. 12, pp. 40-63.

Salverson, Laura Goodman (1939 [1981]: *Confessions of an Immigrant's Daughter*. Toronto: University of Toronto Press.

Salverson, Laura Goodman (1975 [1923]): *The Viking Heart*. Toronto: McClelland and Stewart.

Sigurjónsson, Arnór (1947): 'Guttormur J. Guttormsson og kvæði hans', in Sigurjónsson (ed.): *Kvæðasafn*. Reykjavík: Iðunn, pp. 5-36.

Stephansson, Stephan G. (1988): *Selected Prose and Poetry* (translated by Kristjana Gunnars). Red Deer, Alberta: Red Deer College Press.

Trinh T. Minh-ha (1991): *When the Moon Waxes Red: Representation, Gender and Cultural Politics*. New York: Routledge.

Valgardson, W. D. (1990): *What Can't Be Changed Shouldn't Be Mourned*. Vancouver: Douglas & McIntyre.

Valgardson, W. D. (2001): 'The Myth of Homogeneity – or Deconstructing Amma', in Gudsteins (ed.): *Rediscovering Canadian Difference*. Reykjavík: University of Iceland Press, pp. 209-13.

Notes

1. Salverson's relationship to the Icelandic-Canadian community is more complex than is possible to explain here. See also Neijmann (2000).
2. The American sociologist Herman Gans has called this third-generation-plus ethnicity 'symbolic ethnicity' (1979).

Stepping off the Map?
Greenlandic Literature between
Nation and Globalisation

Kirsten Thisted

Seen from an external perspective, the Nordic countries may themselves be very exotic, 'the far North' – but then again, viewed from within the Nordic countries, the Arctic North certainly constitutes a periphery! As far as the relation between Greenland and Denmark is concerned, Greenland has made the otherwise small, thoroughly agricultural and well-organized Denmark seem so much greater. Greenland has – both symbolically and in reality – played the part of the Danes' private wilderness, serving as an arena for all kinds of fantasies which cannot be realised in Denmark. Part of this wilderness has been the Greenlanders, who have been seen as symbiotically connected to the surrounding nature. The relationship between Denmark and Greenland is thus mired in a Western concept of 'us' and 'them', where the idea of a common Western European culture has arisen from the alienation of 'the others'. It is for these reasons that Greenland – having long since become a political and administrative reality – can also be seen as a kind of geopolitical construction like that of the 'Orient'. I call this process 'Arctic Orientalism'. In the same way that Edward Said demonstrates how Renan, for instance, working in his 'philological laboratory', does not simply concoct the scholarly topos of the Semitic Orient but in the same process also produces a conception of what it means to be European and modern, Danish writers and scholars have been involved in a similar process when describing Eskimo language, culture, marriage rituals, the so-called 'adaption problems', etc.[1]

However, this very asymmetrical relationship is slowly changing. In 1979 Greenland gained home rule. This was a revision of the Constitutional Law of 1953 according to which Greenland had changed its status from being a colony to being a county in the kingdom of Denmark. The recent negotiations about the US army's continued possession of the Thule Airbase have brought the whole question of who has the power to represent Greenland into focus. By law, Denmark still holds this right, since the question of the airbase falls under foreign affairs and national security; but nevertheless an agreement was negotiated between three parties: the USA, Denmark and Greenland. The agreement, which grants the USA the right to retain the airbase, was signed in Igaliku in South Greenland in the summer of 2004. Practically from the start of home rule, Greenland initiated a development towards self-representation, which, strictly speaking, goes beyond the letter of the law. In January 2000 a Home Rule Commission was set up to draw up the principles of a revised law more in step with reality. Its goal was to expand Greenland's self-government, but still within the framework of the present union. From the Greenlandic side the wish for a renewed *partnership* was expressed, with a special view to a more symmetrical distribution of power. The Home Rule Commission presented its report in 2003. In 2004 a new, joint commision was set up by the Greenlandic Home Rule and the Danish Parliament. Also this commission works within the frames of the present union; but in Greenland the question that is discussed is whether (or rather when) Greenland will be able to form a separate national state.

In the following, I will try to describe the centre-periphery relationship as seen from the perspective of Greenlandic literature – but since no such thing as one unified 'Greenlandic literature' exists, I shall introduce two different writers, each with their own very different perspective.

Ole Korneliussen and Hans Anthon Lynge

Ole Korneliussen was born in 1947 in Nanortalik in southern Greenland. He has been living in Denmark since 1967. Korneliussen is one of the very few Greenlandic writers – if not the only one – who has made his name in Denmark, and this has happened quite recently, with the novel *Saltstøtten* (The Pillar of Salt), published in 2000. The novel was first published in Greenlandic in 1999, under the title *Tarrarsuummi tarraq*, which means something like 'The Shadow in the Mirror'. Korneliussen writes both in Danish and in Greenlandic, and prefers translating his texts himself. According to his own description, none of his books are translations – all are independently written texts – although some of them may have the same theme in Danish and in Greenlandic. Actually, the texts *are* always quite different in Danish and Greenlandic, and bilingual readers would benefit from reading both versions – since it can sometimes be argued that the two versions together establish the *complete* text. Also, it is not always the Greenlandic version that is the first version – the first draft of *Tarrarsuummi tarraq/ Saltstøtten*, for instance, was written in Danish; the draft was finished in 1988 and sent to several Danish publishers, but was not accepted for publication at that time.

Hans Anthon Lynge was born in 1945 in Qullissat in northern Greenland. He now lives in Nuuk, and always writes in Greenlandic. Lynge, however, is one of the very few Greenlandic writers who does get translated into Danish. The Danish versions are also published by the Greenlandic publishing firm Atuakkiorfik, and this might be part of the reason why his name is not known in Denmark. Lynge made his debut in 1970 with a short story in a Greenlandic anthology. His first novel was published in 1976. He was co-writer and consultant on the film *Lysets Hjerte* (Heart of Light) from 1997, which got quite a lot of attention both in Greenland and in Denmark, being the first movie with Greenlandic actors and in Greenlandic.

Lynge's novel *Allaqqitat/Bekendelser* (Confessions) was nominated for the Nordic Literature Prize in 2001, and Korneliussen the following year for *Saltstøtten*. Neither of them actually won, but at least their names were mentioned and Scandinavia was reminded that modern Greenlandic literature does exist! Making Greenlandic literature known to the outside world is an important step in Greenland's drive towards self-representation.

Felling the family tree with a chain saw

With his access to two languages and two cultures, Korneliussen himself is a good example of the modern migrated, diasporic elite which forms the basis of postcolonial studies. From his borderline perspective he views *both* societies from the double perspective of the insider/outsider and so he takes up the position of the *in-between*. From this position he establishes an alternate reality, a third space, from which he tries to displace the usual binary logic of primordial polarities through which the cultural encounter between Denmark and Greenland is usually constructed: Denmark *v.* Greenland, modernity *v.* tradition, self *v.* other. Especially in Korneliussen's later texts, these binary opposites are denied, since the differences are not differences *between* but differences *within* – not leading to the traditional discourse of a tragic *split* between cultures in such a person, but to a third dimension.

One thing that many of these so-called post-colonial, bi-lingual and bi-cultural authors have in common is a lack of belief in the usual connection between 'roots', language, identity and 'culture' that support the idea of the nation. The main character in Salman Rushdie's novel *The Ground Beneath Her Feet* (1999) dreams of letting go of this whole idea that has become a straitjacket to the modern, migrating individual:

> ... let's just suppose. What if the whole deal – orientation, knowing where you are, and so on, – what if it's all a scam? What if all of it – home, kinship, the whole enchilada – is just the biggest, most truly global, and centuries-oldest

piece of brainwashing? Suppose that it's only when you dare to let go that your real life begins? When you are whirling free of the mother ship, when you cut the ropes, slip your chain, step off the map, go absent without leave, scram, vamoose, whatever: suppose that it is then, and only then, that you're actually free to act! To lead the life nobody tells you how to live, or when, or why. (Rushdie 1999:176-77)

Ole Korneliussen expresses the same thought in this way:

Inuup kinarpiaanera aatsaat paasinarsisarpa siulini kinguaanilu ilanngullugit ilisaritikkuni? Inuk siuleqanngitsoq kinguaaqanngitsorlu kinaassuseqannginnami? Inuk siuliminik qimatsisoq kinaassuseerukkami? Naamik, naamivik, taamaaliguni aatsaat kinaassuserpiani takutissinnaanngortarpaa siulini ajappissatut napaniutitut atorunnaassagamigit. Inuk kisimiittoq kinaassuserpiaminik takutitsisinnaasutuaavoq. (Korneliussen 1999:14)

Har mennesket kun en identitet, hvis det blander forfædre og efterkommere ind i billedet? Har et menneske uden fortid og fremtid ingen identitet. Har et menneske, der har forladt sine forfædre, ingen identitet? Jo og atter jo, det er først nu, den personlige identitet virkelig dukker frem, nu er han sig selv, klamrer sig ikke længere til sine forfædre. For lang tid siden væltede jeg mit stamtræ med en motorsav og sprængte dets rødder med dynamit. (Korneliussen 2000:14)

(Does a human being only have an identity if he draws ancestors and descendants into the equation? Does a human being without a past and a future have no identity? Does a human being who has left his ancestors behind have no identity? Quite the contrary, it is not until this moment his personal identity really emerges, now he is himself, no longer clinging to his ancestors. I long ago felled my family tree with a chain saw and blew up its roots with dynamite.)[2]

In the opening of Korneliussen's novel the first person narrator is burning his old boat on a beach which we might believe is situated in Greenland. But the main action takes place in a big city which we might believe is Copenhagen. One day the narrator wakes up and immediately realises that this day is not just any day, but a very special day. No mark has been put on the calendar yet, but the pencil has been hanging there, beside the calendar, waiting to be used.

Without looking back the narrator leaves his apartment and starts walking towards an unknown goal or destination. Underneath or beside the city landscape we sense another landscape: a landscape with high mountains, deep fjords, wide open spaces and glaciers. The narrator is walking in *both* these dimensions or geographies at the same time – since both are part of his consciousness – although the one dimension may be more a landscape of remembrance.

On his way the narrator encounters literally half of Copenhagen's population, from the most marginalised, ostracised characters to more well-to-do citizens. Through these encounters a picture is drawn of Denmark which has no resemblance to the picture drawn by the colonial and post-colonial Danish administration in Greenland. In this 'colonial' picture the Danes are rich, efficient, hard-working, goal-oriented, rational, open-minded, and modern – as opposed to the poor, inefficient, intuitive, emotional, narrow-minded, 'traditional' Greenlanders. Seen through Korneliussen's looking glass, the picture appears somewhat different. However, this does not mean that his own background is held up as an alternative – basically the first-person narrator is content with his life in Denmark: 'Nunami inuuffiginngisanni najugaqarpunga, nunalu najoruminarmat akunniffigisutut najorpara, naluara najortuassanerlugu' (Korneliussen 1999:14) / 'Nu lever jeg i et land, hvor jeg ikke er født. Landet er gavmildt og behageligt at bo i, og jeg betragter det som en mellemstation på min rejse' (Korneliussen 2000:14) (At present I live in a country I was not born in. The country is bountiful and pleasant to live in, and I consider it a temporary stop on my journey).

Greenlandic myths and traditions play an important role in the story – but in contrast to the usual description, the Greenlandic past is not used as any kind of corrective to the culture of present-day Denmark. In the Danish/Greenlandic context there exists a more or less hegemonic discourse shared between Danes and Greenlanders according to which Greenland – or rather the Greenland of the 'good old days' – is depicted as the perfect natural idyll in which the Danes have intruded to distort and destroy the so-called 'aboriginal' culture. This culture is seen as the essence of the Greenlandic character, something indestructible in the Greenlander's mind which is both the Greenlander's strength and his limitation. Korneliussen rejects any such primordialism or essentialism. In his universe these depictions are mere *constructions*, just like any depictions or so-called 'recollections' of the pre-colonial past are constructions. Korneliussen's first person narrator dare not even talk about his ancestors, but emphasises his constructivist – or what Homi Bhabha would call 'enunciative' – starting point with the cautious expression: 'siuaasaartukkakka' (Korneliussen 1999:12) / 'dem jeg er oplært at kalde mine forfædre' (Korneliussen 2000:12) (those I have been brought up to call my ancestors).

Actually, Korneliussen's first-person narrator introduces himself in the very same way Korneliussen has often introduced himself in interviews, when giving a lecture etc. He tells this story: A long, long time ago the ancestors lived on the other side of the globe. At some point the place where they were living was no longer a good place to live. So the ancestors started walking. Those who stayed were those who did not have the ability to travel. Sluggards and stay-at-homes. Those who continued, even when others settled down along the way, were the ones who had the courage and the energy, and the most courageous and enduring did not settle down until they reached the big ocean at the end of the world.

You have to envision the long journey from Alaska through Canada to Thule in the extreme North, and from there down to Cape Farewell at the southernmost tip of Greenland, close to Nanortalik where Korneliussen was born. This journey has a mythical quality in a Danish/Greenlandic context, where the Arctic explorer Knud Rasmussen is famous for having repeated the journey in the opposite direction, from Greenland to the Bering Straits, to document and to revive interest in the Greenlanders' common origin with the other Inuit of Canada and Alaska. The myth is fundamental in Greenlandic nation building, as it simultaneously testifies to the Greenlanders close relationship with the other Inuit, *and* sets the Greenlanders apart as being something special and unique.

However, Korneliussen does not end the journey here. As soon as the big ocean was no longer the utmost border, the most enterprising individuals carried on where the ancestors had to stop and continued to Denmark – whence they journey on to populate the world! (Korneliussen 1999/2000:12-14, my resumé).

By this somewhat humorous and self-ironic introduction Korneliussen turns the underlying premise of the usual story of the ancestors' journey on its head: far from using the Greenlanders' close connection with Greenland to claim it as 'their' natural country, Korneliussen uses the story to dismantle this type of mythology. Not only does he refuse to choose between the two countries which through colonialism have come to share one another's history, but he also denies the very idea of nationalism. No people are predestined by their so-called 'culture', no people are 'meant' to live in the very place they were born, and the narrator hopes for his own offspring that they will never feel tied to one particular country, but be able to consider the whole globe as their country. In a Greenlandic context – in the middle of home rule and nation building – this is a very avante-garde and rather provocative statement.

The positive aspects of being a Greenlander

Hans Anthon Lynge's texts are usually set in Greenland – often in the smaller towns or settlements. In *Allaqqitat/Bekendelser* the main character is living a pleasant, quiet life in just such a small city. He has a job, a nice home, a wife. Suddenly, however, his idyllic lifestyle is disturbed. One day he gets a visitor: an old friend from his childhood. The two went to school together, although they were not very close, and lost contact afterwards. The friend is not happy, he is not healthy and he is not at peace with himself. Before he leaves, he extorts from his host the promise that he will go through a huge pile of letters that he leaves behind. The main character, called the 'host' or the 'reader', is left in his nice and comfortable home with all these papers, and not having the guts to break his promise feels more and more frustrated and shaken in his beliefs, as he reads through what turns out to be not only the writings of his friend, but also all sorts of old press cuttings etc. – texts which force him to remember and to rethink history. The visit takes place in the beginning of 1976, and the last page of the main character's reflections on the writings of his friend is written 'Apriilip ulluisa naggataat 1979' (Lynge 1997:147) (the last day of April 1979). This is not just any day – it is the last day before home rule.

The novel insists on the kind of dialogue that the host/reader hates. According to his own words, the reluctance to get involved, instead of just keeping one's peace of mind and letting others sort out the problems, is 'inuiattut ilisarnaatitta ilagaat (Lynge 1997:107) (one of the characteristics of my people). First, the writing friend is in a constant dialogue with himself in all his papers and notes – and he forces his reading friend to take part in this dialogue. Second, the novel attempts to play the same trick on its own reader: never coming to any conclusions, but raising an immense number of questions. Questions such as: What exactly is Greenlandic 'culture'? How tightly or openly must it be defined? What happens when the respect for the elders, which was previously so important in Greenlandic society, disappears? Can the traditional upbringing of children be adapted to the new society or is it damaging to a child who is to live in a totally different society to be brought up in that way? Does religion have any role to play in this new society, or is it also just a relic of tradition? The point is that we, the actual readers, are reading this twenty or thirty years later. So while the fictional reader is reflecting upon thirty years as 'equal Danish citizens' from 1953-1979, the actual reader is reflecting upon these reflections, seen from the perspective of twenty years with home rule. A rather complicated, but interesting plot.

Even though Lynge raises all these questions, he never gives up operating with a common 'we', 'we the Greenlanders'. The great synthesis of nation and people that Korneliussen rejects still seems to give meaning in Lynge's context, where it is still possible to speak about 'Greenlandic culture' and 'Greenlandic identity'. In spite of the self-criticism levelled towards Greenlandic society in his text, and the above-mentioned Greenlandic 'illness', Lynge holds on to the idea of the nation. Being Greenlandic is also seen as a source of great pride, and the book concludes in a list of 'kalaaliussutsip nuannersui' (Lynge 1997:146) (all the positive aspects of being Greenlandic).

On the other hand, the overall feeling in Lynge's text is this feeling of 'unhomeliness' that creeps in on him as his friend and all his papers with their alarming thoughts enter his home. The feeling of unhomeliness in his own home becomes a downright nuisance – not very unlike the one that also haunts the first person narrator in Korneliussen's novel because, to return to *Tarrarsuummi tarraq/Saltstøtten*, the narrator may not be so happily integrated as he claims to be in the opening of the novel. In fact, if we read beneath his own statements, a different picture emerges. Right from the very beginning, a similar feeling of 'unhomeliness' creeps up on the narrator. It is as if he has never really taken his own apartment into possession, as if he is not really 'at home' in his own house, and sometimes a strange shadow on the wall indicates a door, as if to a different apartment with other, unknown inhabitants. And as we follow the narrator on his wandering through the big city, we cannot help but notice that he is not once recognised for what he is by the people who are supposed to be his fellow citizens. Whenever he enters a bar or a restaurant, people take him for an immigrant from Turkey or some other Muslim country. He is constantly advised not to eat this and that because it is pork meat etc. – and he is definitely not made to feel welcome.

Stepping off the map?

Postcolonial literature has been enormously successful in the western world. Not only in those areas which were colonised, but seemingly to an even higher degree in those countries which were formerly imperial powers. According to postcolonial theory, this is due to the ability of postcolonial literature to capture the general postmodern feeling of living in a borderland after the breakdown of stable identities and traditions (Rushdie 1991, Bhabha 1994). At the same time, this kind of literature seems to be a literature of the 'jet set' – written by and for an international, globalised elite, travelling as privileged 'tourists' as opposed to the underprivileged 'vagabonds', to use Zygmunt Bauman's metaphors. Aijaz Ahmad has expressed the critique in this way:

> Among the migrants themselves, only the privileged can live a life of constant mobility and surplus pleasure, between Whitman and Warhol as it were. Most migrants tend to be poor and experience displacement not as cultural plenitude but as torment; what they seek is not displacement but, precisely, a place from where they might begin anew, with some sense of a stable future. Postcoloniality is also, like most things, a matter of class. (Ahmad 1995:16)

Even though migration is a defining characteristic of our times (as it has been in previous times as well), a fact that tends to get overlooked in the discussion is that most people still tend to spend their lives in the area they are born. Therefore, there is a gap between the denial of the nation state often advocated by the globalised elite, and the conviction of the ordinary people who still, to an often dangerous degree, believe in the nation state. Therefore:

> To reject nationalism absolutely or to refuse to discriminate between nationalisms is to accede to a way of thought by which intellectuals – especially postcolonial intellectuals – cut themselves off from effective action. (During 1990:139, quoted in Gandhi 1998:166)

Or, as an Indian journalist expressed it during the controversy surrounding Salman Rushdie:

> No dear Rushdie, we do not wish to build a repressive India. On the contrary, we are doing our best to build a liberal India, where we can all breathe freely. But in order to build this India, we have to preserve the India that exists. That may not be a pretty India, but it's the only India we have. (Appignasesi & Maitland 1990, quoted in Gandhi 1998:166)

It is interesting that the very same author, Ole Korneliussen, who so explicitly rejects his own cultural roots, is at the same time one of the Greenlandic authors who draws most frequently both explicitly and implicitly on these very same roots in his art. You may appreciate the novel *Tarrarsuummi tarraq/Saltstøtten* without ever having heard of a *qivittoq*, a mountain wanderer, but some knowledge about the cultural background does help the reader understand what is going on in the novel. Only in this case it will enable the reader to detect how the negative role of the *qivittoq* symbolically changes into the positive role of the *angakkok*, the shaman, at the end of the novel.

Having read Korneliussen one may want to ask if it is *actually* possible to 'step off the map'. Is this not just a vision, a fantasy? On the other hand, reading Hans Anthon Lynge one may want to ask if it is possible NOT to step off the map at least to some degree, since modernisation and globalisation are realities we cannot escape, not even in the most remote places on earth.

So in spite of their widely differing starting points, the two Greenlandic novels should not be seen as poles apart, but rather as different voices in the same dialogue. These are questions raised not only by and of relevance for an 'exotic' periphery or minority, but the very same questions that have to be dealt with by the majorities and centres of Scandinavia.

References

Ahmad, Aijaz (1995): *In Theory: Classes, Nations, Literatures*. Oxford: Verso.
Appignanesi, L. & Maitland, S. (1990): *The Rushdie File*. Syracuse: Syracuse Univeristy Press.
Bauman, Zygmunt (1998): *Globalization. The Human Consequences*. Cambridge: Polity Press.
Bhabha, Homi K. (1994): *The Location of Culture*. London & New York: Routledge.
During, Simon (1990): 'Literature – nationalism's Other? The case for revision', in Homi Bhabha (ed.): *Nation and Narration*. London: Routledge, pp. 135-53.
Gandhi, Leela (1998): *Postcolonial Theory. A critical introduction*. Edinburgh: Edinburgh University Press.
Hall, Stuart (1991): 'Old and New Identities, Old and New Ethnicities', in Anthony D. King (ed.): *Culture, Globalization and the World-System. Contemporary Conditions for the Representation of Identity*. New York & London: Macmillan in association with Department of Art and Art History. State University of New York at Binghampton, pp. 41-68.
Korneliussen, Ole (1999): *Tarrarsuummi tarraq*. Nuuk: Atuakkiorfik.
Korneliussen, Ole (2000): *Saltstøtten. Roman*. Nuuk & Copenhagen: Atuakkiorfik i samarbejde med Lindhardt og Ringhof.
Lynge, Hans Anthon (1997): *Allaqqitat*. Nuuk: Atuakkiorfik.
Lynge, Hans Anthon (1998): *Bekendelser. Roman*. Nuuk: Atuakkiorfik.
Lynge, Hans Anthon & Grønlykke, Jacob (1997): *Qaamarngup uummataa. Lysets hjerte*. Nuuk: Atuakkiorfik.
Rushdie, Salman (1991 [1982]): 'Imaginary Homelands', in *Imaginary Homelands. Essays and Criticism 1981-1991*. Harmondsworth: Penguin, pp. 9-21.
Rushdie, Salman (1999): *The Ground Beneath Her Feet. A Novel*. New York: Henry Holt & Co.
Said, Edward W. (1991 [1978]): *Orientalism. Western Conceptions of the Orient*. Harmondsworth: Penguin.
Thisted, Kirsten (2001): 'Stepping off the map? Grønlandsk litteratur mellem globalisering og nation. Om Ole Korneliussen: Tarrarsuummi tarraq/ Saltstøtten og Hans Anthon Lynge: Allaqqitat/ Bekendelser', in *Edda* 01/04, pp. 419-36.
Thisted, Kirsten (2002a): 'Som spæk og vand? Om forholdet mellem Grønland og Danmark set fra den grønlandske litteraturs synsvinkel', in Satu Gröndahl (ed.): *Litteraturens gränsland. Invandrar- och minoritetslitteratur i nordiskt perspektiv*. Uppsala: Centrum för multietnisk forskning. Uppsala Universitet, pp. 201-23.
Thisted, Kirsten (2002b): 'Grønlandske relationer', in Alberdi *et al.* (eds): *Transkulturel psykiatri*. Copenhagen: Hans Reitzels Forlag, pp. 87-111.
Thisted, Kirsten (2002c): 'The power to represent. Intertextuality and discourse in Miss Smilla's Sense of Snow', in Michael Bravo & Sverker Sörlin (eds): *Narrating the Arctic. A Cultural History of Nordic Scientific Practices*. USA: Science History Publications, pp. 311-42.

Notes

1. For a further introduction to the postcolonial relationship between Denmark and Greenland, see Thisted 2002a, 2002b, 2002c. The rest of this paper is a shortened version of Thisted 2001.
2. Unless otherwise stated, all translations are by the author. The last sentence of this translation is only found in the Danish version, not in the Greenlandic.

Notes on Contributors

Aileen Christianson is Senior Lecturer in the Department of English Literature at the University of Edinburgh. She is a senior editor of the Duke-Edinburgh edition of *The Collected Letters of Thomas and Jane Welsh Carlyle*, vols 1-34 (1970-2006, ongoing). She also specialises in nineteenth- and twentieth-century Scottish women's writing, particularly Jane Welsh Carlyle and Willa Muir.

Cairns Craig is Glucksman Professor of Irish and Scottish Studies at the University of Aberdeen and Director of the AHRC Centre for Irish and Scottish Studies. He was general editor of the four volume *History of Scottish Literature* (1987-89) and has published widely on Scottish and on modernist literature, including *Yeats, Eliot, Pound and the Politics of Poetry* (1982), *Out of History: Narrative Paradigms in Scottish and English Culture* (1996) and *The Modern Scottish Novel* (1999).

Bill Findlay was, until his death in 2005, Reader in the School of Drama and Creative Industries at Queen Margaret University, Edinburgh. He published widely on the use of Scots in stage translations and translated into Scots for the professional stage over a dozen classic and contemporary plays. He was editor of *A History of Scottish Theatre* (1998), *Scots Plays of the Seventies* (2001), *Frae Ither Tongues. Essays on Modern Translations into Scots* (2004) and (with John Corbett) *Serving Twa Maisters: Five Classic Plays in Scots Translation* (2005).

Baldur Hafstað is Professor of Icelandic Literature at the Iceland University of Education in Reykjavik. He has published works on Saga literature as well as on Icelandic folk tales and fairy tales. He was the co-editor (with Haraldur Bessason) of *Heiðin minni* (1999) and *Úr manna minnum* (2002).

R. D. S. Jack is Professor Emeritus of Scottish and Medieval Literature at the University of Edinburgh having held that chair from 1987 until 2004. His books include *The Italian Influence on Scottish Literature* (1972), *Patterns of Divine Comedy* (1989) and *The Road to the Never Land* (1991). Most recently he has co-edited a collection of essays entitled *Scotland in Europe*.

Donald E. Meek is a native of the Inner Hebridean island of Tiree, which he still regards as 'home', although he has spent most of his life on the Scottish mainland. He has worked in the Celtic Departments of the Universities of Glasgow, Edinburgh, and Aberdeen. At Aberdeen he was Professor of Celtic from 1993 to 2001. He has been Professor of Scottish and Gaelic Studies at the University of Edinburgh since 2002. He has written extensively on Gaelic language, literature and history, with some forays into the wider Celtic field. His most recent books are *The Quest for Celtic Christianity* (2000), *Caran an t-Saoghail / The Wiles of the World: An Anthology of Nineteenth-century Scottish Gaelic Verse* (2003), and (with Nick S. Robins) *The Kingdom of MacBrayne: From Steamships to Car-ferries in the West Highlands and Hebrides 1820-2005* (2006).

Daisy Neijmann is Halldór Laxness Lecturer in Icelandic Language and Literature in the Department of Scandinavian Studies at University College London. She has worked in the areas of Icelandic-Canadian studies and contemporary Icelandic fiction. Her current research interests are in the areas of nationalism and literature, magical realism, and changing perceptions of the Second World War in Icelandic fiction. Her publications include *The Icelandic Voice in Canadian Letters* (1997), *Colloquial Icelandic* (2000), *Perkensian Rambles: A Collection of Essays in Honour of Richard Perkins* (ed., 2005), *A History of Icelandic Literature* (ed., 2006), and a variety of articles on the representation of Icelandic identity in literature.

Steinvör Pálsson is of Icelandic parentage and born and educated in Edinburgh. The only daughter of the eminent scholar Hermann Pálsson, she pursued a career in dance before returning to her native city in 1992. She commenced her studies at the University of Edinburgh the following year and in 2006 she gained a PhD in Norwegian literature. Her main area of research interest is the representation of sexual violence in Norwegian fiction.

Anders Persson is Senior Lecturer in Comparative Literature at Umeå University. His doctoral thesis from 1998 was entitled *'Försonarn vid sitt bröst, en stjernkrönt Qvinna'. Jungfru- och moderstematiken hos C. J. L. Almqvist och P. D. A. Atterbom.* At present he is writing a book on Norrlandic revivalism as a theme in Swedish fiction.

Anne-Kari Skarðhamar is Senior Lecturer in the Faculty of Education at Oslo University College. She has published *Poetikk og livstolkning i Christian Matras' lyrikk. Med et tillegg om Matras og færøysk lyrikk* (2002),

Fyrvokteren ved verdens ende og hans laterna magica. Ti artikler om William Heinesens forfatterskap (2005), *Periferi og sentrum. Tolv artikler om færøysk litteratur* (2006), as well as articles on the representation of childhood in Nordic literature, on children's literature, and books on didactic approaches to literature.

Kirsten Thisted is Senior Lecturer in the Department of Minority Studies at the University of Copenhagen. Her research interests include linquistic and cultural intersections, cultural translation, colonial history, postcolonialism, migration and literature, orality and writing. She has treated and translated traditional Greenlandic narrative and modern Greenlandic literature in numerous publications, including the main work *Således skriver jeg, Aron* (1999). She has edited *Postkolonialisme* (*SPRING*, vol. 22, 2004; with Morten Gaustad) and *Grønlandsforskning* (2005).

Bjarne Thorup Thomsen is Senior Lecturer in Scandinavian Literature at the University of Edinburgh. He was a co-editor of *Dansk litteraturhistorie* (1983-85) and has published widely on Scandinavian nineteenth- and early twentieth-century literature. He also has a research interest in early Scandinavian cinema. His most recent publication is the monograph *Lagerlöfs litterære landvinding* (2007).

C. Claire Thomson teaches Scandinavian Studies and Film Studies at University College London. Her PhD (University of Edinburgh, 2003) focused on time, space and history in Danish literature of the 1990s, and she has written on Nordic and Scottish literature and film for a range of journals, including *Scandinavica*, *Language & Literature*, *New Cinemas*, and *Textualities*. She is editor of *Northern Constellations: New Readings in Nordic Cinema* (Norvik Press, 2006).

Nalle Valtiala is a Finland-Swedish author who has published numerous works in a variety of genres between 1961 and the present. His novels include *Nationens hjälte* (1986), *Tang* (1995), *På min mammas gata* (1999) and *Anna* (2005). His doctoral thesis (1998) was on James Fenimore Cooper's landscapes.

Clas Zilliacus is Professor in the Department of Comparative Literature at Åbo Akademi University. His books include *Beckett and Broadcasting* (1976), *Opinionens tryck. En studie över pressens bildningsskede i Finland* (1985), *Finlands svenska litteraturhistoria*, vol. II (ed., 2000), and *Eftertankar om Finlands svenska litteraturhistoria II* (ed., 2001).

Anders Öhman is Professor in the Department of Comparative Literature at Umeå University and Director of the Centre for the Study of Science and Values. His research interests include the Swedish nineteenth-century novel, Norrlandic literature, and cultural studies. His books include *Äventyrets tid. Den sociala äventyrsromanen i Sverige 1841-1859* (1990), *Apologier. En linje i den svenska romanen från August Strindberg till Agnes von Krusenstjerna* (2001), *Populärlitteratur. De populära genrernas estetik och historia* (2002), and *De förskingrade. Norrland, moderniteten och Gustav Hedenvind-Eriksson* (2004).

Index

The Scandinavian letters æ/ä, ø/ö, and å are alphabetised after z, according to Scandinavian convention.

C. CLAIRE THOMSON (ED.)

Northern Constellations
New Readings in Nordic Cinema

What happens when a camera gets trapped in a Swedish elevator, or when the body of the tourist meets the snow of an Icelandic winter? How is Lars von Trier re-working Carl Th. Dreyer's images of flesh and spirit for a digital age? How can filmic space re-negotiate local, national, and global forms of belonging?

Northern Constellations features interventions from leading cinema studies scholars and Scandinavian specialists from the UK, the US and the Nordic world. Engaging with contemporary film and cultural theory – particularly on affect, embodiment, memory, place, interculturality, and realism – the essays explore the potential of cinema to map space, body, and community. Older Nordic classics by Carl Th. Dreyer, Ingmar Bergman and Victor Sjöström are re-interpreted in constellation with the themes and concerns of established and emerging contemporary filmmakers, including Lars von Trier, Aki Kaurismäki, Liv Ullmann, Suzanne Taslimi and Max Kestner.

As the seventh art forges on towards its second century, *Northern Constellations* bears witness to the fertile interdisciplinarity and maturity of the discipline of film studies, and celebrates the diversity and dynamism of film-making in the Nordic world. It should appeal to the general cinema-goer as well as to film scholars and students. The volume includes black-and-white illustrations, and each chapter is supported by bibliographical references.

ISBN 978 1 870041 63 8

UK £16.95
(paperback, 248 pages)

MARIE WELLS (ED.)

The Discovery of Nineteenth-Century Scandinavia

This volume brings together a range of articles about travel to, and within, Scandinavia in the nineteenth century. The articles cover topics ranging from a study of the way in which accounts by intrepid travellers, who faced all sorts of hardships with regard to transport and accommodation in Finland, were gradually replaced in the course of the century by guidebooks for tourists, to an exploration of how it was foreign interest in Iceland that helped develop the Icelanders' pride in the natural features of their own country. An account of Sabine Baring-Gould's fascination for the culture of Iceland sits next to an account of the difficult lot of the ordinary Icelander at the time. One article compares the very different reactions to Norway of two travellers who lived seventy years apart, while another traces the role Norwegian parsonages played in providing board and lodging for well-to-do travellers. Marmier's account of the French Expedition du Nord's voyage to Spitsbergen (Svalbard) and northern Norway sits alongside three articles on Hans Christian Andersen as travel-writer, and a fascinating account of Anglo-Swedish contacts from the seventeenth century onwards shows how lively contacts between the two countries had started long before the nineteenth century.

In addition the articles in this volume show how travel-writing has become a genre which may be approached from a variety of theoretical angles, most obviously those of cultural and post-colonial theory, but also translation theory.

The volume is a fascinating read for anyone interested in Scandinavia, Scandinavian history, travel-writing, and literary and cultural theory.

ISBN 978 1 870041 69 0

UK £19.95
(paperback, c.244 pages) (2007)

JANET GARTON & MICHAEL ROBINSON (EDS)

On the Threshold:
New Studies in Nordic Literature

This collection of essays by scholars of Nordic literature from around the world is focused upon two central themes. The first relates to periods of transition in Nordic writing, the growth of new directions, the turn of a century or a millennium, and investigates phenomena such as fin-de-siècle writing, decadence and millennium myths, ragnarok and apocalypse.

The second major theme of this volume explores the writing of texts – poetry, prose, drama – and, in particular, ways of beginning and ending narrative. Among the authors who are the subjects of closer study are August Strindberg, Knut Hamsun, J. P. Jacobsen, William Heinesen, Kerstin Ekman, Cora Sandel and Tom Kristensen.

This is a multi-lingual volume, with essays in English, Danish, Norwegian and Swedish.

ISBN 978 1 870041 50 8

UK £19.95
(paperback, 490 pages)

HELENA FORSÅS-SCOTT (ED.)

Gender – Power – Text
Nordic Culture in the Twentieth Century

The Nordic countries are often imagined by the outside world to be a haven of sexual equality and exemplary gender relations. *Gender – Power – Text: Nordic Culture in the Twentieth Century* presents a more nuanced picture to the English-speaking world, interrogating the constructions, negotiations and transformations of gender and power in a diversity of texts and textual practices.

GENDER theory informs all sixteen essays in this volume, and a productive and provocative juxtaposition of disciplinary and theoretical boundaries is in evidence throughout. The contributors draw on the work of theorists including Roland Barthes, Judith Butler, Jacques Derrida, Michel Foucault, Julia Kristeva and Hayden White, reading this against texts by Nordic writers, filmmakers and artists such as Edith Södergran, Ellen Key, Knut Hamsun, Gunvor Hofmo, Ingmar Bergman, Liv Ullmann and Vibeke Grønfeldt.

POWER and its distribution in society are analysed both as a problem central to the construction of the nation-state and welfare society, and as a dynamic underlying the cultural texts which function as sites where social practice, political engagement and aesthetic creativity meet and merge.

TEXT is understood in this volume in a wide sense, encompassing painting, handicrafts, film, and photography, as well as poetry, the novel, and drama. The texts explored by the contributors belong to the Danish, Finnish, Finland-Swedish, Norwegian, Sámi and Swedish traditions, but the cross-currents that constitute a wider 'Nordic' cultural community are also investigated.

ISBN 978 1 870041 60 7

UK £19.95
(paperback, 292 pages)

ELLEN REES

On the Margins
Nordic Women Modernists of the 1930s

This study examines the work of six women prose writers of the 1930s, placing them for the first time within the broader context of European and American literary modernism. These writers – Stina Aronson, Karen Blixen, Karo Espeseth, Hagar Olsson, Cora Sandel and Edith Øberg – have been doubly marginalized. Their work has long been viewed as anomalous within the Scandinavian literary canon, but, apart from Karen Blixen, it also remains marginalized from examinations of women writers produced outside Scandinavia. This is a 'connective study' which examines the literary strategies, preoccupations, and responses to changes in society shared across national boundaries by these writers. They all sought inspiration from foreign literature and culture, and made themselves literal or figurative exiles from their homelands.

Ellen Rees is Assistant Professor of Scandinavian Studies at the University of Oregon. She has published widely on Scandinavian prose fiction and cinema, and is currently researching a monograph on Cora Sandel.

ISBN 978 1 870041 59 1

UK £14.95
(paperback, 204 pages)

MATS JANSSON, JAKOB LOTHE & HANNU RIIKONEN (EDS.)

European and Nordic Modernisms

This collection of essays explores the growth and development of Nordic
Modernisms in a European context. Modernism is a truly international movement
that cuts across many boundaries – geographical, cultural, and linguistic. Modernism
involves the literatures of several countries; indeed, as these thematically
homogenous but methodologically diverse essays demonstrate, cross-fertilization is
a prerequisite for its very existence. The essays gathered here discuss the diverse
forms of Modernism that emerged in the Nordic countries at widely differing
moments. Modernist forerunners such as Friedrich Nietzsche, and key
representatives of Modernism such as T. S. Eliot and Franz Kafka, are linked to a
number of writers who all contributed to the development of a Nordic Modernism.
This book demonstrates that the emergence of Modernism in the Nordic literatures
is closely related to, and inspired by, the modernizing works and movements in early
twentieth-century Europe.

ISBN 978 1 870041 58 4

UK £24.95
(hardback, 258 pages)

For further information, or to request a catalogue, please contact:
Norvik Press, University of East Anglia (LLT), Norwich NR4 7TJ, England
or visit our website at www.norvikpress.com